ASVAB
ARMED SERVICES VOCATIONAL APTITUDE BATTERY

ASVAB
ARMED SERVICES VOCATIONAL APTITUDE BATTERY

Third Edition

NEW YORK

Copyright © 2005 LearningExpress

All rights reserved under International and Pan-American Copyright Conventions.
Published in the United States by LearningExpress, LLC, New York.

Library of Congress Cataloging-in-Publication Data:
ASVAB.—3rd ed.
    p. cm.
  ISBN 978-1-57685-482-2
  1. Armed Services Vocational Aptitude Battery—Study guides. I. LearningExpress
(Organization)
U408.5.A83 2005
355'.00973—dc22

                                                          2004027515

Printed in the United States of America

9 8 7 6 5

Third Edition

Regarding the Information in This Book
We attempt to verify the information presented in our books prior to publication. It is always a
good idea. however, to double-check such important information as minimum requirements,
application and testing procedures, and deadlines with your local recruitment agncy, as such
information can change from time to time.

For more information or to place an order, contact LearningExpress at:
 2 Rector Street
 26th Floor
 New York, NY 10006

Or visit us at:
 www.learnatest.com

Contents

Contributors

The following individuals contributed to the content of this book.

Elizabeth Chesla is the author of *501 Vocabulary Questions, TOEFL Exam Success, Reading Comprehension Success, Write Better Essays,* and contributing author of *GMAT Exam Success, ACT Exam Success, GED Exam Success,* and many other writing and reading guides and test-preparation books. She lives in Harleysville, Pennsylvania.

Pamela Harrell is an editor and writer living in New York City; she has a master of science degree in entomology.

Mary Hesalroad, a police officer for the Austin, Texas, Police Department, consults with police departments on recruiting efforts and is a freelance writer.

Clay McGann is an electrical engineer who designs electrical systems for space launch vehicles.

Judith N. Meyers is director of the Two Together Tutorial Program of the Jewish Child Care Association in New York City and formerly an Adult Basic Education Practitioner at City University of New York.

Judith Robinovitz is an independent educational consultant and director of Score at the Top, a comprehensive test preparation program in Vero Beach, Florida.

Jo Lynn Southard is a freelance writer and editor living in Portland, Maine.

Shirley Tarbell is a test development specialist and writer living in Portland, Maine.

Steven Truitt, P.E., is a civil engineer and technical writer specializing in environmental engineering and pollution control in Golden, Colorado.

ASVAB
ARMED SERVICES
VOCATIONAL
APTITUDE BATTERY

1 ▶ About the ASVAB

CHAPTER SUMMARY

This chapter will introduce the Armed Services Vocational Aptitude Battery, or ASVAB, describe what is contained in it, and explain how this book can help you prepare to achieve maximum success when you take it.

The ASVAB is a multiple-aptitude test battery consisting of eight subtests on various subjects. The eight subtests that make up the ASVAB, each covering a different subject area and each carefully timed, are shown on the table on the next page. (A more complete description of each test will follow later in this chapter.) The ASVAB is used for two main purposes:

- As a military recruiting tool of the U.S. Department of Defense to test potential recruits to determine their developed abilities (that is, to gauge what they already know about certain subjects); to measure their general learning ability and vocational aptitude; and to predict performance in certain academic areas
- As a guide for high school and post-secondary school students, to help them decide on the career paths for which they might best be suited, whether in the military or in some other field

Depending on where you take the ASVAB, you will take either the computer version or the paper-and-pencil version. Candidates for enlistment taking the ASVAB at a Military Entrance Processing Station (MEPS) will take the computer version, while candidates for enlistment taking the ASVAB at a reserve center or Mobile Examination Team (MET) site will take the paper-and-pencil version. The content of the test is the same on both versions; only the format, the mechanics of scoring, and the numbers of questions asked are different. The LearningExpress CD-ROM for the ASVAB, included with this book, provides plenty of review material (which

NUMBER OF ITEMS AND TESTING TIME FOR THE ASVAB

Subtest	Number of Questions	Time (Minutes)
General Science (GS)	25	11
Arithmetic Reasoning (AR)	30	36
Word Knowledge (WK)	25	11
Paragraph Comprehension (PC)	15	13
Auto and Shop Information (AS)	25	11
Mathematics Knowledge (MK)	35	24
Mechanical Comprehension (MC)	25	19
Electronics Information (EI)	20	9
Total	200 Items	134 Minutes

will be useful no matter which version of the ASVAB you take) and also prepares you to take the computer-based test.

Most sections of the ASVAB—General Science, Arithmetic Reasoning, Word Knowledge, Auto and Shop Information, Mathematics Knowledge, Mechanical Comprehension, and Electronics Information—depend on your knowing about the subject from your high school courses or other reading.

The one section that does not depend on your knowing the subject in advance is the Paragraph Comprehension section. For the Paragraph Comprehension questions, you will be able to find the answers using only the information given in the paragraph and questions that accompany it.

▶ The Eight ASVAB Subtests

Following is a more detailed description of each of the eight subtests in the ASVAB. There's a chapter in this book on each of the subtests.

Part 1: General Science

The General Science subtest of the ASVAB consists of 25 questions that are designed to measure your ability to recognize, apply, and analyze basic scientific principles in the areas of:

- **Life science:** botany, zoology, anatomy and physiology, ecology
- **Physical science:** force and motion, energy, fluids and gases, atomic structure, chemistry
- **Earth and space science:** astronomy, geology, meteorology, oceanography

General Science questions are covered in Chapter 6 of this book.

Part 2: Arithmetic Reasoning

The Arithmetic Reasoning subtest consists of 30 word problems describing everyday life situations, which are designed to measure your reasoning skills and understanding of:

- Operations with whole numbers
- Operations with fractions and decimals or money
- Ratio and proportion
- Interest and percentage
- Measurement of perimeters, areas, volumes, and time and temperature

Chapter 7 will show you how to deal with the word problems on this subtest.

Part 3: Word Knowledge

The Word Knowledge subtest consists of 25 questions that ask you to choose the correct definitions of verbs, nouns, adjectives, and adverbs. These questions come in two forms:

- Definitions presented alone, with no context
- Words in the context of a short sentence

The vocabulary skills you need for the Word Knowledge subtest are presented in Chapter 8.

Part 4: Paragraph Comprehension

The Paragraph Comprehension subtest is 15 questions based on several short passages written on a variety of topics. No prior knowledge of the subject will be required—all the information you will need to answer the questions will be found in the passage. The questions are designed to test your ability to obtain the following kinds of information from written material:

- **Literal comprehension:** your ability to identify stated facts, identify reworded facts, and determine sequence of events
- **Implicit, inferential, or critical comprehension:** your ability to draw conclusions; identify the main idea of a paragraph; determine the author's purpose, mood, or tone; and identify style and technique

Chapter 9 gives you the skills you need to do well in this subtest.

Part 5: Auto and Shop Information

The Auto and Shop Information subtest includes 25 questions on automotive repair and building construction. General shop practices are also included. The questions are on the following topics:

- Automotive components
- Automotive systems
- Automotive tools
- Automotive troubleshooting and repair
- Shop tools
- Building materials
- Building and construction procedures

Auto and Shop Information is covered in Chapter 10 of this book.

Part 6: Mathematics Knowledge

The Mathematics Knowledge subtest consists of 35 questions designed to measure your understanding of mathematical concepts, principles, and procedures. The emphasis is on your ability to recognize and apply basic mathematical principles. The questions cover:

- **Number theory:** factors, multiples, reciprocals, number properties, primes, integers
- **Numeration:** fractional parts, decimals, percentages, and conversions; order of operations; exponents; rounding; reducing fractions; roots and radicals; signed numbers
- **Algebraic operations and equations:** solving or determining equations, factoring, simplifying algebraic expressions, converting a sentence to an equation
- **Geometry and measurement:** coordinates and slope, Pythagorean theorem, angle measurement, properties of polygons and circles, perimeter, area, volume, unit conversion
- **Probability**

These mathematical concepts are covered in Chapter 7 of this book.

Part 7: Mechanical Comprehension

The Mechanical Comprehension subtest consists of 25 problems, many of them illustrated, on general mechanics and physical principles. The questions will cover the principles of simple machines such as gears, pulleys, and levers, as well as force and fluid dynamics. Problems involving basic properties of materials are also included. The questions may consist of knowledge, application, and analysis questions on:

- **Basic compound machines:** gears, cams, pistons, cranks, linkages, belts, chains
- **Simple machines:** levers, planes, pulleys, screws, wedges, wheels, axles

- **Mechanical motion:** friction, velocity, direction, acceleration, centrifugal force
- **Fluid dynamics:** hydraulic forces, compression
- **Properties of materials:** weight, strength, expansion/contraction, absorption, center of gravity
- **Structural support**

See Chapter 11 for everything you need to know about Mechanical Comprehension.

Part 8: Electronics Information

The Electronics Information subtest consists of 20 questions on electrical and electronics systems. These questions are designed to measure basic knowledge and principles of electrical and electronics systems:

- Electrical tools, symbols, devices, and materials
- Electrical circuits
- Electricity and electronic systems
- Electrical current: voltage, conductivity, resistance, grounding

Chapter 12 covers Electronics Information.

▶ Arranging to Take the ASVAB

If you are in high school, ask your guidance counselor about taking the ASVAB. Many high schools offer the ASVAB at a specific time during the school year.

If you're on your own, go to the nearest recruiter of the branch of the armed services you're interested in. There is no charge to take the ASVAB. Taking the exam doesn't obligate you to join the military, although you can probably expect a persuasive sales pitch for the many job opportunities available through the Army, Air Force, Navy, Marine Corps, and U.S. Coast Guard. For more details about the ASVAB, see the Army's ASVAB website at *www.goarmy.com*.

▶ What the ASVAB Means for You

If you're taking the ASVAB as a high school student with no intention of entering the military, the test is, for you, simply an aptitude test that will help you find out what kinds of things you're good at and what things might not make such good career paths. Your ASVAB results can help you decide whether or not to go to college or whether to get training for a specialized career in an area such as electronics. Your scores may also show you areas that you should probably avoid—things you have less aptitude or training for than would be required by many jobs in that area. Your guidance counselor will explain your score report and how to use it.

If you want to enter the military, more is riding on your ASVAB score. Approximately 500,000 people each year take the ASVAB in order to enlist in the military. Your scores on certain subtests of the ASVAB determine whether you can get in at all. Once you're in, scores on the various subtests determine which jobs, or Military Occupational Specialities, you'll be allowed to train for. For instance, if you want to learn to be a computer operator, you need good scores in Paragraph Comprehension, Word Knowledge, Mathematics Knowledge, General Science, and Mechanical Comprehension. See Chapter 3 for more details on what your score means to your choice of military careers.

The bottom line is that you want to score well on the ASVAB if you're looking toward a career with the armed forces. And this book is here to help.

▶ How to Use This Book to Increase Your Score

The key to success in almost any field is, of course, to prepare for all you're worth. And one of the very best ways to prepare for the ASVAB is to read and study this book, take the practice tests, and measure how you're doing as you pass each milestone.

To ensure you are clear on the basic information, start by reading Chapter 2, which explains the recruitment and enlistment process, and how the ASVAB fits into that process. To learn more about the score you need for the job you want, read Chapter 3 next.

Next, Chapter 4 takes you through the Learning-Express Test Preparation System. The 9 steps in this chapter will ensure you are in top physical and mental shape to do your best on test day.

Armed with the knowledge you have gained in the first four chapters, take the first of three practice tests in Chapter 5. By taking this test, you will be able to see how you would perform if it were test day. Based on your score, you can also recognize your strengths and weaknesses and tailor the rest of your preparation before the actual test. Chapters 6 through 12 include targeted review and practice for each of eight subtests of the ASVAB.

Finally, Chapters 13 and 14 include two additional practice tests. Use these two tests to track your progress since the first test. You can return to the review and practice chapters as needed to ensure that you are focusing on the material that you find hardest.

Practice and preparation are the keys to doing well on this or any exam. This book will give you everything you need to score your best. Good luck!

2 ▶ Getting into the Military

CHAPTER SUMMARY

You may find joining the military an appealing career choice. Once you have made the decision that the military is where you are headed, you will need to be armed with information about the enlistment process. That is what this chapter has to offer.

Your introduction to the enlistment process usually starts with a visit to your local recruiting office. A look in the yellow pages of your phone book under "Recruiting" should give you the phone numbers and addresses of the nearest offices, or you can look in the blue government pages for one of the specific branches, if you have already decided on one.

Don't narrow your options too soon, though. If you are thinking of a career in the military, visiting a recruiter from each of the five branches—Army, Navy, Air Force, Marines, and Coast Guard. There are lots of similarities, but the subtle differences in what each branch of service has to offer you could make a lot of difference in your career.

▶ Basic Requirements

There are certain requirements you will have to meet in order to enlist in any branch of the military. You must:

- be between 17 and 34 years of age, and have a parent or guardian's permission if you are under 18
- be a U.S. citizen
- have a high school diploma or GED
- be drug-free
- have a clean arrest record

It is important to be truthful with your recruiter about any trouble you have had in the past with drugs or with the law. Criminal history checks are conducted on applicants. However, some kinds of problems can be overcome, if they are really *in the past,* not current difficulties. Check with your recruiter.

▶ Working with Your Recruiter

The recruiter is there to help you. In speaking with him or her, you will have the opportunity to ask as many questions as you want and to get a detailed picture of what each branch has to offer if you shop around. All recruiters will have brochures, videotapes, pamphlets, and years of personal experience to offer as resources. Don't be afraid to bring along a parent or a trusted friend to help you ask questions. A professional military recruiter won't mind the extra set of eyes and ears.

You can ask about the service and its benefits—salaries and fringe benefits, postings, and educational opportunities, including financial aid for college once you get out. (See the table on pages 10–11 for the basic salary for various grades of enlisted personnel in all the services.) The recruiter will also ask about you: your education, your physical and mental health, and all sorts of in-depth questions about your goals, interests, hobbies, and life experience.

Before you take the Armed Services Vocational Aptitude Battery (ASVAB), you will be given a brief test designed to give the recruiter an idea of how well you will perform on the real test. This pretest covers math and vocabulary. Although the ASVAB has eight different subtests, it's the math and verbal portions that determine whether or not you pass the test. The other sections are designed to discover what your aptitudes are for different jobs. There is no limit to how many times you can take this brief test in the recruiter's office.

Your recruiter will talk to you about the benefits of enlisting: the pay, the travel, the experience, the training. You and your recruiter can also start to discuss the kinds of jobs available to you in the military. But before that discussion can go very far, you will have to be tested to see, first, if you can enlist, and second, what specialties you qualify for. That's where your trip to the Military Entrance Processing Station comes in.

▶ Military Entrance Processing Station (MEPS)

Your recruiter will schedule you for a trip to a MEPS in your area—there is one in almost every state—for a day of written and physical testing. You will travel as a guest of Uncle Sam by plane, train, bus, or car, depending on how far away you live from the nearest facility. MEPS schedules may vary a little from area to area, but they all operate five days per week and are open a few Saturdays during the year. If for any reason you are required to stay overnight for testing, then the military will pay for your hotel room and meals.

The MEPS is where all applicants for every branch of the military begin the enlistment process. So, even if the Marine Corps is your future employer, you can expect to see staff wearing Navy blue, Army green, or Air Force blue. When you walk through the door, you will check in at the control desk and be sent to the liaison office for your branch of the service.

Important Documents

Throughout the enlistment process, you will have to present certain documents. Have the following available to ensure you are prepared:

- birth certificate or other proof of citizenship and date of birth
- valid Social Security card or two other pieces of Social Security identification
- high school diploma or GED certificate
- letter or transcript documenting your midterm graduation from high school, if applicable
- college transcript, if applicable, showing credits earned
- parental or guardian consent form if you are under 18 years old
- doctor's letter if you have, or have a history of, special medical condition(s)
- marriage certificate, if applicable
- divorce papers, if applicable

Your MEPS Day at a Glance

During your day at MEPS you will go through three phases:

- mental (aptitude) testing
- medical exam
- administrative procedures

Your schedule may vary from the one outlined here, depending on how much of the process you have completed in advance. Some applicants, for example, may have already taken the ASVAB at a Mobile Examining Team (MET) site near their hometown recruiting station.

Mental (Aptitude) Testing

Your day at MEPS will most likely begin with the ASVAB, if you haven't already taken it. (See Chapter 1, "About the ASVAB") Don't underestimate the impact the ASVAB will have on your entry into the military. Results of the ASVAB test and the physical and mental exam you receive during the entrance process are used to determine whether or not you can join the branch of the military you prefer and which training programs you are qualified to enter.

Some MEPS are now conducting ASVAB testing on computer. The computer version of the test takes one hour and forty minutes to complete, as opposed to over two hours for the paper-and-pencil version. The computer ASVAB still consists of eight subtests, but it works a little differently than the paper version. The computer will give you the first question, and, if you get this question right, it gives you another question on the same subject—but this question is a bit harder than the first one. The questions get harder as you progress, and, after you answer a certain number correctly, the computer skips to the next subtest. So, you could get eight questions right, for example, and then the computer might go to the next subtest instead of requiring you to answer all 25 questions in that one subtest.

Most MEPS do not have enough computers to test everyone. If you notice that some applicants are taken to a room with the computer testing and the others are required to take the ASVAB with pencil and paper, don't worry. Either way, the information and skills you need remain the same.

COMMISSIONED OFFICERS

FY 2005 Military base pay is based upon grade (rank) and years of service:

Rank	<2	2	3	4	6	8	10	12	14	16	18	20	22	24	26
O-10												12963.00	13026.60	13297.50	13769.40
O-9												11337.90	11501.10	11737.20	12149.10
O-8	8022.30	8285.10	8459.40	8508.30	8725.50	9089.40	9173.70	9519.00	9618.00	9915.30	10345.50	10742.40	11007.60	11007.60	11007.60
O-7	6666.00	6975.60	7119.00	7233.00	7439.10	7642.50	7878.30	8113.50	8349.00	9089.40	9714.60	9714.60	9714.60	9714.60	9763.80
O-6	4940.70	5427.90	5784.00	5784.00	5805.90	6054.90	6087.90	6087.90	6433.80	7045.50	7404.60	7763.40	7967.70	8174.10	8575.50
O-5	4118.70	4639.80	4961.10	5021.40	5221.50	5341.80	5605.50	5799.00	6048.60	6431.10	6613.20	6793.20	6997.50	6997.50	6997.50
O-4	3553.80	4113.90	4388.40	4449.60	4704.30	4977.60	5317.50	5582.70	5766.60	5872.20	5933.70	5933.70	5933.70	5933.70	5933.70
O-3	3124.50	3542.10	3823.20	4168.20	4367.70	4586.70	4728.60	4962.00	5083.20	5083.20	5083.20	5083.20	5083.20	5083.20	5083.20
O-2	2699.40	3074.70	3541.20	3660.90	3736.20	3736.20	3736.20	3736.20	3736.20	3736.20	3736.20	3736.20	3736.20	3736.20	3736.20
O-1	2343.60	2439.00	2948.10	2948.10	2948.10	2948.10	2948.10	2948.10	2948.10	2948.10	2948.10	2948.10	2948.10	2948.10	2948.10

Commissioned Officers with Over Four Years of Active Duty Service as an Enlisted Member or Warrant Officer

Rank	4	6	8	10	12	14	16	18	20	22	24	26
O-3E	4168.20	4367.70	4586.70	4728.60	4962.00	5158.50	5271.00	5424.60	5424.60	5424.60	5424.60	5424.60
O-2E	3660.90	3736.20	3855.30	4055.70	4211.10	4326.60	4326.60	4326.60	4326.60	4326.60	4326.60	4326.60
O-1E	2948.10	3148.80	3264.90	3383.70	3500.70	3660.90	3660.90	3660.90	3660.90	3660.90	3660.90	3660.90

WARRANT OFFICERS

FY 2005 Military base pay is based upon grade (rank) and years of service:

Rank	<2	2	3	4	6	8	10	12	14	16	18	20	22	24	26
W-5												5548.20	5738.40	5929.20	6121.20
W-4	3228.60	3473.40	3573.30	3671.40	3840.30	4007.10	4176.30	4341.00	4511.70	4779.00	4950.00	5117.40	5290.80	5461.80	5636.40
W-3	2948.40	3071.70	3197.40	3238.80	3371.10	3522.30	3721.80	3918.90	4128.30	4285.50	4442.10	4509.30	4578.90	4730.10	4881.30
W-2	2593.50	2741.70	2871.30	2965.50	3046.20	3268.20	3438.00	3564.00	3687.00	3771.30	3842.40	3977.40	4111.50	4247.40	4247.40
W-1	2290.20	2477.70	2603.10	2684.40	2900.40	3030.90	3146.40	3275.40	3360.90	3438.30	3564.30	3659.70	3659.70	3659.70	3659.70

ENLISTED MEMBERS

FY 2005 Military base pay is based upon grade (rank) and years of service:

Rank	<2	2	3	4	6	8	10	12	14	16	18	20	22	24	26
E-9							3901.20	3989.70	4101.00	4232.40	4364.10	4575.90	4755.00	4943.70	5231.70
E-8						3193.50	3334.80	3422.10	3527.10	3640.50	3845.40	3949.20	4125.90	4224.00	4465.20
E-7	2220.00	2423.10	2515.80	2638.80	2734.50	2899.50	2992.20	3084.60	3249.60	3332.40	3410.70	3458.70	3620.40	3725.10	3990.00
E-6	1920.30	2112.60	2205.90	2296.50	2391.00	2604.30	2687.10	2779.20	2859.90	2888.70	2908.20	2908.20	2908.20	2908.20	2908.20
E-5	1759.50	1877.10	1967.70	2060.70	2205.30	2329.80	2421.60	2450.70	2450.70	2450.70	2450.70	2450.70	2450.70	2450.70	2450.70
E-4	1612.80	1695.60	1787.10	1877.70	1957.80	1957.80	1957.80	1957.80	1957.80	1957.80	1957.80	1957.80	1957.80	1957.80	1957.80
E-3	1456.20	1547.70	1641.00	1641.00	1641.00	1641.00	1641.00	1641.00	1641.00	1641.00	1641.00	1641.00	1641.00	1641.00	1641.00
E-2	1384.50	1384.50	1384.50	1384.50	1384.50	1384.50	1384.50	1384.50	1384.50	1384.50	1384.50	1384.50	1384.50	1384.50	1384.50
E-1	1235.17	1235.10	1235.10	1235.10	1235.17	1235.10	1235.10	1235.10	1235.17	1235.17	1235.10	1235.17	1235.17	1235.10	1235.10

E-1 with less than 4 months of service $1142.70

Medical Exam

Next is the medical exam. All of the doctors you will see at this point are civilians. You will see them at least three times during the day. During the first visit, you and the medical staff will thoroughly pore over your medical prescreening form, your medical history form, and all of the medical records you have been told by your recruiter to bring along. This meeting will be one-on-one.

After this meeting, you will move on to the examining room. You'll strip down to your underwear and perform a series of about 20 exercises that will let the medical staff see how your limbs and joints work. You may be with a group of other applicants of the same sex during this examination or you may be alone with the doctor.

Your third meeting with the doctor will be where you receive a routine physical. Among the procedures you can expect are:

- blood pressure evaluation
- pulse rate evaluation
- heart and lung check
- evaluation of blood and urine samples
- eye exam
- hearing exam
- height-proportional-to-weight check
- chest X-ray
- HIV test

Female applicants will be given a pelvic/rectal examination. Another woman will be present during this procedure, but otherwise this exam will be conducted in private.

After these checks, you will find out whether your physical condition is adequate. If the medical staff uncovers a problem that will keep you from joining the service, they will discuss the matter with you. In some cases the doctor may tell you that you are being disqualified at the moment, but that you can come back at a later date to try again. For example, if you are over-weight, you could lose a few pounds and then come back to the MEPS for another try.

If the doctor wants to have a medical specialist examine you for some reason, you may have to stay overnight, or the doctor may schedule an appointment for a later date—at the military's expense, of course. Unless you do need to see a specialist, the medical exam should take no more than three hours.

Paper Work

The rest of your day will be taken up with administrative concerns. First you will meet with the guidance counselor for your branch of the service. He or she will take the results of your physical test, your ASVAB scores, and all the other information you have provided and enter this information into a computer system. The computer will show which military jobs are best suited to you. Then you can begin asking questions about your career options. Before you leave the room you will know:

- for which jobs you are qualified
- which jobs suit your personality, abilities, and interests
- which jobs are available
- when that training is available

You will also be able to decide whether you prefer to enter the military on this very day or to go in under the Delayed Entry Program. Some applicants raise their right hand during swearing-in ceremonies at the end of the processing day, while others prefer to go home and decide what they want to do.

Either way, it's critical that you ask as many questions as possible during this visit with the counselor. Take your time, and be sure you know what you want before you go any further in the process. Be aware, though, that the seats in the popular training programs go fast. The earlier you make your decision, the more likely you will have a chance to get what you really want.

▶ Delayed Entry Programs

Delayed Entry Programs allow you to enlist with your chosen branch of the military and report for duty up to 365 days later. This is a popular program for students who are still in high school or for those who have other obligations that prevent them from leaving for Basic Training right away.

▶ Basic Training

Everything you have done has been leading up to this moment—the day you leave for Basic Training. You will report back to the MEPS to prepare to leave for Basic Training. If you have been in the Delayed Entry Program, you will get a last-minute mini-physical to make sure your condition is still up to par. You will also be asked about any changes that might affect your eligibility since the last time you were at MEPS. If you have been arrested or had any medical problems, now is the time to speak up.

Your orders and records will be completed at MEPS, and then you are on your way to Basic, by plane, bus, or car—it will all be at military expense. Where you train will depend on the branch of service. The Air Force, Navy, and Coast Guard each have only one training facility. The Marines have two, and the Army has quite a few because where the Army sends you will depend on the specialized training you signed up for at MEPS.

The First Few Days

No matter which branch of service you join, the first few days of Basic Training are pretty much the same. You will spend time at an intake facility, where you will be assigned to a basic training unit and undergo a quick-paced introduction to your branch of the service. Your days will include:

- orientation briefings
- uniform distribution
- records processing
- I.D. card preparation
- barracks upkeep training
- drill and ceremony instruction
- physical training (PT)

BASIC TRAINING (BY BRANCH)		
Branch	**Location of Basic Training Facility**	**Length of Training**
Army	Fort Jackson, Columbia, SC; Fort Knox, Louisville, KY; Fort Leonard Wood, Waynesville, MO; Fort McClellan, Anniston, AL; Fort Sill, Lawton, OK	9 weeks
Navy	Salvage Training Center (NDSTC) in Panama City, FL	9 weeks
Air Force	Lackland Air Force Base, TX	6 weeks
Marine Corps	Parris Island, SC,* or San Diego, CA	13 weeks
Coast Guard	Cape May, NJ	$7\frac{1}{2}$ weeks

*All female Marines attend Basic at Parris Island. All men from the East Coast attend Parris Island. All men from the West Coast attend San Diego.

You will be assigned to a group of recruits ranging from 35 to 80 people. The Navy calls this training group a "company," the Army and Marine Corps call it a "platoon," and the Air Force calls it a "flight." And let's not forget your "supervisor" for these early days of your military career—the drill instructor. This is your primary instructor throughout the day.

The Following Weeks

From the intake facility, you will go to your Basic Training site. You can expect your training day to start around 5 A.M. and officially end around 9 P.M. Most Saturdays and Sundays are light training days. You won't have much free time, and your ability to travel away from your unit on weekends will be very limited, if you get this privilege at all. In most cases you will not be eligible to take leave (vacation time) until after Basic Training, although exceptions can sometimes be made in case of family emergency.

The subjects you learn in Basic Training include:

- military courtesy
- military regulations
- military rules of conduct
- hygiene and sanitation
- organization and mission
- handling and care of weapons
- tactics and training related specifically to your service

While you are in Basic Training, you can expect plenty of physical training. Physical fitness is critical for trainees, and your drill instructor will keep tabs on your progress throughout Basic Training by giving you tests periodically. Your best bet is to start a running and weight-lifting program *the instant* you make your decision to join the military. Recruits in all branches of the service run mile after mile, perform hundreds of sit-ups and push-ups, and become closely acquainted with obstacle courses. These courses differ in appearance from facility to facility, but they all require the same things: plenty of upper body strength and overall endurance, as well as the will to succeed.

ENLISTMENT DURATIONS BY BRANCH	
Branch of Service	Terms of Enlistment
Army	2, 3, 4, 5, or 6 years
Navy	3, 4, 5, or 6 years
Air Force	4 or 8 years
Marine Corps	3, 4, or 5 years
Coast Guard	4 or 6 years

Lifetime Opportunities

Basic Training, no matter which branch of the service you choose, is a time in your life that you will never forget. No one is promising you it will be pleasant, but during this time you will forge friendships you will keep for the rest of your life. And the opportunities you will have during and after your military service will be unparalleled. You may choose a lifetime career in the military, or you may use it as a springboard to a rewarding career in the private sector. Either way, your future starts now and this book is designed to prepare you for it.

3 ▶ The Score You Need for the Job You Want

CHAPTER SUMMARY

To get the most out of this book, you need to know the score you need to get into the service branch of your choice, and the score you need to get the specialties that interest you. This chapter walks you step-by-step through the process of converting your scores on the practice tests in this book into the scores the military uses. Reading this chapter, you will also learn what scores you need for selected Military Occupational Specialties.

When you take the three practice tests in this book, you will want to know whether your scores measure up. You will also probably want to know what kinds of jobs or Military Occupational Specialties (MOSs), your score will enable you to select. You will need some patience here. There are several different kinds of composite scores you will need to compute from your raw scores on the individual parts of the ASVAB.

▶ About Your Scores

Your first step is to convert the raw scores you got on your practice exam to the scores the military uses to compute the various composites—the composite score that says whether or not you can enlist, and the composite scores that show which MOSs you qualify for.

In the table on the following page, write your scores on ASVAB Practice Test 1 in the column that says "Raw Score" under Practice Test 1. Your raw score is simply the number you got right on that subtest. For the raw score in the last blank, Verbal Equivalent, add together your raw scores on both the Word Knowledge (WK) and Paragraph Comprehension (PC) subtests.

Note that blanks are also provided for ASVAB Practice Test 2 and ASVAB Practice Test 3; you can fill in those blanks when you take those tests. This table will help you keep track of your improvement as you work through the practice tests in this book.

All of the score conversions throughout this chapter are approximate. Different versions of the ASVAB vary in their score conversions, and your scores on the practice tests in this book will not be exactly the same as your score on the real ASVAB. Use the exams in this book to get an *approximate* idea of where you stand and how much you're improving.

Now you need to fill in the column on this page labelled "Scaled Score." On the following page is a table that shows you approximate correlations between raw scores and scaled scores for each subtest. On the left are raw scores. The other columns show the equivalent scaled score for each test. (Make sure you're using the column for the proper subtest! The subtests are labelled with the abbreviations shown in the left-hand column of the table below.)

▶ Do You Qualify?

Now that you have your scaled score for each subtest filled in on the table on this page, you're ready for the next steps: finding out if your score will get you in to the military and finding out which MOSs your scores may qualify you for. Remember to use only your *scaled scores*, not your raw scores, for these conversions.

The Armed Forces Qualifying Test (AFQT) Score

All five branches of the military compute your AFQT score—the one that determines whether or not you can enlist—in the same way. Only the Verbal Equivalent (which you determined by adding Word Knowledge and Paragraph Comprehension scores and then converting to a scaled score), Arithmetic Reasoning, and Mathematics Knowledge scaled scores count toward your AFQT. The military just wants to know if you have basic reading and arithmetic skills. The score conversion goes like this:

$$2(VE) + AR + MK = AFQT$$

YOUR SCORES						
	Practice Test 1		Practice Test 2		Practice Test 3	
Subtest	Raw Score	Scaled Score	Raw Score	Scaled Score	Raw Score	Scaled Score
General Science (GS)						
Arithmetic Reasoning (AR)						
Word Knowledge (WK)						
Paragraph Comprehension (PC)						
Auto and Shop Information (AS)						
Mathematics Knowledge (MK)						
Mechanical Comprehension (MC)						
Electronics Information (EI)						
Verbal Equivalent (VE = WK + PC)						

RAW SCORE TO SCALED SCORE CONVERSION

Raw	GS	AR	WK	PC	AS	MK	MC	EI	VE
0–1	20	26	20	20	27	30	24	24	20
2–3	23	29	21	23	31	33	28	28	20
4–5	27	32	22	28	33	36	32	33	21
6–7	31	34	25	35	36	39	35	38	22
8–9	35	37	28	41	40	42	38	42	23
10–11	39	39	30	48	43	45	42	47	25
12–13	43	42	33	54	47	48	46	52	27
14–15	46	45	35	60	50	51	50	57	29
16–17	51	48	38		54	54	53	59	31
18–19	54	50	40		57	57	58	66	32
20–21	58	53	43		60	61	61	69	34
22–23	62	56	46		64	64	66		36
24–25	67	60	48		69	67	70		38
26–27		61				70			40
28–29		63				73			42
30–31		66				76			44
32–33						79			45
34–35						82			47
36–37									49
38–39									50
40–41									52
42–43									54
44–45									56
46–47									58
48–49									60
50–51									62

Find the subtest you want to score in the boxes on the top. Then, on the left column, find your raw score for that subtest. Follow the raw-score row to the right until you get to the proper subtest. That number is your scaled score for this subtest.

In other words, your AFQT (scaled score) is your Verbal Equivalent scaled score, doubled, added to your Arithmetic Reasoning and Mathematics Knowledge scaled scores. Fill in the blanks below to find your AFQT on ASVAB Practice Test 1.

VE score   _____ ×2 = _____
AR score   _____
MK score   + _____
AFQT (scaled score)   _____

Now use the table "AFQT Scaled Score to Percentile Conversion" on page 19. Look up the score you wrote in the blank for AFQT scaled score above, and next to it, you'll find your approximate percentile score.

If your AFQT on Practice Test 1 isn't up to 31, don't despair. You're using this book to help you improve your score, after all, and you've just gotten started. Remember, too, that your score on these practice exams may not be exactly the same as your score on the actual test.

On the other hand, a higher score makes you more attractive to recruiters, and depending on your score on individual subtests, it may qualify you for more of the occupational specialities you want.

Military Occupational Specialty Qualifying Scores

If your AFQT is high enough to get you in, the next thing your scores will be used for is to help determine which Military Occupational Specialities (MOSs) you qualify for. For this purpose, the branches of the military use composite scores—different from the AFQT—made up of scores on various subtests.

Each branch of the military has its own way of computing composites and its own classification system for the MOSs. The tables here use the Army's MOSs and composites. All of the branches offer similar MOSs, and the composite scores required are also similar. So if you're considering another branch of the service, you can still use these tables to get a good idea of where you stand.

Turn to pages 20–23 to find a list of selected MOSs and the requirements for each job. If you're using the ASVAB for career guidance rather than for entrance into the military, pay special attention to the column labelled Equivalent Civilian Occupations.

In the column Minimum ASVAB Composite Score, you'll see which composite is used to determine if you're qualified for a given MOS and the minimum score required on that composite. Go on to the section "Computing Your Composites" on page 24 to find out whether you match that minimum score.

AFQT SCALED SCORE TO PERCENTILE CONVERSION

Standard Score	Percentile	Standard Score	Percentile	Standard Score	Percentile
80–120	1	186	34	221	67
121–124	2	187–188	35	222	68
125–127	3	189	36	223	69
128–131	4	190	37	224	70
132–134	5	191	38	225	71
135–137	6	192	39	226	72
138–139	7	193	40	227	73
140–142	8	194	41	228	74
143–144	9	195	42	229	75
145–146	10	196	43	230	76
147–148	11	197	44	231	77
149–150	12	198	45	232	78
151–153	13	199	46	233	79
154	14	200	47	234–235	80
155–156	15	201	48	236	81
157–158	16	202	49	237	82
159–160	17	203	50	238	83
161–162	18	204	51	239	84
163–164	19	205	52	240	85
165	20	206	63	241	86
166–167	21	207–208	54	242	87
168–169	22	209	55	243	88
170–171	23	210	56	244	89
172	24	211	57	245	90
173–174	25	212	58	246	91
175	26	213	59	247	92
176–177	27	214	60	248	93
178	28	215	61	249	94
179–180	29	216	62	250	95
181	30	217	63	251	96
182	31	218	64	252	97
183–184	32	219	65	253	98
185	33	220	66	254–320	99

REQUIREMENTS FOR SELECTED MILITARY OCCUPATIONAL SPECIALITIES

Military Occupational Speciality	Physical Demands	Minimum ASVAB Composite Score	Other Requirements	Equivalent Civilian Occupations
Infantryman*	very heavy	CO 90	red/green color discrimination, vision correctable to 20/20 in one eye and 20/100 in the other	none
Combat Engineer*	very heavy	CO 90	normal color vision	truck driver, construction worker, laborer, blaster, others
PATRIOT Missile Crewmember	moderately heavy	OF 100	red/green color discrimination, SECRET security clearance	none
M1 Armor (tank) Crewman*	very heavy	CO 90	normal color vision, vision correctable to 20/20 in one eye and 20/100 in the other, maximum height of 6' 1"	none
Multimedia Illustrator	moderately heavy	ST 95, EL 95	nomal color vision	illustrator, sign painter
PATRIOT System Repairer	not applicable	EL 110	normal color vision, SECRET security clearance	radar mechanic, electronics technician
Radio Repairer	heavy	EL 110	normal color vision, SECRET security clearance, one year of high school algebra and science	radio mechanic, electronics mechanic
Single Channel Radio Operator	very heavy	SC 100, EL 100	SECRET security clearance, ability to enunciate English, ability to type 25 WPM	radio operator, communications equipment operator, radio installer
Aviation Systems Repairer	moderately heavy	ST 115	normal color vision, TOP SECRET security clearance, completion of high school algebra course; certain restrictions on foreign ties	automatic equipment technician, radio repairer, teletypewriter installer
Psychological Operations Specialist	medium	ST 105	normal color vision, SECRET security clearance, minimum score on language test	editor, intelligence specialist

REQUIREMENTS FOR SELECTED MILITARY OCCUPATIONAL SPECIALITIES (continued)

Military Occupational Speciality	Physical Demands	Minimum ASVAB Composite Score	Other Requirements	Equivalent Civilian Occupations
Dental Laboratory Specialist	moderately heavy	GM 100, ST 95	normal color vision	dental laboratory technician
Fabric Repair Specialist	very heavy	GM 85	civilian acquired skills (i.e., prior training in fabric repair)	sewing machine operator, automobile upholsterer, tailor, canvas worker
Machinist	heavy	GM 100	normal color vision, visual acuity of 20/30 without correction, minimum score on other visual tests	machinist, welder, drop hammer operator
Broadcast Journalist	light	GT 110	ability to type 20 WPM, completion of at least 2 years of high school English, driver's license	announcer, continuity writer, reader, screen writer
Carpentry and Masonry Specialist	very heavy	GM 90	normal color vision, freedom from vertigo	carpenter, bricklayer, cement mason, stonemason, rigger, structural steel worker
Interior Electrician	heavy	EL 95	normal color vision	electrician
Ammunition Specialist	very heavy	ST 100	normal color vision, CONFIDENTIAL security clearance, not allergic to explosive components, not claustrophobic	accounting clerk, stock control supervisor, supply clerk, explosives operator
Crane Operator	very heavy	GM 90	red/green color discrimination, driver's license	crane operator, power shovel operator
Light-Wheel Vehicle Mechanic	very heavy	MM 90	normal color vision, equipment qualifications	automobile mechanic, diesel mechanic
UH-60 Helicopter Repairer	very heavy	MM 105	normal color vision, no history of alcohol or drug abuse	aircraft mechanic

REQUIREMENTS FOR SELECTED MILITARY OCCUPATIONAL SPECIALITIES (continued)

Military Occupational Speciality	Physical Demands	Minimum ASVAB Composite Score	Other Requirements	Equivalent Civilian Occupations
Executive Administrative Assistant	not applicable	ST 105	SECRET security clearance, ability to type 35 WPM, minimum score on English test	stenographer, administrative assistant, secretary
Legal Specialist	light	CL 110	ability to type 35 WPM, no civil convictions	court clerk, law clerk
Administrative Specialist	medium	CL 95	ability to type 25 WPM	administrative assistant, clerk typist, office helper, mail clerk
Finance Specialist	light	CL 95	no record of dishonesty or moral turpitude	bookkeeper, cashier, payroll clerk
Information Systems Operator	moderately heavy	ST 100	normal color vision, SECRET security clearance	computer operator, data processing technician, coding clerk
Personnel Administration Specialist	medium	CL 95	ability to type 20 WPM	personnel clerk
Cartographer	light	ST 85	normal color vision, other visual tests	drafter, cartographic technician
Watercraft Operator	very heavy	MM 100	normal color vision, vision correctable to 20/20 in one eye and 20/40 in the other, prior training	boat operator, seaman
Motor Transport Operator	very heavy	OF 90	red/green color discrimination, driver's license	chauffeur, truck driver, dispatcher
Medical Specialist	moderately heavy	ST 95	normal color vision	medical assistant, first aid attendant, emergency medical technician, nurse's aide
Practical Nurse	not applicable	ST 95	normal color vision; ability to complete licensure training or already licensed	licensed practical nurse

REQUIREMENTS FOR SELECTED MILITARY OCCUPATIONAL SPECIALTIES (continued)

Military Occupational Speciality	Physical Demands	Minimum ASVAB Composite Score	Other Requirements	Equivalent Civilian Occupations
Behavioral Science Specialist	light	ST 105		caseworker
X-Ray Specialist	moderately heavy	ST 100		X-ray technician, radiologic technologist
Animal Care Specialist	moderately heavy	ST 95	normal color vision, completion of high school course in biology	animal health technician
Food Service Specialist	heavy	OF 90	normal color vision, driver's license, possess or be qualified for food handler's license	chef, cook, butcher, baker
Military Police	moderately heavy	ST 95	red/green color discrimination, minimum height 5' 8" for males, 5' 4" for females, CONFIDENTIAL security clearance, driver's license, no record of civilian convictions	police officer, guard
Intelligence Analyst	medium	ST 105	normal color vision, TOP SECRET security clearance, no record, certain restrictions on foreign ties	editor, intelligence specialist

Computing Your Composites

Maybe you looked at the table of MOSs and said, "Wow, I didn't know the Army had Animal Care Specialists!"—or Broadcast Journalists or Legal Specialists or whatever MOSs caught your eye. The Air Force, Navy, Marines, and Coast Guard have all these specialities, too. You might think, "I could go for Animal Care Specialist training, and then when I get out I could use my G. I. Bill money to go to veterinary school and become a vet. I could work as an assistant in a vet's office while I go to school. This is great! But what does this ST 95 score mean? Can I make it?"

This is absolutely the last score computation you'll have to do, but it's a complicated one. Stick with it, and be patient. Your future may depend on your performance on the ASVAB.

ST 95, like the other letter-number combinations in the Minimum ASVAB Composite Score column, is the composite score the Army uses to determine your eligibility for the given MOS. The composite scores used by the other branches of the service are similar, though not identical. Here's a key to the meaning of the composite scores listed in the MOS table:

- FA: Field Artillery
- OF: Operations and Food Handling
- ST: Skilled Technical
- GT: General Technical
- CL: Clerical
- GM: General Maintenance
- EL: Electronics Repair
- MM: Mechanical Maintenance
- SC: Surveillance/Communications
- CO: Combat

So, if you want to be an Animal Care Specialist, you need to know your ST, or Skilled Technical, composite score. (You'll also, of course, have to meet the other requirements listed in the MOS table. Check with your recruiter.)

Here's how to compute the composites. Look for the composite(s) for the MOS(s) you want in the list below. After the name of the composite is a list of the subtest scores you have to add together. Go back to the table on page 16, where you filled in your subtest scores, and get your scores on those subtests. (Remember to use your scaled scores, not your raw scores!) Adding them up gives you a sum called a Subtest Standard Score (SSS). When you have the SSS for the composite you want, turn to the table on pages 26–27. That table lists SSSs in the left column. Find the SSS you computed for the composite you want, and then follow the line to the right until you get to the composite you're looking for. That's your composite for this subtest, and you should write it on page 000 in the blank next to the appropriate abbreviation. Now you can compare your composite score to the minimum requirement listed in the MOS table. You don't have to compute all the composite scores, just the ones that are required for the jobs you're interested in.

FA: AR _____ + CS _____ + MC _____ + MK _____ = SSS_____ FA composite: _____

OF: NO _____ + AS _____ + MC _____ + VE _____ = SSS_____ OF composite: _____

ST: VE _____ + MK _____ + MC _____ + GS _____ = SSS_____ ST composite: _____

GT: VE _____ + AR _____ = SSS_____ GT composite: _____

CL: AR _____ + MK _____ + VE _____ = SSS_____ CL composite: _____

GM: MK _____ + EI _____ + AS _____ + GS _____ = SSS_____ GM composite: _____

EL: AR _____ + MK _____ + EI _____ + GS _____ = SSS_____ EL composite: _____

MM: NO _____ + AS _____ + MC _____ + EI _____ = SSS_____ MM composite: _____

SC: AR _____ + AS _____ + MC _____ + VE _____ = SSS_____ SC composite: _____

CO: CS _____ + AR _____ + MC _____ + AS _____ = SSS_____ CO composite: _____

Suppose you want to be an Animal Care Specialist. The composite score you need for this MOS is ST 95. So you look at the ST line above and find you need to add your scores for VE, MK, MC, and GS. You go back to the table on page 16 and find your *scaled scores* (not raw scores) for these subtests. Let's say you did pretty well in Mechanical Comprehension and General Science, and not as well in Paragraph Comprehension and Word Knowledge (your Verbal Equivalent score) or Mathematics Knowledge. So you fill in line ST above like this:

ST: VE _40_ + MK _3_ + MC _61_ + GS _54_ = SSS_____   ST composite: _____

Add up your four subtest scores to get the SSS:

ST: VE _40_ + MK _3_ + MC _61_ + GS _54_ = SSS_194_   ST composite: _____

Now go to the table on the next page. Find ST at the top of the table, and follow that column down until you get to the row for 190–194. You find that your ST composite score is in the range of 95–97; in fact, it's probably about 97, since your SSS is near the top of its range.

ST: VE _40_ + MK _3_ + MC _61_ + GS _54_ = SSS_194_   ST composite: _97_

Is your score good enough to get you Animal Care Specialist training? Well, maybe just. Since you're so close to the minimum of 95, you would want some insurance. Remember, your scores on the exams in this book are only an *approximation* of your scores on the real ASVAB. So you would want to study hard on the subtests that make up your chosen composite, in this case, Paragraph Comprehension, Word Knowledge, Mathematics Knowledge, Mechanical Comprehension, and General Science.

You can use this procedure to find the composite score for whatever job you want. If your score is well above the minimum required for the MOS you want, you don't have much to worry about, though you'll probably want to work through this book just to make sure. If your score is below the minimum required, you know where to concentrate your efforts as you study the chapters in this book and take the practice exams.

STANDARD SUBTEST SCORE (SSS) TO COMPOSITE SCORE CONVERSION										
SSS	FA	OF	ST	GT	CL	GM	EL	MM	SC	CO
45–49				41–45						
50–54				46–50						
55–59				52–56						
60–64				57–61	40					
65–69				62–67	41					
70–74				68–72	42–44					
75–79				73–77	45–48					
80–84	40	40	40	78–83	49–52	40	40	40	40	
85–89	40	40	40	84–88	53–55	40	40	40	40	
90–94	40	40	40	89–94	56–59	40	40	40	40	
95–99	40	40	41–42	95–99	60–63	40–41	41–43	40	40	
100–104	41–42	40	43–45	100–104	64–66	42–44	44–46	40–41	41–44	40
105–109	43–45	41–44	46–48	105–110	67–70	45–47	47–49	42–44	45–47	41–43
110–114	46–48	45–47	49–51	111–115	71–74	48–50	50–51	45–48	48–50	44–46
115–119	49–51	48–50	52–54	116–121	75–77	51–53	52–55	49–51	51–52	47–49
120–124	52–54	51–53	55–56	122–126	78–81	54–56	56–57	52–54	53–55	50–52
125–129	55–57	54–56	57–59	127–131	82–85	57–59	58–60	55–57	56–58	53–55
130–134	58–60	57–59	60–62	132–137	86–88	60–61	61–63	58–60	59–61	56–59
135–139	61–63	60–62	63–65	138–142	89–92	62–64	64–66	61–63	62–64	60–62
140–144	64–66	63–65	66–68	143–148	93–96	65–67	67–68	64–66	65–67	63–65
145–149	67–69	66–68	69–71	149–153	96–99	68–70	69–71	67–69	68–70	66–68
150–154	70–72	69–71	72–74	154–158	100–103	71–73	72–74	70–72	71–73	69–71
155–159	73–75	72–75	75–77	159–160	104–107	74–76	75–77	73–75	74–76	72–74
160–164	76–78	76–78	78–79	160	107–110	77–79	78–80	76–78	77–79	75–77
165–169	79–81	79–81	80–82		111–114	80–82	81–83	79–81	80–82	78–81
170–174	82–84	82–84	83–85		115–118	83–85	84–85	82–84	83–85	82–84

SSS TO COMPOSITE SCORE CONVERSION (continued)

SSS	FA	OF	ST	GT	CL	GM	EL	MM	SC	CO
175–179	85–87	85–87	86–88		119–121	86–88	86–88	85–87	86–88	85–87
180–184	88–90	88–90	89–91		122–125	89–91	89–91	88–90	89–91	88–90
185–189	91–93	91–93	92–94		126–129	92–94	92–94	91–93	92–94	91–93
190–194	94–96	94–96	95–97		130–132	95–97	95–97	94–96	95–97	94–96
195–199	97–99	97–99	98–99		133–136	98–100	98–100	97–99	98–99	97–99
200–204	100–102	100–102	100–102		137–140	101–102	101–102	100–102	100–102	100–103
205–209	103–105	103–106	103–105		141–143	103–105	103–105	103–106	103–105	104–106
210–214	106–108	107–109	106–108		144–147	106–108	106–108	107–109	106–108	107–109
215–219	109–111	110–112	109–111		148–151	109–111	109–111	110–112	109–111	110–112
220–224	112–115	113–115	112–114		152–154	112–114	112–114	113–115	112–114	113–115
225–229	116–118	116–118	115–117		155–158	115–117	115–116	116–118	115–117	116–118
230–234	119–121	119–121	118–120		159–160	118–120	117–119	119–121	118–120	119–121
235–239	122–124	122–124	121–122		160	121–123	120–122	122–124	121–123	122–125
240–244	125–127	125–127	123–125			124–126	123–125	125–127	124–126	126–128
245–249	128–130	128–130	126–128			127–129	126–128	128–130	127–129	129–131
250–254	131–133	131–134	129–131			130–132	129–131	131–133	130–132	132–134
255–259	134–136	135–137	132–134			133–135	132–133	134–136	133–135	135–137
260–264	137–139	138–140	135–137			136–138	134–136	137–139	136–138	138–140
265–269	140–142	141–143	138–140			139–140	137–139	140–142	139–141	141–143
270–274	143–145	144–146	141–143			141–143	140–142	143–145	142–144	144–147
275–279	146–148	147–149	144–145			144–146	143–145	146–148	145–146	148–150
280–284	149–151	150–152	146–148			147–149	146–148	149–151	147–149	151–153
285–289	152–154	153–155	149–151			150–152	149–150	152–154	150–152	154–156
290–294	155–157	156–158	152–154			153–155	151–153	155–157	153–155	157–159
295–299	158–160	159–160	155–157			156–158	154–156	158–160	156–158	160
300–304	160	160	158–160			159–160	157–159	160	159–160	
305–309			160			160	159–160		160	

CHAPTER

4

▶ The
LearningExpress
Test Preparation
System

CHAPTER SUMMARY

Taking the ASVAB can be tough. It demands a lot of preparation if you want to achieve a top score. Whether or not you get into the military depends on how well you do on the AFQT portion of the exam. The LearningExpress Test Preparation System, developed exclusively for LearningExpress by leading test experts, gives you the discipline and attitude you need to be a winner.

Fact: Taking the ASVAB isn't easy, and neither is getting ready for it. Your future military career depends on you passing the core section of the ASVAB—Arithmetic Reasoning, Word Knowledge, Paragraph Comprehension, and Mathematics Knowledge. By focusing on these four subtests, you have taken your first step to getting into the military. However, there are all sorts of pitfalls that can prevent you from doing your best on this all-important portion of the exam. Here are some of the obstacles that can stand in the way of your success:

- being unfamiliar with the format of the exam
- being paralyzed by test anxiety
- leaving your preparation to the last minute
- not preparing at all!
- not knowing vital test-taking skills: how to pace yourself through the exam, how to use the process of elimination, and when to guess
- not being in tip-top mental and physical shape
- messing up on test day by arriving late at the test site, having to work on an empty stomach, or shivering through the exam because the room is cold

What is the common denominator in all these test-taking pitfalls? One word: *control.* Who is in control, you or the exam?

Here is some good news: The LearningExpress Test Preparation System puts you in control. In just nine easy-to-follow steps, you will learn everything you need to know to make sure that you are in charge of your preparation and your performance on the exam. Other test-takers may let the test get the better of them; other test-takers may be unprepared or out of shape, but not you. You will have taken all the steps you need to take to get a high score on the ASVAB.

Here's how the LearningExpress Test Preparation System works: Nine easy steps lead you through everything you need to know and do to get ready to master your exam. Each of the steps listed below includes both reading about the step and one or more activities. It's important that you do the activities along with the reading, or you won't be getting the full benefit of the system. Each step tells you approximately how much time that step will take you to complete.

Step 1. Get Information	30 minutes
Step 2. Conquer Test Anxiety	20 minutes
Step 3. Make a Plan	50 minutes
Step 4. Learn to Manage Your Time	10 minutes
Step 5. Learn to Use the Process of Elimination	20 minutes
Step 6. Know When to Guess	20 minutes
Step 7. Reach Your Peak Performance Zone	10 minutes
Step 8. Get Your Act Together	10 minutes
Step 9. Do It!	10 minutes
Total	**3 hours**

We estimate that working through the entire system will take you approximately three hours, though it's perfectly fine if you work faster or slower than the time estimates assume. If you can take a whole afternoon or evening, you can work through the whole LearningExpress Test Preparation System in one sitting. Otherwise, you can break it up, and do just one or two steps a day for the next several days. It's up to you—remember, you are in control.

▶ Step 1: Get Information

Time to complete: 30 minutes
Activity: Read Chapter l, "About the ASVAB"
Knowledge is power. The first step in the LearningExpress Test Preparation System is finding out everything you can about the ASVAB. Once you have your information, the next steps in the LearningExpress Test Preparation System will show you what to do about it.

Part A: Straight Talk about the ASVAB

Basically, the United States military invented the whole idea of standardized testing, starting around the time of World War I. The Department of Defense wanted to make sure that its recruits were trainable—not that they already knew the skills they needed to serve in the armed forces, but that they could learn them.

The ASVAB started as an intelligence test, but now it is a test of specific aptitudes and abilities. While some of these aptitudes, such as reading and math problem-solving skills, are important in almost any job, others, such as electronics or automotive principles, are quite specialized. These more specialized subtests don't count toward your Armed Forces Qualifying Test (AFQT) score, which determines your eligibility to enlist in the military. Only the four subtests covered in this book count toward the AFQT score.

It's important for you to realize that your score on the ASVAB does not determine what kind of person you are. There are all kinds of things a written exam like this can't test: whether you can follow orders, whether you can become part of a unit that works together to accomplish a task, and so on. Those kinds of things are hard to evaluate, while a test is easy to evaluate.

This is not to say that the exam is not important! Your chances of getting into the military still depend on your getting a good score on the subtests of the ASVAB core. And that's why you're here—using the LearningExpress Test Preparation System to achieve control over the exam.

Part B: What Is on the Test

If you haven't already done so, stop here and read Chapter 1 of this book, which gives you an overview of the ASVAB.

▶ Step 2: Conquer Test Anxiety

Time to complete: 20 minutes
Activity: Take the Test Stress Test

Having complete information about the exam is the first step in getting control of the exam. Next, you have to overcome one of the biggest obstacles to test success: test anxiety. Test anxiety not only impairs your performance on the exam itself, but also keeps you from preparing! In Step 2, you will learn stress management techniques that will help you succeed on your exam. Learn these strategies now, and practice them as you work through the exams in this book, so they will be second nature to you by exam day.

Combating Test Anxiety

The first thing you need to know is that a little test anxiety is a good thing. Everyone gets nervous before a big exam—and if that nervousness motivates you to prepare thoroughly, so much the better. It's said that Sir Laurence Olivier, one of the foremost British actors of last century, felt ill before every performance. His stage fright didn't impair his performance; in fact, it probably gave him a little extra edge—just the kind of edge you need to do well, whether on a stage or in an examination room.

On page 33 is the Test Stress Test. Stop and answer the questions, to find out whether your level of test anxiety is something you should worry about.

Stress Management before the Test

If you feel your level of anxiety getting the best of you in the weeks before the test, here is what you need to do to bring the level down again:

- **Get prepared.** There is nothing like knowing what to expect and being prepared for it to put you in control of test anxiety. That's why you're reading this book. Use it faithfully, and remind yourself that you are better prepared than most of the people taking the test.

- **Practice self-confidence.** A positive attitude is a great way to combat test anxiety. This is no time to be humble or shy. Stand in front of the mirror and say to your reflection, "I'm prepared. I'm full of self-confidence. I'm going to ace this test. I know I can do it." Say it into a tape recorder and play it back once a day. If you hear it often enough, you will believe it.

- **Fight negative messages.** Every time someone starts telling you how hard the exam is or how it's almost impossible to get a high score, start telling them your self-confidence messages above. Don't listen to the negative messages. Turn on your tape recorder and listen to your self-confidence messages.

- **Visualize.** Imagine yourself reporting for duty on your first day as a military trainee. Think of yourself wearing your uniform and learning skills you will use for the rest of your life. Visualizing success can help make it happen—and it reminds you of why you are going to all this work in preparing for the exam.

- **Exercise.** Physical activity helps calm your body down and focus your mind. Besides, being in good physical shape can actually help you do well on the exam. Go for a run, lift weights, go swimming—and do it regularly.

Stress Management on Test Day

There are several ways you can bring down your level of test anxiety on test day. They will work best if you practice them in the weeks before the test, so you know which ones work best for you.

- **Deep breathing.** Take a deep breath while you count to five. Hold it for a count of one, then let it out on a count of five. Repeat several times.

- **Move your body.** Try rolling your head in a circle. Rotate your shoulders. Shake your hands from the wrist. Many people find these movements very relaxing.

- **Visualize again.** Think of the place where you are most relaxed: lying on a beach in the sun, walking through the park, or whatever. Now close your eyes and imagine you are actually there. If you practice in advance, you will find that you only need a few seconds of this exercise to experience a significant increase in your sense of well-being.

When anxiety threatens to overwhelm you right there during the exam, there are still things you can do to manage the stress level:

- **Repeat your self-confidence messages.** You should have them memorized by now. Say them silently to yourself, and believe them!

- **Visualize one more time.** This time, visualize yourself moving smoothly and quickly through the test answering every question right and finishing just before time is up. Like most visualization techniques, this one works best if you have practiced it ahead of time.

- **Find an easy question.** Skim over the test until you find an easy question, and answer it. Getting even one question finished gets you into the test-taking groove.

- **Take a mental break.** Everyone loses concentration once in a while during a long test. It's normal, so you shouldn't worry about it. Instead, accept what has happened. Say to yourself, "Hey, I lost it there for a minute. My brain is taking a break." Put down your pencil, close your eyes, and do some deep breathing for a few seconds. Then you're ready to go back to work.

Try these techniques ahead of time, and see if they work for you!

You only need to worry about test anxiety if it is extreme enough to impair your performance. The following questionnaire will provide a diagnosis of your level of test anxiety. In the blank before each statement, write the number that most accurately describes your experience.

0 = Never   1 = Once or twice   2 = Sometimes   3 = Often

_____ I have gotten so nervous before an exam that I simply put down the books and didn't study for it.

_____ I have experienced disabling physical symptoms such as vomiting and severe headaches because I was nervous about an exam.

_____ I have simply not showed up for an exam because I was scared to take it.

_____ I have experienced dizziness and disorientation while taking an exam.

_____ I have had trouble filling in the little circles because my hands were shaking too hard.

_____ I have failed an exam because I was too nervous to complete it.

_____ **Total: Add up the numbers in the blanks above.**

Your Test Stress Score

Here are the steps you should take, depending on your score. If you scored:

- **Below 3,** your level of test anxiety is nothing to worry about; it's probably just enough to give you that little extra edge.
- **Between 3 and 6,** your test anxiety may be enough to impair your performance, and you should practice the stress management techniques listed in this section to try to bring your test anxiety down to manageable levels.
- **Above 6,** your level of test anxiety is a serious concern. In addition to practicing the stress management techniques listed in this section, you may want to seek additional, personal help. Call your community college and ask for the academic counselor. Tell the counselor that you have a level of test anxiety that sometimes keeps you from being able to take an exam. The counselor may be willing to help you or may suggest someone else you should talk to.

▶ Step 3: Make a Plan

Time to complete: 50 minutes
Activity: Construct a study plan
Maybe the most important thing you can do to get control of yourself and your exam is to make a study plan. Too many people fail to prepare simply because they fail to plan. Spending hours on the day before the exam poring over sample test questions not only raises your level of test anxiety, it also is simply no substitute for careful preparation and practice over time.

On the following pages are three sample schedules, based on the amount of time you have before you take the ASVAB. If you are the kind of person who needs deadlines and assignments to motivate you for a project, here they are. If you are the kind of person who doesn't like to follow other people's plans, you can use the suggested schedules here to construct your own.

Even more important than making a plan is making a commitment. You can't improve your skills in the four areas tested on the ASVAB core overnight. You have to set aside some time every day for study and practice. Try for at least 30 minutes a day. Thirty minutes daily will do you much more good than two hours on Saturday.

Don't put off your study until the day before the exam. Start now. A few minutes a day, with half an hour or more on weekends, can make a big difference in your score.

▶ Step 4: Learn to Manage Your Time

Time to complete: 10 minutes to read, many hours of practice!
Activities: Practice these strategies as you take the sample tests in this book

Steps 4, 5, and 6 of the LearningExpress Test Preparation System put you in charge of your exam by showing you test-taking strategies that work. Practice these strategies as you take the sample tests in this book, and then you will be ready to use them on test day.

First, you will take control of your time on the exam. Each of the four subtests of the ASVAB core is timed separately. Most allow you enough time to complete the section, though none allows a lot of extra time. You should use your time wisely to avoid making errors. Here are some general tips for the whole exam.

- **Listen carefully to directions.** By the time you get to the exam, you should know how all the subtests work, but listen just in case something has changed.
- **Pace yourself.** Glance at your watch every few minutes, and compare the time to how far you have gotten in the subtest. When one-quarter of the time has elapsed, you should be a quarter of the way through the sub-test, and so on. If you're falling behind, pick up the pace a bit.
- **Keep moving.** Don't waste time on one question. If you don't know the answer, skip the question and move on. Circle the number of the question in your test booklet in case you have time to come back to it later.
- **Keep track of your place on the answer sheet.** If you skip a question, make sure you skip on the answer sheet too. Check yourself every 5–10 questions to make sure the question number and the answer sheet number are still the same.
- **Don't rush.** Though you should keep moving, rushing won't help. Try to keep calm and work methodically and quickly.

Schedule A: 30 Days to Getting the Score You Need for the Job You Want

If you have at least a month before you take the ASVAB, you have plenty of time to prepare—as long as you don't waste it! This schedule will help you achieve the score you need to enlist as well as the score you need for the job you want. If you have less than a month, turn to Schedule B.

TIME	PREPARATION
Day 1	Take the first practice exam in Chapter 5. Score the exam and identify two areas that you will concentrate on before you take the second practice exam.
Days 2–5	Study the areas you identified as your weaknesses. Use the review lessons in Chapters 6–12. Review these chapters in detail to improve your score on the next practice test.
Day 6	Study Chapter 6, General Science Review.

Day 7	Study Chapter 7, Math Review.
Day 8	Study Chapter 8, Word Knowledge Review.
Day 9	Study Chapter 9, Paragraph Comprehension Review.
Day 10	Study Chapter 10, Auto and Shop Information Review.
Day 11	Study Chapter 11, Mechanical Comprehension Review.
Day 12	Study Chapter 12, Electronics Information Review.
Day 13	Take a day off, or if you feel up to it, go back and review a chapter that you found difficult.
Day 14	Take the second practice exam in Chapter 13 and calculate your score. Identify three areas to concentrate on before you take the third practice exam.
Days 15–19	Study one of the areas that gave you the most trouble on Practice Test 2.
Days 20–23	Study another one of the areas that gave you the most trouble on Practice Test 2.
Days 24–27	Study another one of the areas that gave you the most trouble on Practice Test 2.
Day 28	Take the last practice exam in Chapter 14. Score the test. Note how much you have improved!
Day 29	Take an overview of all your study materials, consolidating your strengths and improving on your weaknesses.
Day before the exam	Relax. Do something unrelated to the exam and go to bed at a reasonable hour.

Schedule B: 14 Days to Getting the Score You Need

If you have two weeks or less before you take the exam, use this schedule to focus on getiing an AFQT score needed to enlist and to help boost your score to get the job you want.

TIME	PREPARATION
Day 1	Take the first practice exam in Chapter 5. Score the exam and identify two areas that you will concentrate on before you take the second practice exam.
Days 2–5	Study the areas you identified as your weaknesses. Review the lessons and practice questions on Math, Vocabulary, and Reading in Chapters 7–9.

Day 6	Take the second practice exam in Chapter 13 and calculate your score. Identify areas to concentrate on before you take the third practice exam.
Days 7–9	Review the lessons and practice questions on Science, Auto and Shop Information, Mechanical Comprehension, and Electronic Information in Chapters 6, 10, 11, and 12.
Day 10	Take the last practice exam in Chapter 14. Score the test. Note how much you have improved!
Days 11–13	Take an overview of all your study materials, consolidating your strengths and improving on your weaknesses.
Day before the exam	Relax. Do something unrelated to the exam and go to bed at a reasonable hour.

Schedule C: Only 7 Days Until Exam Day

If you have a week or less before you take the exam, use this 7-day schedule to focus on getting a high AFQT score needed to enlist.

TIME	PREPARATION
Day 1	Take the first practice exam in Chapter 5. Score the exam and identify two areas that you will concentrate on before you take the second practice exam.
Days 2–3	Study the areas you identified as your weaknesses. Don't forget, there are review lessons for Math, Vocabulary, and Reading in Chapters 7–9. Review these chapters in detail to improve your score on the next practice test.
Day 4	Take the second practice exam in Chapter 13 and calculate your score. Identify one area to concentrate on before you take the third practice exam.
Day 5	Study the one area you identified for further review. Again, use the Math, Vocabulary, and Reading chapters for help. Take the last practice exam in Chapter 14. Score the test. Note how much you have improved!
Day 6	Take an overview of all your study materials, consolidating your strengths and improving on your weaknesses.
Day before the exam	If you feel comfortable with the four subtests that determine your eligibility for enlistment, spend a couple of hours reviewing for the other four subtests using the lessons in Chapters 6, 10, 11, and 12. Otherwise, relax. Do something unrelated to the exam and go to bed at a reasonable hour.

► Step 5: Learn to Use the Process of Elimination

Time to complete: 20 minutes
Activity: Complete worksheet on Using the Process of Elimination

After time management, your next most important tool for taking control of your exam is using the process of elimination wisely. It's standard test-taking wisdom that you should always read all the answer choices before choosing your answer. This helps you find the right answer by eliminating wrong answer choices. And, sure enough, that standard wisdom applies to your exam, too.

You should always use the process of elimination on tough questions, even if the right answer jumps out at you. Sometimes the answer that jumps out isn't right after all. You should always proceed through the answer choices in order. You can start with answer choice **a** and eliminate any choices that are clearly incorrect.

Let's say you're facing a vocabulary question that goes like this:

"Biology uses a *binomial* system of classification."
In this sentence, the word *binomial* most nearly means
  a. understanding the law.
  b. having two names.
  c. scientifically sound.
  d. having a double meaning.

If you happen to know what *binomial* means, of course, you don't need to use the process of elimination, but let's assume you don't. So, you look at the answer choices. "Understanding the law" sure doesn't sound very likely for something having to do with biology. So you eliminate choice **a**—and now you only have three answer choices to deal with. Mark an X next to choice a so you never have to read it again.

Now, move on to the other answer choices. If you know that the prefix *bi-* means *two*, as in *bicycle*, you will flag answer **b** as a possible answer. Mark a check mark beside it, meaning "good answer, I might use this one."

Choice **c**, "scientifically sound," is a possibility. At least it's about science, not law. It could work here, though, when you think about it, having a "scientifically sound" classification system in a scientific field is kind of redundant. You remember the *bi-* in *binomial*, and probably continue to like answer **b** better. But you're not sure, so you put a question mark next to **c**, meaning "well, maybe."

Now, choice **d**, "having a double meaning." You're still keeping in mind that *bi-* means *two*, so this one looks possible at first. But then you look again at the sentence the word belongs in, and you think, "Why would biology want a system of classification that has two meanings? That wouldn't work very well!" If you're really taken with the idea that *bi-* means *two*, you might put a question mark here. But if you're feeling a little more confident, you'll put an X. You have already got a better answer picked out.

Now your question looks like this:

"Biology uses a *binomial* system of classification."
In this sentence, the word *binomial* most nearly means
  X **a.** understanding the law.
  ✓ **b.** having two names.
  ? **c.** scientifically sound.
  ? **d.** having a double meaning.

You've got just one checkmark for a good answer. If you're pressed for time, you should simply mark answer **b** on your answer sheet. If you have the time to be extra careful, you could compare your check-mark answer to your question-mark answers to make sure that it's better. (It is: the *binomial* system in biology is the one that gives a two-part genus and species name like *homo sapiens*.)

It's good to have a system for marking good, bad, and maybe answers. Here's one recommendation:

  X = bad
  ✓ = good
  ? = maybe

If you don't like these marks, devise your own system. Just make sure you do it long before test day—while you're working through the practice exams in this book—so you won't have to worry about it during the test.

Even when you think you are absolutely clueless about a question, you can often use the process of elimination to get rid of one answer choice. If so, you are better prepared to make an educated guess, as you will see in Step 6. More often, the process of elimination allows you to get down to only *two* possibly right answers. Then, you're in a strong position to guess.

And sometimes, even though you don't know the right answer, you find it simply by getting rid of the wrong ones, as you did in the example above.

Try using your powers of elimination on the questions in the worksheet Using the Process of Elimination beginning on this page. The answer explanations show one possible way you might use the process to arrive at the right answer.

The process of elimination is your tool for the next step, which is knowing when to guess.

Using the Process of Elimination

Use the process of elimination to answer the following questions.

1. Ilsa is as old as Meghan will be in five years. The difference between Ed's age and Meghan's age is twice the difference between Ilsa's age and Meghan's age. Ed is 29. How old is Ilsa?
   a. 4
   b. 10
   c. 19
   d. 24

2. "All drivers of commercial vehicles must carry a valid commercial driver's license whenever operating a commercial vehicle." According to this sentence, which of the following people need NOT carry a commercial driver's license?
   a. a truck driver idling his engine while waiting to be directed to a loading dock
   b. a bus operator backing her bus out of the way of another bus in the bus lot
   c. a taxi driver driving his personal car to the grocery store
   d. a limousine driver taking the limousine to her home after dropping off her last passenger of the evening

3. Smoking tobacco has been linked to
   a. increased risk of stroke and heart attack.
   b. all forms of respiratory disease.
   c. increasing mortality rates over the past ten years.
   d. juvenile delinquency.

4. Which of the following words is spelled correctly?
   a. incorrigible
   b. outragous
   c. domestickated
   d. understandible

Answers

Here are the answers, as well as some suggestions as to how you might have used the process of elimination to find them.

1. d. You should have eliminated answer **a** off the bat. Ilsa can't be four years old if Meghan is going to be Ilsa's age in five years. The best way to eliminate other answer choices is to try plugging them in to the information given in the problem. For instance, for answer **b**, if Ilsa is 10, then Meghan must be 5. The difference in their ages is 5. The difference between Ed's age, 29, and Meghan's age, 5, is 24. Is 24 two times 5? No. Then answer **b** is wrong. You could eliminate answer **c** in the same way and be left with answer **d**.

2. c. Note the word *not* in the question, and go through the answers one by one. Is the truck driver in choice **a** "operating a commercial vehicle"? Yes, idling counts as "operating," so he needs to have a commercial driver's license. Likewise, the bus operator in answer **b** is operating a commercial vehicle; the question doesn't say the operator has to be on the street. The limo driver in **d** is operating a commercial vehicle, even if it doesn't have passenger in it. However, the cabbie in answer **c** is *not* operating a commercial vehicle, but his own private car.

3. a. You could eliminate answer **b** simply because of the presence of the word *all*. Such absolutes hardly ever appear in correct answer choices. Choice **c** looks attractive until you think a little about what you know—aren't fewer people smoking these days, rather than more? So how could smoking be responsible for a higher mortality rate? (If you didn't know that *mortality rate* means the rate at which people die, you might keep this choice as a possibility, but you'd still be able to eliminate two answers and have only two to choose from.) Choice **d** is plain silly, so you could eliminate that one, too. You're left with the correct choice, **a**.

4. a. How you used the process of elimination here depends on which words you recognized as being spelled incorrectly. If you knew that the correct spellings were *outrageous, domesticated*, and *understandable*, then you were home free. You probably knew that at least one of those words was wrong.

▶ Step 6: Know When to Guess

Time to complete: 20 minutes
Activity: Complete worksheet on Your Guessing Ability

Armed with the process of elimination, you are ready to take control of one of the big questions in test-taking: Should I guess? The first and main answer is Yes. Some exams have what is called a "guessing penalty," in which a fraction of your wrong answers is subtracted from your right answers—but the ASVAB isn't one of them. The number of questions you answer correctly yields your raw score. So you have nothing to lose and everything to gain by guessing.

The more complicated answer to the question "Should I guess?" depends on you—your personality and your "guessing intuition." There are two things you need to know about yourself before you go into the exam:

- Are you a risk-taker?
- Are you a good guesser?

You will have to decide about your risk-taking quotient on your own. To find out if you're a good guesser, complete the worksheet "Your Guessing Ability" that begins on this page. Frankly, even if you're a play-it-safe person with lousy intuition, you are still safe in guessing every time. The best thing would be if you could overcome your anxieties and go ahead and mark an answer. But you may want to have a sense of how good your intuition is before you go into the exam.

Your Guessing Ability

The following are ten really hard questions. You are not supposed to know the answers. Rather, this is an assessment of your ability to guess when you don't have a clue. Read each question carefully, just as if you did expect to answer it. If you have any knowledge at all about the subject of the question, use that knowledge to help you eliminate wrong answer choices.

ANSWER GRID

1. (a) (b) (c) (d)
2. (a) (b) (c) (d)
3. (a) (b) (c) (d)
4. (a) (b) (c) (d)

5. (a) (b) (c) (d)
6. (a) (b) (c) (d)
7. (a) (b) (c) (d)
8. (a) (b) (c) (d)

9. (a) (b) (c) (d)
10. (a) (b) (c) (d)

1. September 7 is Independence Day in
   a. India.
   b. Costa Rica.
   c. Brazil.
   d. Australia.

2. Which of the following is the formula for determining the momentum of an object?
   a. $p = mv$
   b. $F = ma$
   c. $P = IV$
   d. $E = mc^2$

3. Because of the expansion of the universe, the stars and other celestial bodies are all moving away from each other. This phenomenon is known as
   a. Newton's first law.
   b. the big bang.
   c. gravitational collapse.
   d. Hubble flow.

4. American author Gertrude Stein was born in
   a. 1713.
   b. 1830.
   c. 1874.
   d. 1901.

5. Which of the following is NOT one of the Five Classics attributed to Confucius?
   a. the *I Ching*
   b. the *Book of Holiness*
   c. the *Spring and Autumn Annals*
   d. the *Book of History*

6. The religious and philosophical doctrine that holds that the universe is constantly in a struggle between good and evil is known as
   a. Pelagianism.
   b. Manichaeanism.
   c. neo-Hegelianism.
   d. Epicureanism.

7. The third Chief Justice of the U.S. Supreme Court was
   a. John Blair.
   b. William Cushing.
   c. James Wilson.
   d. John Jay.

8. Which of the following is the poisonous portion of a daffodil?
   a. the bulb
   b. the leaves
   c. the stem
   d. the flowers

9. The winner of the Masters golf tournament in 1953 was
   a. Sam Snead.
   b. Cary Middlecoff.
   c. Arnold Palmer.
   d. Ben Hogan.

10. The state with the highest per capita personal income in 1980 was
   a. Alaska.
   b. Connecticut.
   c. New York.
   d. Texas.

Answers

Check your answers against the correct answers below.

1. c.
2. a.
3. d.
4. c.
5. b.
6. b.
7. b.
8. a.
9. d.
10. a.

How Did You Do?

You may have simply gotten lucky and actually known the answer to one or two questions. In addition, your guessing was more successful if you were able to use the process of elimination on any of the questions. Maybe you didn't know who the third Chief Justice was (question 7), but you knew that John Jay was the first. In that case, you would have eliminated choice **d** and therefore improved your odds of guessing correctly from one in four to one in three.

According to probability, you should get $2\frac{1}{2}$ answers correct, so getting either two or three right would be average. If you got four or more right, you may be a really terrific guesser. If you got one or none right, you may be a really bad guesser.

Keep in mind, though, that this is only a small sample. You should continue to keep track of your guessing ability as you work through the sample questions in this book. Circle the numbers of questions you guess on as you make your guess; or, if you don't have time while you take the practice exams, go back afterward and try to remember which questions you guessed at. Remember, on an exam with four answer choices, your chances of getting a right answer is one in four. So keep a separate "guessing" score for each exam. How many questions did you guess on? How many did you get right? If the number you got right is at least one-fourth of the number of questions you guessed on, you are at least an average guesser, maybe better—and you should always go ahead and guess on a real exam. If the number you got right is significantly lower than one-fourth of the number you guessed on, you would, frankly, be safe in guessing anyway, but maybe you would feel more comfortable if you guessed only selectively, when you can eliminate a wrong answer or at least have a good feeling about one of the answer choices.

▶ Step 7: Reach Your Peak Performance Zone

Time to complete: 10 minutes to read; weeks to complete

Activity: Complete the Physical Preparation Checklist

To get ready for a challenge like a big exam, you have to take control of your physical, as well as your mental, state. Exercise, proper diet, and rest will ensure that your body works with, rather than against, your mind on test day, as well as during your preparation.

Exercise

If you don't already have a regular exercise program going, the time during which you are preparing for an exam is actually an excellent time to start one. You will have to be pretty fit to make it through the first weeks of Basic Training anyway. And if you're already keeping fit—or trying to get that way—don't let the pressure of preparing for an exam fool you into quitting now. Exercise helps reduce stress by pumping wonderful good-feeling hormones called endorphins into your system. It also increases the oxygen supply throughout your body, including your brain, so you will be at peak performance on test day.

A half hour of vigorous activity—enough to raise a sweat—every day should be your aim. If you are really pressed for time, every other day is OK. Choose an activity you like and get out there and do it. Jogging with a friend always makes the time go faster, or take a radio.

But don't overdo it. You don't want to exhaust yourself. Moderation is the key.

Diet

First of all, cut out the junk. Go easy on caffeine and nicotine, and eliminate alcohol and any other drugs from your system at least two weeks before the exam. Promise yourself a treat the night after the exam, if need be.

What your body needs for peak performance is simply a balanced diet. Eat plenty of fruits and vegetables, along with protein and carbohydrates. Foods that are high in lecithin (an amino acid), such as fish and beans, are especially good brain foods.

The night before the exam, you might "carbo-load" the way athletes do before a contest. Eat a big plate of spaghetti, rice and beans, or whatever your favorite carbohydrate is.

Rest

You probably know how much sleep you need every night to be at your best, even if you don't always get it. Make sure you do get that much sleep, though, for at least a week before the exam. Moderation is important here, too. Extra sleep will just make you groggy.

If you are not a morning person and your exam will be given in the morning, you should reset your internal clock so that your body doesn't think you're taking an exam at 3:00 A.M. You have to start this process well before the exam. The way it works is to get up half an hour earlier each morning, and then go to bed half an hour earlier that night. Don't try it the other way around: You will just toss and turn if you go to bed early without having gotten up early. The next morning, get up another half an hour earlier, and so on. How long you will have to do this depends on how late you're used to getting up. Use the Physical Preparation Checklist on page 43 to make sure you are in tip-top form.

▶ Step 8: Get Your Act Together

Time to complete: 10 minutes to read; time to complete will vary

Activity: Complete Final Preparations worksheet

You are in control of your mind and body; you are in charge of test anxiety, your preparation, and your test-taking strategies. Now it's time to take charge of external factors, like the testing site and the materials you need to take the exam.

Getting to the MEPS

You will be the guest of the Department of Defense in your trip to the Military Entrance Processing Station (MEPS). You will probably be scheduled to spend a full day at the MEPS, though if it's far from your hometown you may have to go the night before. Your recruiter will tell you when and where you will be picked up for your trip to the MEPS. Make sure you know how to get to that location, if it's not your recruiting station, and how long it will take to get there. Figure out how early you will have to get up that morning, and get up that early every day for a week before your MEPS day.

Physical Preparation Checklist

For the week before the test, write down 1) what physical exercise you engaged in and for how long and 2) what you ate for each meal. Remember, you're trying for at least half an hour of exercise every other day (preferably every day) and a balanced diet that's light on junk food.

Exam minus 7 days

Exercise: _____ for _____ minutes

Breakfast: _____

Lunch: _____

Dinner: _____

Snacks: _____

Exam minus 6 days

Exercise: _____ for _____ minutes

Breakfast: _____

Lunch: _____

Dinner: _____

Snacks: _____

Exam minus 5 days

Exercise: _____ for _____ minutes

Breakfast: _____

Lunch: _____

Dinner: _____

Snacks: _____

Exam minus 4 days

Exercise: _____ for _____ minutes

Breakfast: _____

Lunch: _____

Dinner: _____

Snacks: _____

Exam minus 3 days

Exercise: _____ for _____ minutes

Breakfast: _____

Lunch: _____

Dinner: _____

Snacks: _____

Exam minus 2 days

Exercise: _____ for _____ minutes

Breakfast: _____

Lunch: _____

Dinner: _____

Snacks: _____

Exam minus 1 day

Exercise: _____ for _____ minutes

Breakfast: _____

Lunch: _____

Dinner: _____

Snacks: _____

Gather Your Materials

The night before the exam, lay out the clothes you will wear and the materials you have to bring with you to the MEPS. Plan on dressing in layers; you won't have any control over the temperature of the examination room. Have a sweater or jacket you can take off if it's warm. Use the checklist on the Final Preparations worksheet on this page to help you pull together what you will need.

Don't Skip Breakfast

Even if you don't usually eat breakfast, do so on exam morning. A cup of coffee doesn't count. Don't do doughnuts or other sweet foods, either. A sugar high will leave you with a sugar low in the middle of the exam. A mix of protein and carbohydrates is best: cereal with milk and just a little sugar, or eggs with toast, will do your body a world of good.

▶ Step 9: Do It!

Time to complete: 10 minutes, plus test-taking time
Activity: Ace the ASVAB!

Fast forward to exam day. You are ready. You made a study plan and followed through. You practiced your test-taking strategies while working through this book. You are in control of your physical, mental, and emotional state. You know when and where to show up and what to bring with you. In other words, you are better prepared than most of the other people taking the ASVAB with you. You are psyched.

Just one more thing. When you're done with your day at the MEPS, you will have earned a reward. Plan a celebration. Call up your friends and plan a party, or have a nice dinner for two—whatever your heart desires. Give yourself something to look forward to.

And then do it. Take the ASVAB, full of confidence, armed with the test-taking strategies you have practiced until they are second nature. You are in control of yourself, your environment, and your performance on the exam. You are ready to succeed. So do it. Go in there and ace the exam. And look forward to your future military career!

Final Preparations

Getting to the MEPS Pickup Site

Location of pickup site: _____

Date: _____

Departure time: _____

Do I know how to get to the pickup site?   Yes ___   No ___
If no, make a trial run.

Time it will take to get to the pickup site: _____

Things to lay out the night before

Clothes I will wear   ___   Photo ID   ___

Sweater/jacket   ___   4 No. 2 pencils   ___

Watch   ___

CHAPTER

5 ▶ ASVAB Practice Test 1

CHAPTER SUMMARY

This is the first of three practice test batteries in this book based on the Armed Services Vocational Aptitude Battery (ASVAB). Use this test to see how you would do if you were to take the exam today.

The ASVAB consists of the following eight tests: General Science, Arithmetic Reasoning, Word Knowledge, Paragraph Comprehension, Auto and Shop Information, Mathematics Knowledge, Mechanical Comprehension, and Electronics Information. These eight tests are timed. The amount of time allowed for each test will be found at the beginning of that test.

The practice battery that follows consists of the above eight tests, for a total of 200 items. For now, do not worry too much about timing. Just take the tests in as relaxed a manner as you can. The answer sheet you should use for answering the questions is on pages 47–48. After you take the test, use the detailed answer explanations that follow to review any questions you missed.

▶ Part 1: General Science

1.	ⓐ	ⓑ	ⓒ	ⓓ	10.	ⓐ	ⓑ	ⓒ	ⓓ	19.	ⓐ	ⓑ	ⓒ	ⓓ
2.	ⓐ	ⓑ	ⓒ	ⓓ	11.	ⓐ	ⓑ	ⓒ	ⓓ	20.	ⓐ	ⓑ	ⓒ	ⓓ
3.	ⓐ	ⓑ	ⓒ	ⓓ	12.	ⓐ	ⓑ	ⓒ	ⓓ	21.	ⓐ	ⓑ	ⓒ	ⓓ
4.	ⓐ	ⓑ	ⓒ	ⓓ	13.	ⓐ	ⓑ	ⓒ	ⓓ	22.	ⓐ	ⓑ	ⓒ	ⓓ
5.	ⓐ	ⓑ	ⓒ	ⓓ	14.	ⓐ	ⓑ	ⓒ	ⓓ	23.	ⓐ	ⓑ	ⓒ	ⓓ
6.	ⓐ	ⓑ	ⓒ	ⓓ	15.	ⓐ	ⓑ	ⓒ	ⓓ	24.	ⓐ	ⓑ	ⓒ	ⓓ
7.	ⓐ	ⓑ	ⓒ	ⓓ	16.	ⓐ	ⓑ	ⓒ	ⓓ	25.	ⓐ	ⓑ	ⓒ	ⓓ
8.	ⓐ	ⓑ	ⓒ	ⓓ	17.	ⓐ	ⓑ	ⓒ	ⓓ					
9.	ⓐ	ⓑ	ⓒ	ⓓ	18.	ⓐ	ⓑ	ⓒ	ⓓ					

▶ Part 2: Arithmetic Reasoning

1.	ⓐ	ⓑ	ⓒ	ⓓ	11.	ⓐ	ⓑ	ⓒ	ⓓ	21.	ⓐ	ⓑ	ⓒ	ⓓ
2.	ⓐ	ⓑ	ⓒ	ⓓ	12.	ⓐ	ⓑ	ⓒ	ⓓ	22.	ⓐ	ⓑ	ⓒ	ⓓ
3.	ⓐ	ⓑ	ⓒ	ⓓ	13.	ⓐ	ⓑ	ⓒ	ⓓ	23.	ⓐ	ⓑ	ⓒ	ⓓ
4.	ⓐ	ⓑ	ⓒ	ⓓ	14.	ⓐ	ⓑ	ⓒ	ⓓ	24.	ⓐ	ⓑ	ⓒ	ⓓ
5.	ⓐ	ⓑ	ⓒ	ⓓ	15.	ⓐ	ⓑ	ⓒ	ⓓ	25.	ⓐ	ⓑ	ⓒ	ⓓ
6.	ⓐ	ⓑ	ⓒ	ⓓ	16.	ⓐ	ⓑ	ⓒ	ⓓ	26.	ⓐ	ⓑ	ⓒ	ⓓ
7.	ⓐ	ⓑ	ⓒ	ⓓ	17.	ⓐ	ⓑ	ⓒ	ⓓ	27.	ⓐ	ⓑ	ⓒ	ⓓ
8.	ⓐ	ⓑ	ⓒ	ⓓ	18.	ⓐ	ⓑ	ⓒ	ⓓ	28.	ⓐ	ⓑ	ⓒ	ⓓ
9.	ⓐ	ⓑ	ⓒ	ⓓ	19.	ⓐ	ⓑ	ⓒ	ⓓ	29.	ⓐ	ⓑ	ⓒ	ⓓ
10.	ⓐ	ⓑ	ⓒ	ⓓ	20.	ⓐ	ⓑ	ⓒ	ⓓ	30.	ⓐ	ⓑ	ⓒ	ⓓ

▶ Part 3: Word Knowledge

1.	ⓐ	ⓑ	ⓒ	ⓓ	10.	ⓐ	ⓑ	ⓒ	ⓓ	19.	ⓐ	ⓑ	ⓒ	ⓓ
2.	ⓐ	ⓑ	ⓒ	ⓓ	11.	ⓐ	ⓑ	ⓒ	ⓓ	20.	ⓐ	ⓑ	ⓒ	ⓓ
3.	ⓐ	ⓑ	ⓒ	ⓓ	12.	ⓐ	ⓑ	ⓒ	ⓓ	21.	ⓐ	ⓑ	ⓒ	ⓓ
4.	ⓐ	ⓑ	ⓒ	ⓓ	13.	ⓐ	ⓑ	ⓒ	ⓓ	22.	ⓐ	ⓑ	ⓒ	ⓓ
5.	ⓐ	ⓑ	ⓒ	ⓓ	14.	ⓐ	ⓑ	ⓒ	ⓓ	23.	ⓐ	ⓑ	ⓒ	ⓓ
6.	ⓐ	ⓑ	ⓒ	ⓓ	15.	ⓐ	ⓑ	ⓒ	ⓓ	24.	ⓐ	ⓑ	ⓒ	ⓓ
7.	ⓐ	ⓑ	ⓒ	ⓓ	16.	ⓐ	ⓑ	ⓒ	ⓓ	25.	ⓐ	ⓑ	ⓒ	ⓓ
8.	ⓐ	ⓑ	ⓒ	ⓓ	17.	ⓐ	ⓑ	ⓒ	ⓓ					
9.	ⓐ	ⓑ	ⓒ	ⓓ	18.	ⓐ	ⓑ	ⓒ	ⓓ					

▶ Part 4: Paragraph Comprehension

1.	ⓐ	ⓑ	ⓒ	ⓓ	6.	ⓐ	ⓑ	ⓒ	ⓓ	11.	ⓐ	ⓑ	ⓒ	ⓓ
2.	ⓐ	ⓑ	ⓒ	ⓓ	7.	ⓐ	ⓑ	ⓒ	ⓓ	12.	ⓐ	ⓑ	ⓒ	ⓓ
3.	ⓐ	ⓑ	ⓒ	ⓓ	8.	ⓐ	ⓑ	ⓒ	ⓓ	13.	ⓐ	ⓑ	ⓒ	ⓓ
4.	ⓐ	ⓑ	ⓒ	ⓓ	9.	ⓐ	ⓑ	ⓒ	ⓓ	14.	ⓐ	ⓑ	ⓒ	ⓓ
5.	ⓐ	ⓑ	ⓒ	ⓓ	10.	ⓐ	ⓑ	ⓒ	ⓓ	15.	ⓐ	ⓑ	ⓒ	ⓓ

▶ Part 5: Auto and Shop Information

1.	ⓐ	ⓑ	ⓒ	ⓓ
2.	ⓐ	ⓑ	ⓒ	ⓓ
3.	ⓐ	ⓑ	ⓒ	ⓓ
4.	ⓐ	ⓑ	ⓒ	ⓓ
5.	ⓐ	ⓑ	ⓒ	ⓓ
6.	ⓐ	ⓑ	ⓒ	ⓓ
7.	ⓐ	ⓑ	ⓒ	ⓓ
8.	ⓐ	ⓑ	ⓒ	ⓓ
9.	ⓐ	ⓑ	ⓒ	ⓓ

10.	ⓐ	ⓑ	ⓒ	ⓓ
11.	ⓐ	ⓑ	ⓒ	ⓓ
12.	ⓐ	ⓑ	ⓒ	ⓓ
13.	ⓐ	ⓑ	ⓒ	ⓓ
14.	ⓐ	ⓑ	ⓒ	ⓓ
15.	ⓐ	ⓑ	ⓒ	ⓓ
16.	ⓐ	ⓑ	ⓒ	ⓓ
17.	ⓐ	ⓑ	ⓒ	ⓓ
18.	ⓐ	ⓑ	ⓒ	ⓓ

19.	ⓐ	ⓑ	ⓒ	ⓓ
20.	ⓐ	ⓑ	ⓒ	ⓓ
21.	ⓐ	ⓑ	ⓒ	ⓓ
22.	ⓐ	ⓑ	ⓒ	ⓓ
23.	ⓐ	ⓑ	ⓒ	ⓓ
24.	ⓐ	ⓑ	ⓒ	ⓓ
25.	ⓐ	ⓑ	ⓒ	ⓓ

▶ Part 6: Mathematics Knowledge

1.	ⓐ	ⓑ	ⓒ	ⓓ
2.	ⓐ	ⓑ	ⓒ	ⓓ
3.	ⓐ	ⓑ	ⓒ	ⓓ
4.	ⓐ	ⓑ	ⓒ	ⓓ
5.	ⓐ	ⓑ	ⓒ	ⓓ
6.	ⓐ	ⓑ	ⓒ	ⓓ
7.	ⓐ	ⓑ	ⓒ	ⓓ
8.	ⓐ	ⓑ	ⓒ	ⓓ
9.	ⓐ	ⓑ	ⓒ	ⓓ
10.	ⓐ	ⓑ	ⓒ	ⓓ
11.	ⓐ	ⓑ	ⓒ	ⓓ
12.	ⓐ	ⓑ	ⓒ	ⓓ

13.	ⓐ	ⓑ	ⓒ	ⓓ
14.	ⓐ	ⓑ	ⓒ	ⓓ
15.	ⓐ	ⓑ	ⓒ	ⓓ
16.	ⓐ	ⓑ	ⓒ	ⓓ
17.	ⓐ	ⓑ	ⓒ	ⓓ
18.	ⓐ	ⓑ	ⓒ	ⓓ
19.	ⓐ	ⓑ	ⓒ	ⓓ
20.	ⓐ	ⓑ	ⓒ	ⓓ
21.	ⓐ	ⓑ	ⓒ	ⓓ
22.	ⓐ	ⓑ	ⓒ	ⓓ
23.	ⓐ	ⓑ	ⓒ	ⓓ
24.	ⓐ	ⓑ	ⓒ	ⓓ

25.	ⓐ	ⓑ	ⓒ	ⓓ
26.	ⓐ	ⓑ	ⓒ	ⓓ
27.	ⓐ	ⓑ	ⓒ	ⓓ
28.	ⓐ	ⓑ	ⓒ	ⓓ
29.	ⓐ	ⓑ	ⓒ	ⓓ
30.	ⓐ	ⓑ	ⓒ	ⓓ
31.	ⓐ	ⓑ	ⓒ	ⓓ
32.	ⓐ	ⓑ	ⓒ	ⓓ
33.	ⓐ	ⓑ	ⓒ	ⓓ
34.	ⓐ	ⓑ	ⓒ	ⓓ
35.	ⓐ	ⓑ	ⓒ	ⓓ

▶ Part 7: Mechanical Comprehension

1.	ⓐ	ⓑ	ⓒ	ⓓ
2.	ⓐ	ⓑ	ⓒ	ⓓ
3.	ⓐ	ⓑ	ⓒ	ⓓ
4.	ⓐ	ⓑ	ⓒ	ⓓ
5.	ⓐ	ⓑ	ⓒ	ⓓ
6.	ⓐ	ⓑ	ⓒ	ⓓ
7.	ⓐ	ⓑ	ⓒ	ⓓ
8.	ⓐ	ⓑ	ⓒ	ⓓ
9.	ⓐ	ⓑ	ⓒ	ⓓ

10.	ⓐ	ⓑ	ⓒ	ⓓ
11.	ⓐ	ⓑ	ⓒ	ⓓ
12.	ⓐ	ⓑ	ⓒ	ⓓ
13.	ⓐ	ⓑ	ⓒ	ⓓ
14.	ⓐ	ⓑ	ⓒ	ⓓ
15.	ⓐ	ⓑ	ⓒ	ⓓ
16.	ⓐ	ⓑ	ⓒ	ⓓ
17.	ⓐ	ⓑ	ⓒ	ⓓ
18.	ⓐ	ⓑ	ⓒ	ⓓ

19.	ⓐ	ⓑ	ⓒ	ⓓ
20.	ⓐ	ⓑ	ⓒ	ⓓ
21.	ⓐ	ⓑ	ⓒ	ⓓ
22.	ⓐ	ⓑ	ⓒ	ⓓ
23.	ⓐ	ⓑ	ⓒ	ⓓ
24.	ⓐ	ⓑ	ⓒ	ⓓ
25.	ⓐ	ⓑ	ⓒ	ⓓ

▶ Part 8: Electronics Information

1.	ⓐ	ⓑ	ⓒ	ⓓ
2.	ⓐ	ⓑ	ⓒ	ⓓ
3.	ⓐ	ⓑ	ⓒ	ⓓ
4.	ⓐ	ⓑ	ⓒ	ⓓ
5.	ⓐ	ⓑ	ⓒ	ⓓ
6.	ⓐ	ⓑ	ⓒ	ⓓ
7.	ⓐ	ⓑ	ⓒ	ⓓ

8.	ⓐ	ⓑ	ⓒ	ⓓ
9.	ⓐ	ⓑ	ⓒ	ⓓ
10.	ⓐ	ⓑ	ⓒ	ⓓ
11.	ⓐ	ⓑ	ⓒ	ⓓ
12.	ⓐ	ⓑ	ⓒ	ⓓ
13.	ⓐ	ⓑ	ⓒ	ⓓ
14.	ⓐ	ⓑ	ⓒ	ⓓ

15.	ⓐ	ⓑ	ⓒ	ⓓ
16.	ⓐ	ⓑ	ⓒ	ⓓ
17.	ⓐ	ⓑ	ⓒ	ⓓ
18.	ⓐ	ⓑ	ⓒ	ⓓ
19.	ⓐ	ⓑ	ⓒ	ⓓ
20.	ⓐ	ⓑ	ⓒ	ⓓ

▶ Part 1: General Science

Time: 11 minutes

1. An element's location on the periodic table is determined by its number of
   a. electrons.
   b. neutrons.
   c. protons.
   d. nuclei.

2. What are atoms of the same element that have different numbers of neutrons called?
   a. alloys
   b. isotopes
   c. alkali metals
   d. ions

3. Which of the following units does NOT express volume?
   a. cc
   b. dm^3
   c. L
   d. mm

4. Which of the following symbols represents a molecule of carbon dioxide?
   a. C
   b. O
   c. CO
   d. CO_2

5. The driver of a car you are riding in loses control in a snowstorm. The car spins 360 degrees and you are thrown against the car door. Which of the following is the best description of what you are experiencing?
   a. fundamental forces
   b. center of mass
   c. centrifugal force
   d. Coriolis effect

6. If particles of food coloring are dropped into a glass of hot water, they will spread rapidly. This is an example of
   a. osmosis.
   b. diffusion.
   c. evaporation.
   d. active transport.

7. Which of the following represents a chemical change?
   a. tearing a piece of paper
   b. melting an ice cube
   c. cooking a hamburger
   d. dissolving sugar in water

8. Carbohydrates are much better foods for quick energy than fats because they
   a. are digested more easily and absorbed more quickly.
   b. supply essential amino acids, which provide energy.
   c. are high in both protein and iron.
   d. carry oxygen to the blood.

9. The function of a leukocyte, or white blood cell, is to
   a. carry oxygen to the blood.
   b. produce hemoglobin.
   c. protect the body against infection.
   d. help in the clotting of blood.

10. All of the following are characteristics of reptiles EXCEPT
    a. internal development of eggs.
    b. eggs laid on land.
    c. land-dwelling adults.
    d. scaly skin.

11. Which of the following is a vertebrate?
   a. a sponge
   b. a starfish
   c. an octopus
   d. a snake

12. The process by which an organism adapts physiologically to the rigors of a new environment is known as
   a. natural selection.
   b. acclimatization.
   c. evolution.
   d. mutation.

13. Which of the following is the best description of what an omnivore eats?
   a. animal matter only
   b. vegetable matter only
   c. detritus only
   d. both animal and vegetable matter

14. Which of the following has the shortest wavelength?
   a. ultraviolet
   b. X rays
   c. microwave
   d. infrared

15. The fundamental force that is the natural force of attraction acting between objects with mass is which of the following?
   a. electromagnetism
   b. strong nuclear force
   c. weak nuclear force
   d. gravity

16. Where is most of the mass of our solar system?
   a. Sun
   b. Earth
   c. Venus
   d. Jupiter

17. Absolute zero is equal to which of the following?
   a. 0 degrees Fahrenheit
   b. 30 degrees Fahrenheit
   c. 30 degrees Kelvin
   d. –273 degrees Celsius

18. Our Solar System is made up of the Sun and how many planets?
   a. eight
   b. nine
   c. ten
   d. eleven

19. A cell containing chloroplasts would most likely belong to which organism?
   a. rabbit
   b. fern
   c. roach
   d. lizard

20. In animal cells, what organelle contains the DNA?
   a. nucleus
   b. cytoplasm
   c. Golgi apparatus
   d. ribosomes

21. How many chromosomes do normal human sex cells have?
   a. 8
   b. 16
   c. 23
   d. 46

22. In humans, what is the largest bone in the pectoral region?
   a. the scapula
   b. the femur
   c. the ulna
   d. the humerus

23. In vertebrates, which of the following is not controlled by the autonomic nervous system?
   a. speech
   b. salivation
   c. digestion
   d. heart rate

24. What element does the symbol K on the periodic table of the elements represent?
   a. potassium
   b. krypton
   c. calcium
   d. chromium

25. What is the symbol for ozone?
   a. O
   b. O_2
   c. O_3
   d. CO_2

▶ Part 2: Arithmetic Reasoning

Time: 36 minutes

1. It costs $0.75 each to make color copies at a copy center. At this price, how many copies can be purchased with $60.00?
   a. 8
   b. 45
   c. 80
   d. 75

2. An aquarium has a base length of 12 inches and a width of 5 inches. If the aquarium is 10 inches tall, what is the total volume?
   a. 480 cubic inches
   b. 540 cubic inches
   c. 600 cubic inches
   d. 720 cubic inches

3. A man turns in a woman's handbag to the Lost and Found Department of a large downtown store. The man informs the clerk in charge that he found the handbag on the floor beside an entranceway. The clerk estimates that the handbag is worth approximately $150. Inside, the clerk finds the following items:
   - 1 leather makeup case valued at $65
   - 1 vial of perfume, unopened, valued at $75
   - 1 pair of earrings valued at $150
   - cash $178

The clerk is writing a report to be submitted along with the found property. What should he write as the total value of the found cash and property?
   a. $468
   b. $608
   c. $618
   d. $718

Use the following information to answer questions 4–6.

The cost of movie theater tickets is $7.50 for adults and $5 for children ages 12 and under. On Saturday and Sunday afternoons until 4:00 P.M., there is a matinee price: $5.50 for adults and $3 for children ages 12 and under. Special group discounts are available for groups of 30 or more people.

4. Which of these can be determined from the information given in the above passage?
   a. how much it will cost a family of four to buy movie theater tickets on Saturday afternoon
   b. the difference between the cost of two movie theater tickets on Tuesday night and the cost of one ticket on Sunday at 3:00 P.M.
   c. how much movie theater tickets will cost each person if he or she is part of a group of 40 people
   d. the difference between the cost of a movie theater ticket for an adult on Friday night and a movie theater ticket for a 13-year-old on Saturday afternoon at 1:00 P.M.

5. Based on the passage, how much will movie theater tickets cost for two adults, one 15-year-old child and one 10-year-old child at 7:00 P.M. on a Sunday night?
   a. $17.00
   b. $19.50
   c. $25.00
   d. $27.50

6. Using the passage, how can you find the difference in price between a movie theater ticket for an adult and a movie theater ticket for a child under the age of 12 if the tickets are for a show at 3:00 P.M. on a Saturday afternoon?
   a. subtract $3.00 from $5.50
   b. subtract $5.00 from $7.50
   c. subtract $7.50 from $5.50
   d. add $5.50 and $3.00 and divide by 2

7. It takes a typist 0.75 seconds to type one word. At this rate, how many words can be typed in 60 seconds?
   a. 4.5
   b. 8
   c. 45
   d. 80

8. If the average woman burns 8.2 calories per minute while riding a bicycle, how many calories will she burn if she rides for 35 minutes?
   a. 286
   b. 287
   c. 387
   d. 980

9. Dr. Drake charges $36.00 for an office visit, which is $\frac{3}{4}$ of what Dr. Jean charges. How much does Dr. Jean charge?
   a. $48.00
   b. $27.00
   c. $38.00
   d. $57.00

10. Thirty percent of the students at a middle school are involved in the vocal and instrumental music programs. If 15% of the musicians are in the choir, what percentage of the whole school is in the choir?
   a. 4.5%
   b. 9.0%
   c. 15%
   d. 30%

Use the information below to answer questions 11 and 12.

Basic cable television service, which includes 16 channels, costs $15 a month. The initial labor fee to install the service is $25. A $65 deposit is required but will be refunded within two years if the customer's bills are paid in full. Other cable services may be added to the basic service: the movie channel service is $9.40 a month; the news channels are $7.50 a month; the arts channels are $5.00 a month; the sports channels are $4.80 a month.

11. A customer's cable television bill totaled $20 a month. Using the passage above, what portion of the bill was for basic cable service?
   a. 25%
   b. 33%
   c. 50%
   d. 75%

12. A customer's first bill after having cable television installed totaled $112.50. This customer chose basic cable and one additional cable service. Which additional service was chosen?
   a. the news channels
   b. the movie channels
   c. the arts channels
   d. the sports channels

13. Out of 100 shoppers polled, 80 said they buy fresh fruit every week. How many shoppers out of 30,000 could be expected to buy fresh fruit every week?
   a. 2,400
   b. 6,000
   c. 22,000
   d. 24,000

Compact Discs Sold

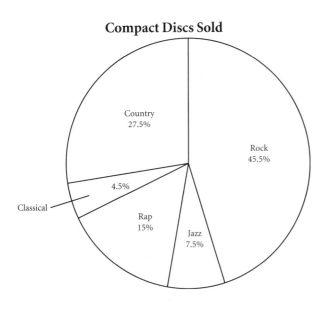

14. If 400 compact discs were sold altogether, how many of the compact discs sold were country music?
   a. 11
   b. 28
   c. 55
   d. 110

15. Based on the graph, which types of music represent exactly half of the compact discs sold?
   a. rock and jazz
   b. classical and rock
   c. rap, classical, and country
   d. jazz, classical, and rap

16. Last year, 220 people bought cars from a certain dealer. Of those, 60 percent reported that they were completely satisfied with their new cars. How many people reported being unsatisfied with their new car?
   a. 36
   b. 55
   c. 88
   d. 132

17. Of 1,125 university students, 135 speak fluent Spanish. What percentage of the student body speaks fluent Spanish?
   a. 7.3%
   b. 8.3%
   c. 12%
   d. 14%

18. The perimeter of a rectangle is 148 feet. Its two longest sides add up to 86 feet. What is the length of each of its two shortest sides?
   a. 31 feet
   b. 42 feet
   c. 62 feet
   d. 74 feet

19. A piece of ribbon 3 feet 4 inches long was divided in 5 equal parts. How long was each part?
   a. 1 foot 2 inches
   b. 10 inches
   c. 8 inches
   d. 6 inches

20. A middle school cafeteria has three different options for lunch.

For $2, a student can get either a sandwich or two cookies.

For $3, a student can get a sandwich and one cookie.

For $4, a student can get either two sandwiches, or a sandwich and two cookies.

If Jimae has $6 to pay for lunch for her and her brother, which of the following is not a possible combination?

a. three sandwiches and one cookie
b. two sandwiches and two cookies
c. one sandwich and four cookies
d. three sandwiches and no cookies

21. A bed is 5 feet wide and 7 feet long. What is the area of the bed?

a. 12 square feet
b. 22 square feet
c. 24 square feet
d. 35 square feet

22. Mr. Beard's temperature is 98 degrees Fahrenheit. What is his temperature in degrees Celsius? $C = \frac{5}{9}(F - 32)$

a. 35.8
b. 36.7
c. 37.6
d. 31.1

23. All of the rooms on the main floor of an office building are rectangular, with 8-foot high ceilings. Keira's office is 9 feet wide by 11 feet long. What is the combined surface area of the four walls of her office, including any windows and doors?

a. 99 square feet
b. 160 square feet
c. 320 square feet
d. 792 square feet

24. A recipe serves four people and calls for $1\frac{1}{2}$ cups of broth. If you want to serve six people, how much broth do you need?

a. 2 cups
b. $2\frac{1}{4}$ cups
c. $2\frac{1}{3}$ cups
d. $2\frac{1}{2}$ cups

25. Plattville is 80 miles west and 60 miles north of Quincy. How long is a direct route from Plattville to Quincy?

a. 100 miles
b. 120 miles
c. 140 miles
d. 160 miles

26. A builder has 27 cubic feet of concrete to pave a sidewalk whose length is 6 times its width. The concrete must be poured 6 inches deep. How long is the sidewalk?

a. 9 feet
b. 12 feet
c. 15 feet
d. 18 feet

27. Which of the following brands is the least expensive?

Brand	W	X	Y	Z
Price	0.21	0.48	0.56	0.96
Weight in ounces	6	15	20	32

a. W
b. X
c. Y
d. Z

28. A salesman drives 2,052 miles in 6 days, stopping at 2 towns each day. How many miles does he average between stops?
a. 171
b. 342
c. 684
d. 1,026

29. A cook spends $540 on silverware. If a place setting includes 1 knife, 1 fork, and 2 spoons, and if knives cost twice as much as forks or spoons, how many place settings did the cook buy?
a. 90
b. 108
c. 135
d. 180

30. An office uses 2 dozen pencils and $3\frac{1}{2}$ reams of paper each week. If pencils cost 5 cents each and a ream of paper costs $7.50, how much does it cost to supply the office for a week?
a. $7.55
b. $12.20
c. $27.45
d. $38.25

▶ Part 3: Word Knowledge

Time: 11 minutes

1. Mediate most nearly means
a. ponder.
b. interfere.
c. reconcile.
d. dissolve.

2. The attorney wanted to expedite the process.
a. accelerate
b. evaluate
c. reverse
d. justify

3. The student gave a plausible explanation for his lateness so it was excused by the teacher.
a. unbelievable
b. credible
c. insufficient
d. apologetic

4. Concurrent most nearly means
a. incidental.
b. simultaneous.
c. apprehensive.
d. substantial.

5. Impromptu most nearly means
a. tactless.
b. passive.
c. rehearsed.
d. spontaneous.

6. Induce most nearly means
a. prompt.
b. withdraw.
c. presume.
d. represent.

7. He based his conclusion on what he inferred from the evidence, not on what he actually observed.
a. intuited
b. imagined
c. surmised
d. implied

8. Saturate most nearly means
a. deprive.
b. construe.
c. soak.
d. verify.

9. <u>Synopsis</u> most nearly means
  a. summary.
  b. abundance.
  c. stereotype.
  d. verify.

10. <u>Hyperbole</u> most nearly means
  a. sincerity.
  b. exaggeration.
  c. understatement.
  d. indignation.

11. <u>Proscribe</u> most nearly means
  a. measure.
  b. recommend.
  c. detect.
  d. forbid.

12. <u>Proponent</u> most nearly means
  a. advocate.
  b. delinquent.
  c. idealist.
  d. critic.

13. <u>Intrepid</u> most nearly means
  a. belligerent.
  b. consistent.
  c. timid.
  d. fearless.

14. <u>Statute</u> most nearly means
  a. replica.
  b. ordinance.
  c. collection.
  d. hypothesis.

15. The general public was <u>apathetic</u> about the verdict.
  a. enraged
  b. indifferent
  c. suspicious
  d. saddened

16. The theories of some astronomers were <u>fortified</u> by the new research.
  a. reinforced
  b. altered
  c. disputed
  d. developed

17. <u>Refrain</u> most nearly means
  a. desist.
  b. secure.
  c. glimpse.
  d. persevere.

18. One of the duties of a captain is to <u>delegate</u> responsibility.
  a. analyze
  b. respect
  c. criticize
  d. assign

19. <u>Spurious</u> most nearly means
  a. prevalent.
  b. false.
  c. melancholy.
  d. actual.

20. The spokesperson must <u>articulate</u> the philosophy of an entire department.
  a. trust
  b. refine
  c. verify
  d. express

21. <u>Disparage</u> most nearly means
  a. endorse.
  b. finalize.
  c. restrict.
  d. criticize.

22. The hospital was an <u>expansive</u> facility.
  a. obsolete
  b. meager
  c. spacious
  d. costly

23. <u>Urbane</u> most nearly means
  a. foolish.
  b. vulgar.
  c. sophisticated.
  d. sentimental.

24. <u>Rationale</u> most nearly means
  a. explanation.
  b. regret.
  c. denial.
  d. anticipation.

25. The ruling proved to be <u>detrimental</u> to the investigation.
  a. decisive
  b. harmful
  c. worthless
  d. advantageous

▶ Part 4: Paragraph Comprehension

Time: 13 minutes

Hearsay evidence, which is the secondhand reporting of a statement, is allowed in court only when the truth of the statement is irrelevant. Hearsay that depends on the statement's truthfulness is inadmissible because the witness does not appear in court and swear an oath to tell the truth. Because his or her demeanor when making the statement is not visible to the jury, the accuracy of the statement cannot be tested under cross-examination, and to introduce it would be to deprive the accused of the constitutional right to confront the accuser. Hearsay is admissible, however, when the truth of the statement is unimportant. If, for example, a defendant claims to have been unconscious at a certain time, and a witness claims that the defendant actually spoke to her at that time, this evidence would be admissible because the truth of what the defendant actually said is irrelevant.

1. The main purpose of the passage is to
  a. explain why hearsay evidence abridges the rights of the accused.
  b. question the probable truthfulness of hearsay evidence.
  c. argue that rules about the admissibility of hearsay evidence should be changed.
  d. specify which use of hearsay evidence is inadmissible and why.

2. Which of the following is NOT a reason given in the passage for the inadmissibility of hearsay evidence?
  a. Rumors are not necessarily credible.
  b. The person making the original statement was not under oath.
  c. The jury should be able to watch the gestures and facial expressions of the person making the statement.
  d. The person making the statement cannot be cross-examined.

3. How does the passage explain the proper use of hearsay evidence?
  a. by listing a set of criteria
  b. by providing a hypothetical example
  c. by referring to the Constitution
  d. by citing case law

4. The passage suggests that the criterion used for deciding that most hearsay evidence is inadmissible was most likely
   a. the unreliability of most hearsay witnesses.
   b. the importance of physical evidence to corroborate witness testimony.
   c. concern for discerning the truth in a fair manner.
   d. doubt about the relevance of hearsay testimony.

During the next ten months, all bus operators with two or more years of service will be required to have completed twenty hours of refresher training on one of the Vehicle Maneuvering Training Buses.

   Instructors who have used this new technology report that trainees develop skills more quickly than with traditional training methods. In refresher training, this new system reinforces defensive driving skills and safe driving habits. Drivers can also check their reaction times and hand-eye coordination.

5. All bus operators are required to do which of the following?
   a. receive training in defensive driving and operating a computer
   b. complete ten months of refresher driver training
   c. train new drivers on how to operate a simulator
   d. complete twenty hours of training on a simulator

6. The main purpose of the refresher training course on the simulator is to
   a. make sure that all bus operators are maintaining proper driving habits.
   b. give experienced bus operators an opportunity to learn new driving techniques.
   c. help all bus operators to develop hand-eye coordination.
   d. reduce the city's operating budget.

The city has distributed standardized recycling containers to all households with directions that read: "We would prefer that you use this new container as your primary recycling container. Additional recycling containers may be purchased from the city."

7. According to the directions, each household
   a. may only use one recycling container.
   b. must use the new recycling container.
   c. should use the new recycling container.
   d. must buy a new recycling container.

8. According to the directions, which of the following is true about the new containers?
   a. The new containers are better than other containers.
   b. Households may use only the new containers for recyclable items.
   c. The new containers hold more than the old containers did.
   d. Households may use other containers besides the new ones if they wish.

After a snow or ice fall, the city streets are treated with ordinary rock salt. In some areas, the salt is combined with calcium chloride, which is more effective in below-zero temperatures and which melts ice better. This combination of salt and calcium chloride is also less damaging to foliage along the roadways.

9. In deciding whether to use ordinary rock salt or the salt and calcium chloride on a particular street, which of the following is NOT a consideration?
   a. the temperature at the time of treatment
   b. the plants and trees along the street
   c. whether there is ice on the street
   d. whether the street is a main or secondary road

10. According to the snow treatment directions, which of the following is true?
   a. If the temperature is below zero, salt and calcium chloride is effective in treating snow- and ice-covered streets.
   b. Crews must wait until the snow or ice stops falling before salting streets.
   c. The city always salts major roads first.
   d. If the snowfall is light, the city will not salt the streets as this would be a waste of the salt supply.

On February 3, 1956, Autherine Lucy became the first African-American student to attend the University of Alabama, although the dean of women refused to allow Autherine to live in a university dormitory. White students rioted in protest of her admission, and the federal government had to assume command of the Alabama National Guard in order to protect her. Nonetheless, on her first day in class, Autherine bravely took a seat in the front row. She remembers being surprised that the professor of the class appeared not to notice she was even in class. Later she would appreciate his seeming indifference, as he was one of only a few professors to speak out in favor of her right to attend the university.

11. This passage is most likely from a book called
   a. *20th Century United States History.*
   b. *A Collection of Favorite Children's Stories.*
   c. *A History of the Civil War.*
   d. *How to Choose the College That Is Right for You.*

12. According to the passage, Autherine Lucy
   a. lived in a dormitory.
   b. sat in the front row of her class.
   c. became a lawyer.
   d. majored in history.

Detectives who routinely investigate violent crimes can't help but become somewhat jaded. Paradoxically, the victims and witnesses with whom they work closely are often in a highly vulnerable and emotional state. The emotional fallout from a sexual assault, for example, can be complex and long-lasting. Detectives must be trained to handle people in emotional distress and must be sensitive to the fact that for the victim the crime is not routine. At the same time, detectives must recognize the limits of their role and resist the temptation to act as therapists or social workers, instead referring victims to the proper agencies.

13. What is the main idea of the passage?
   a. Detectives who investigate violent crime must not become emotionally hardened by the experience.
   b. Victims of violent crime should be referred to therapists and social workers.
   c. Detectives should be sensitive to the emotional state of victims of violent crime.
   d. Detectives should be particularly careful in dealing with victims of sexual assault.

14. According to the passage, what is "paradoxical" about the detective's relationship to the victim?
   a. Detectives know less about the experience of violent crime than do victims.
   b. What for the detective is routine is a unique and profound experience for the victim.
   c. Detectives must be sensitive to victims' needs but can't be social workers or psychologists.
   d. Not only must detectives solve crimes, but they must also handle the victims with care.

15. Which of the following is NOT advocated by the passage for detectives who investigate violent crimes?

    a. They should refer victims to appropriate support services.

    b. They should be aware of the psychological consequences of being victimized.

    c. They should not become jaded.

    d. They should not become too personally involved with victims' problems.

▶ Part 5: Auto and Shop Information

Time: 11 minutes

1. The purpose of a camshaft in an internal combustion engine is to

    a. provide ignition of the fuel.

    b. provide cooling of the engine.

    c. provide lubrication of the engine.

    d. transfer energy to the drive train.

2. Vernier calipers are used to perform which of the following functions?

    a. tightening

    b. measuring

    c. cutting

    d. drilling

3. Which of the following items is used to gain a mechanical advantage?

    a. a lever

    b. a protractor

    c. a spring

    d. a gear

4. Which of the following wrenches is adjustable?

    a. a crescent wrench

    b. a pipe wrench

    c. channel locks

    d. all of the above

5. What type of gauge would be read in units of mph (miles per hour)?

    a. a speed gauge

    b. a depth gauge

    c. a pressure gauge

    d. a temperature gauge

6. The main purpose of a muffler on a car is to

    a. cool the engine.

    b. conserve fuel.

    c. reduce engine noise.

    d. increase horsepower.

7. Which of the following mechanical devices is typically found on an automobile?

    a. an electric router

    b. a hinge

    c. a skimmer float

    d. a drill

8. Of the definitions below, which one best describes "preventative maintenance"?

    a. fixing a device after it fails for the first time

    b. periodically making small adjustments to a device to prevent failure

    c. purchasing a new device in anticipation of the old one's wearing out

    d. purchasing a new device after an old one wears out

9. Which tool listed below is the best for cutting metal?
a. a handsaw
b. a circular saw
c. a hacksaw
d. a back saw

10. Which of the following is the type of gauge shown above? (Note: GPM = gallons per minute.)
a. pressure gauge
b. altitude gauge
c. temperature gauge
d. flow meter gauge

11. Gears are used in which of the following automotive systems?
a. the cooling system
b. the suspension system
c. the exhaust system
d. the transmission system

12. In the United States, most speedometers on automobiles have two different scales: mph, which stands for miles per hour, and kph, which stands for
a. kilometers per mile.
b. kilometers per hour.
c. kilograms per hour.
d. kilobytes per hour.

13. The tool shown above would most likely be used to
a. drive nails.
b. weld metal.
c. tighten bolts.
d. carve wood.

14. Which of the following items is typically part of the suspension of a car?
a. the carburetor
b. the wheels
c. the rods
d. the pistons

15. "Stilson," "strap," "torque," and "spanner" all denote types of
a. saws.
b. hammers.
c. pliers.
d. wrenches.

16. The hand tool shown above is a(n)
a. crescent wrench.
b. offset wrench.
c. box wrench.
d. socket wrench.

17. Which of the following portions of a building must be constructed before all the others listed?
   a. flooring
   b. framing
   c. foundation
   d. walls

18. Which of the following building materials may be used for structural purposes?
   a. wood
   b. plasterboard
   c. glass
   d. fiberglass insulation

19. Which construction procedure listed below is most likely to require the use of a saw for cutting wood?
   a. building a foundation for a bridge
   b. building a wall for an apartment building
   c. building a deck for a house
   d. all of the above

20. What is the name of the building procedure that is used to pinpoint the exact location of a corner of a building or the exact elevation of a bridge deck?
   a. forming
   b. surveying
   c. masonry
   d. all of the above

21. The sub-flooring of a typical residential house in the United States is normally made of which of the following materials?
   a. plastic
   b. wood
   c. fiberglass
   d. resin

22. Which of the following are types of screwdrivers?
   a. Phillips
   b. Allen
   c. socket
   d. all of the above

23. Which automotive system uses the following components: water pump, radiator, and thermostat?
   a. the interior heating system
   b. the engine cooling system
   c. the exhaust system
   d. the braking system

24. Which of the following refers to a kind of chisel?
   a. diamond point
   b. dovetail
   c. coping
   d. duck bill

25. If your car will not start due to a dead battery, which of the following measures should be taken to get the car started?
   a. install a new starter
   b. check the fuel level
   c. use jumper cables
   d. replace all of the fuses

▶ Part 6: Mathematics Knowledge

Time: 24 minutes

1. In the figure below, angle *POS* measures 90 degrees. What is the measure of angle *ROQ*?

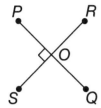

   a. 45 degrees
   b. 90 degrees
   c. 180 degrees
   d. 270 degrees

2. $4\frac{1}{5} + 1\frac{2}{5} + 3\frac{3}{10} =$
   a. $8\frac{9}{10}$
   b. $9\frac{1}{10}$
   c. $8\frac{4}{5}$
   d. $8\frac{6}{15}$

3. $\frac{3}{4}$ is equal to
   a. 0.50
   b. 0.25
   c. 0.75
   d. 0.30

4. $76\frac{1}{2} + 11\frac{5}{6} =$
   a. $87\frac{1}{2}$
   b. $88\frac{1}{3}$
   c. $88\frac{2}{3}$
   d. $88\frac{5}{6}$

5. What is the decimal equivalent of $\frac{1}{3}$, rounded to the nearest hundredth?
   a. 0.13
   b. 0.33
   c. 0.50
   d. 0.67

6. $\frac{1}{6} + \frac{7}{12} + \frac{2}{3} =$
   a. $\frac{10}{24}$
   b. $2\frac{1}{6}$
   c. $1\frac{5}{6}$
   d. $1\frac{5}{12}$

7. What is another name for 20,706?
   a. $200 + 70 + 6$
   b. $2,000 + 700 + 6$
   c. $20,000 + 70 + 6$
   d. $20,000 + 700 + 6$

8. What are the missing integers on this number line?

   a. −4 and 1
   b. −6 and 1
   c. −6 and −1
   d. 4 and 9

9. $1\frac{1}{2}$ is equal to
   a. 0.50
   b. 1.25
   c. 2.50
   d. 1.50

10. If $\frac{x}{54} = \frac{2}{9}$, then x is
   a. 12
   b. 14
   c. 18
   d. 108

11. Which of these is divisible by 6 and 7?
   a. 63
   b. 74
   c. 96
   d. 84

12. What is $\frac{3}{8}$ equal to?
   a. 0.25
   b. 0.333
   c. 0.60
   d. 0.375

13. What is another way to write $4 \times 4 \times 4$?
   a. 3×4
   b. 8×4
   c. 4^3
   d. 3^4

14. Which of the following choices completes this number sentence? $5\_\_\_\_\_ = (10 \times 2) + (5 \times 3)$
   a. $\times (5 + 2)$
   b. $+ (5 + 2)$
   c. $\times (5 \times 2)$
   d. $+ (5 \times 2)$

15. Which of these is equivalent to 35° C?
   $(F = \frac{9}{5}C + 32)$
   a. 105° F
   b. 95° F
   c. 63° F
   d. 19° F

16. What is the volume of a pyramid that has a rectangular base 5 feet by 3 feet and a height of 8 feet? $(V = \frac{1}{3}lwh)$
   a. 16 feet^3
   b. 30 feet^3
   c. 40 feet^3
   d. 120 feet^3

17. What is another way to write 7.25×10^3?
   a. 72.5
   b. 725
   c. 7,250
   d. 72,500

18. How many inches are there in $3\frac{1}{3}$ yards?
   a. 126
   b. 120
   c. 160
   d. 168

19. $\frac{3}{5} =$
   a. 0.60
   b. 0.20
   c. 0.50
   d. 0.80

20. 0.97 is equal to
   a. 97%
   b. 9.7%
   c. 0.97%
   d. 0.097%

21. In a triangle, angle A is 70 degrees and angle B is 30 degrees. What is the measure of angle C?
   a. 90 degrees
   b. 70 degrees
   c. 80 degrees
   d. 100 degrees

22. Which value of x will make the following number sentence true?
   $x + 25 \leq 13$
   a. −13
   b. −11
   c. 12
   d. 38

23. What is $\frac{1}{10}$ in decimal form?
  a. 0.05
  b. 0.20
  c. 0.10
  d. 0.25

24. How many faces does a cube have?
  a. 4
  b. 6
  c. 8
  d. 12

25. $-\frac{1}{2} =$
  a. −0.50
  b. −1.00
  c. −0.25
  d. 0.50

26. What is the length of a rectangle if its width is 9 feet and its area is 117 square feet?
  a. 1.3 feet
  b. 10.5 feet
  c. 12 feet
  d. 13 feet

27. A square is a special case of all of the following geometric figures EXCEPT a
  a. parallelogram.
  b. rectangle.
  c. rhombus.
  d. trapezoid.

28. What is the value of x in the figure below?

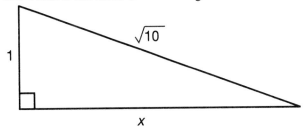

  a. 2
  b. 3
  c. 5
  d. 9

29. $3\frac{1}{4} =$
  a. 3.75
  b. 0.75
  c. 3.5
  d. 3.25

30. If the figure below is a regular decagon with a center at Q, what is the measure of the indicated angle?

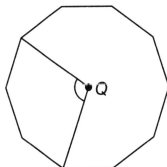

  a. 36 degrees
  b. 45 degrees
  c. 90 degrees
  d. 108 degrees

31. The figure below contains both a circle and a square. What is the area of the entire shaded figure?

8

a. $16 + 4\pi$
b. $16 + 16\pi$
c. $24 + 2\pi$
d. $24 + 4\pi$

32. Negative 1.5 is equal to
a. $1\frac{1}{2}$
b. $-1\frac{1}{5}$
c. $-\frac{2}{5}$
d. $-1\frac{1}{2}$

33. 62.5 percent is equal to
a. $\frac{1}{16}$
b. $\frac{5}{8}$
c. $6\frac{1}{4}$
d. $6\frac{2}{5}$

34. A line intersects two parallel lines in the figure below. If angle P measures 40 degrees, what is the measure of angle Q?

a. 50°
b. 60°
c. 80°
d. 140°

35. 0.05 is equal to
a. $\frac{1}{20}$
b. $\frac{1}{5}$
c. $\frac{1}{10}$
d. $\frac{1}{2}$

► Part 7: Mechanical Comprehension

Time: 19 minutes

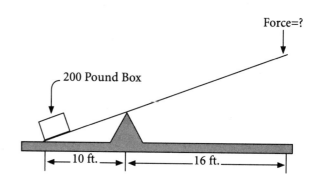

1. In the diagram shown above, Frank must lift a 200-pound box using a lever. How many pounds of force must Frank apply to the right side of the lever to lift the box? $w \times d_1 = f \times d_2$
a. 100 pounds
b. 125 pounds
c. 200 pounds
d. 320 pounds

2. What units are used to measure velocity?
a. feet per minute
b. feet per second
c. miles per hour
d. all of the above

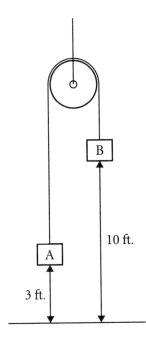

10 ft.

A

3 ft.

3. In the diagram above, how much must block A be raised to allow block B to rest on the floor beneath it?
  a. 3 feet
  b. 10 feet
  c. 13 feet
  d. 7 feet

4. A spring is most likely to be used on which of the following?
  a. a cabinet door
  b. a table
  c. an electric cord
  d. a pogo stick

5. Which of the following items listed below most resembles a lever?
  a. a seesaw
  b. an elevator
  c. a car
  d. a door

6. An elevator uses which of the following mechanical devices?
  a. a cable
  b. a pulley
  c. a motor
  d. all of the above

7. The Earth is a sphere that rotates about an axis that passes through the north pole and the south pole. If one person is standing at the north pole, another at the south pole, and a third at the equator of the Earth, which one will be traveling at a higher tangential velocity? (Tangential velocity means the speed parallel to the surface of the Earth.)
  a. the person at the south pole
  b. the person at the north pole
  c. the person at the equator
  d. all will be traveling at the same tangential velocity

8. Lori and Steve are sitting in separate cars at a stop sign. Lori accelerates at twice the rate that Steve accelerates. After five minutes of constant acceleration, who has traveled a longer distance?
  a. Steve
  b. Lori
  c. they have traveled the same distance
  d. not enough information to answer the question

9. You are in Denver and it is 1:00 P.M. You need to be in Moab, Utah, by 8:00 P.M. Moab is 350 miles from Denver. Assuming you drive straight through with no stops, what must your average speed be in order to arrive in Moab by 8:00 P.M.?
  a. 50 mile per hour
  b. 56 miles per hour
  c. 42 miles per hour
  d. 65 miles per hour

10. Two balls of the same diameter are dropped off the Leaning Tower of Pisa. The first ball is made of lead and weighs 10 pounds. The second ball is made of plastic and weighs 2 pounds. Which of the following statements best describes what happens to the balls after being dropped?
a. The heavier ball hits the ground first.
b. The lighter ball hits the ground first.
c. Both balls hit the ground at the same time.
d. Both balls are heavier after hitting the ground.

11. A block of wood rests on a level surface. What mechanical principle makes it more difficult to push this block sideways if the surface is made of sandpaper than if it is made of glass?
a. centrifugal force
b. gravity
c. wind resistance
d. friction

12. Water is flowing through a piping system. Eventually, due to friction losses and a rise in elevation of the piping, the flow rate of the water becomes very slow. What mechanical device can best be used to increase the flow of the water?
a. a gear
b. a winch
c. a pump
d. a compressor

Chain traveling clockwise around gears

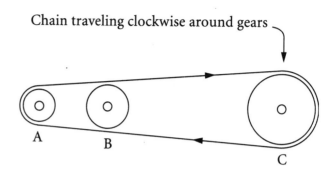

13. In the diagram above, gears A, B, and C are connected by a chain. The diameters of the gears are 1 inch, 2 inches, and 4 inches respectively. If gear A is turning at 20 revolutions per minute (RPM), what is the turning rate of gear C?
a. 5 RPM
b. 20 RPM
c. 40 RPM
d. 80 RPM

14. Water has a density of 62.4 pounds per cubic foot. Mercury has a density of 848.6 pounds per cubic foot. If mercury is poured into a glass of water, what will happen?
a. The mercury will sink.
b. The mercury will float.
c. The weight of the glass of water will decrease.
d. None of the above is true.

15. A steel bar is transferred from a freezer at 30 degrees Fahrenheit to a room at 70 degrees Fahrenheit. The bar will
a. get shorter.
b. break.
c. stay the same length.
d. get longer.

16. A bridge spans 100 feet. It is supported by Pier A on the right and Pier B on the left and has no center or intermediate supports. If a truck is at the center of the bridge, which statement best describes the structural support system of the bridge?

   a. The truck is supported more by Pier A than by Pier B.

   b. The truck is supported more by Pier B than by Pier A.

   c. The truck is supported equally by Pier A and Pier B.

   d. There is not enough information to answer the question.

17. As an object is submerged deeper and deeper in a body of water, what happens to the pressure exerted by the water on the object?

   a. It increases.

   b. It decreases.

   c. It becomes zero.

   d. It stays the same.

18. Why do large steel ships float?

   a. Steel is lighter than water.

   b. The propellers keep the ships afloat.

   c. The ships displace more water than their weight.

   d. Steel is heavier than water.

19. If a truck is traveling at the constant speed of 50 miles per hour for a total time period of 1 hour and 30 minutes, how many miles does it travel? (Distance = rate × time)

   a. 75 miles

   b. 50 miles

   c. 5 miles

   d. 130 miles

20. What common mechanical device is typically used on a push button, such as on a push-button telephone, a computer keyboard, and an electric garage door opener, in order to return the button to its original position?

   a. a wheel

   b. a pulley

   c. a spring

   d. a gear

21. Which of the following types of wire cutters would allow a worker to cut a heavy piece of wire using the least force?

   a. a wire cutter with very thick handles

   b. a wire cutter whose handles are longer than its blades

   c. a wire cutter with finger groves on the grip

   d. a wire cutter whose blades are longer than its handles

22. A bicycle wheel has a diameter of 1.9 feet and a circumference of 6 feet. A girl rides this bicycle for two revolutions of this wheel. How far down the driveway does she travel?

   a. 12 feet

   b. 4 feet

   c. 2 feet

   d. 100 feet

23. What type of gauge is read in units of psi (pounds per square inch)?

   a. a pressure gauge

   b. a depth gauge

   c. a speed gauge

   d. an RPM gauge

24. Newton's First Law of physics says, "A body [such as a car] that is in motion along a straight line will remain in motion, at the same speed, along the same straight line, unless acted upon by an outside force." A car is traveling down a straight, flat road at 30 miles per hour. The operation of all but one of the items listed below can help demonstrate Newton's Second Law. Which item CANNOT be used to demonstrate this Law?
a. the brakes
b. the gas pedal
c. the steering wheel
d. the radiator

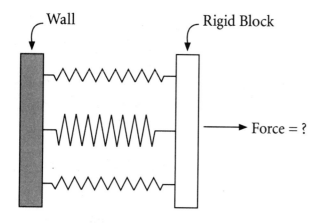

25. Three springs are arranged in parallel between a wall and a rigid block, as shown above. The spring constants are 5 pounds per inch, 12 pounds per inch, and 5 pounds per inch respectively. What force is required to move the block 2 inches to the right?
a. 12 pounds
b. 44 pounds
c. 22 pounds
d. 10 pounds

▶ Part 8: Electronics Information

Time: 9 minutes

1. A power plant that generates two hundred kilowatts generates how many watts?
a. 2,000 watts
b. 20,000 watts
c. 200,000 watts
d. 2,000,000 watts

2. A static charge
a. moves from one terminal of a battery to the other.
b. does not move.
c. does work.
d. is the force between an electron and a proton.

3. Which of the following is the definition of voltage?
a. a moving electric charge
b. the force of gravity on an electric charge
c. the attraction of like charges
d. the potential of electric charge to do work

4. Which of the following is the current when 300 coulombs of charge move through a light bulb in one minute?
a. 5 A
b. 20 A
c. 100 A
d. 300 A

5. Which of the following is NOT a good insulator?
a. a car tire
b. a wooden dowel
c. glass
d. gold

6. Resistance in an electric circuit
  a. forces current to flow.
  b. opposes the flow of current.
  c. is usually harmful.
  d. is usually beneficial.

7. Which of the following is NOT needed to make an electric circuit?
  a. a closed path
  b. resistance
  c. a switch
  d. a potential voltage source

8. Current is measured in
  a. watts.
  b. amperes.
  c. volts.
  d. ohms.

9. Electric charge in motion is
  a. current.
  b. power.
  c. energy.
  d. voltage.

10. Most computer memory chips are made from silicon. Silicon is an example of
  a. an insulator.
  b. a resistor.
  c. a conductor.
  d. a semiconductor.

11. Metals are very good conductors of electricity because they
  a. are high in resistance.
  b. have electrons that are able to move freely.
  c. are inexpensive.
  d. are easily formed into wires.

12. A material with a very large resistance is classified as
  a. an insulator.
  b. a conductor.
  c. a semiconductor.
  d. a transformer.

13. A voltmeter is connected to a circuit as shown. What will the meter read?

  a. 5 volts
  b. 10 volts
  c. 15 volts
  d. 30 volts

14. Two series resistors R_1 and R_2 are connected to a voltage source. If R_1 is equal to R_2, how much current flows through each of the resistors?
  a. The current through R_1 is twice that of R_2.
  b. The current through R_1 is the same as R_2.
  c. The current through R_1 is one-half that of R_2.
  d. The current through R_1 is one-fourth that of R_2.

15. What is the total resistance when two five-ohm light bulbs are connected in series?
  a. 2.5 Ω
  b. 5.0 Ω
  c. 10.0 Ω
  d. 0.2 Ω

16. A voltmeter is connected to a circuit as shown. What will the meter read?

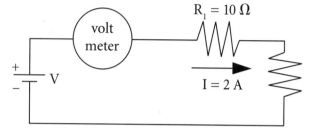

$R_1 = 10 \, \Omega$

volt meter

V

$I = 2 \, A$

   a. 0 volts
   b. 10 volts
   c. 20 volts
   d. 30 volts

17. Two 8-ohm speakers are connected in series to an amplifier with a 24-volt output. What is the voltage across each speaker?
   a. 3 volts
   b. 6 volts
   c. 12 volts
   d. 24 volts

18. Three toasters are plugged into the same outlet. Each toaster draws 3 amperes. What is the total current supplied by the outlet?
   a. 0.33 A
   b. 3.0 A
   c. 6.0 A
   d. 9.0 A

19. Which electronic component can be used to change the value of an alternating voltage?
   a. a diode
   b. a capacitor
   c. a transformer
   d. an inductor

20. When two parallel resistances are combined, the equivalent resistance is
   a. less than either of the two parallel resistances.
   b. equal to the sum of the two parallel resistances.
   c. greater than either of the two parallel resistances.
   d. less than the sum of the two parallel resistances.

► Answers

Part 1: General Science

1. c. An element's number of protons determines its location on the periodic table. For instance, hydrogen (H) has one proton, helium (He) has two protons, and lithium (Li) has three protons, so H, He, Li are numbers 1, 2, and 3 on the periodic table.

2. b. Isotopes are atoms of the same element with varying atomic masses depending how many neutrons are in the nucleus.

3. d. The symbol mm stands for millimeter, a unit that expresses length, not volume. Volume is commonly expressed using cc (cubic centimeter), L (liter), or dm^3 (cubic decimeter).

4. d. A single molecule of any substance must contain the same elements in the same proportions as a larger amount of that substance. Therefore, a molecule of carbon dioxide (CO_2) must have 1 carbon atom and 2 oxygen atoms.

5. c. The concept of centrifugal force suggests that the mass of an object will be pushed in an outward direction when it is spinning in a circular motion. Fundamental forces usually refer to forces between elementary particles such as electromagnetism or gravity. The Coriolis effect is caused by the rotation of the Earth on its axis.

6. b. The food coloring spreading out into the water is an example of diffusion, which is the spreading out of the molecules of a substance from places of greater molecular concentration to places of lower concentration.

7. c. Cooking a hamburger involves a chemical change. The other choices involve physical changes.

8. a. Carbohydrates are digested more easily and absorbed more quickly than fats. Choice **b** is incorrect because amino acids are the building blocks of proteins. Choices **c** and **d** are not true of carbohydrates.

9. c. White blood cells protect the body against foreign invaders such as bacteria and viruses.

10. a. Reptiles lay their eggs on land, so they do not have internal development of eggs.

11. d. The snake is the only vertebrate—that is, it is the only one of the four animals that has a backbone.

12. b. One organism may acclimate itself to the stresses associated with a new environment. Evolution and the process of natural selection occur over several generations.

13. d. Omnivores eat many types of food, including plants and flesh.

14. b. The electromagnetic spectrum contains these wavelengths, from shortest to longest: gamma rays, X rays, ultraviolet, visible, infrared, microwave, radio.

15. d. Gravity is the weakest of the four fundamental forces. Gravity controls the movement of planets, stars, and galaxies, as well as holding objects on Earth.

16. a. The Sun is a star in the center of the Solar System, and it is almost 110 times the diameter of the Earth. Venus is slightly smaller than the Earth. Jupiter is the largest planet in the Solar System (with a diameter 11 times that of the Earth), but it only contains 0.1 percent of a solar mass.

17. d. Absolute zero, when all atoms in solid matter stop vibrating, is −273 degrees Celsius or 0 degrees Kelvin.

18. b. Our Solar System contains nine planets: Mercury, Venus, Earth, Mars, Jupiter, Saturn, Uranus, Neptune, and Pluto.

19. b. Only a plant or algae cell contains chloroplasts, the site of photosynthesis in plants and algae. Therefore, fern (a plant) is the only possible answer.

20. a. Deoxyribonucleic acid (DNA), the genetic blueprint of cells, is located in the nucleus of animal cells.

21. c. Human sex cells (gametes) have 23 chromosomes. All other human cells have 46 chromosomes—23 from the mother and 23 from the father.

22. a. The scapula, also known as the shoulder blade, is the flat triangular bone in the pectoral girdle that anchors the muscles of the forelimb.

23. a. Speech is not controlled by the autonomic nervous system (ANS). The ANS stimulates involuntary muscles and glands in the body.

24. a. K is the symbol for potassium. In animals, potassium and sodium (Na) ions traveling across the nerve-cell membrane initiate the transmission of electrical impulses in the nervous system. Krypton is Kr. Calcium is Ca. Chromium is Cr.

25. c. The symbol for ozone, also known as trioxygen, is O_3. In the atmosphere, the ozone layer occurs 15–50 km above the earth's surface. O_2 is the symbol for the form of oxygen that we need to breathe.

Part 2: Arithmetic Reasoning

1. c. Since the price per copy is $0.75, divide 60 by 0.75 to find the total number that can be purchased with $60; $\frac{60}{0.75} = 80$; 80 copies can be purchased.

2. c. The volume of the aquarium can be found by using the formula $V = l \times w \times h$. Since the length is 12 inches, the width is 5 inches and the height is 10 inches, multiply $V = 12 \times 5 \times 10$ to get a volume of 600 cubic inches.

3. c. The value of the handbag ($150) must be included in the total.

4. d. Both choices **a** and **b** can be ruled out because there is no way to determine how many tickets are for adults or for children. Choice **c** can be ruled out because the price of group tickets is not given.

5. d. Because the 15-year-old requires an adult ticket, there are 3 adult tickets at $7.50 each and one child's ticket at $5.

6. a. The adult price on Saturday afternoon is $5.50; the child's price is $3.00.

7. d. This problem is solved by dividing 60 by 0.75.

8. b. This is a multiplication problem, which is solved by multiplying 35 times 8.2.

9. a. You know the ratio of Drake's charge to Jean's charge is 3 to 4, or $\frac{3}{4}$. To find what Jean charges, you use the equation $\frac{3}{4} = \frac{36}{x}$, or $3x = 4(36)$; $(4)(36) = 144$, which is then divided by 3 to arrive at $x = 48$.

10. a. In this question, you need to find 15% of the 30% of students that are in the music program. To find 15% of 30%, change the percents to decimal form and multiply. Since 30% = 0.30 and 15% = 0.15, multiply $(0.30)(0.15) = 0.045$. As a decimal, this is equivalent to 4.5% which is choice **a**.

11. d. The basic cable service fee of $15 is 75% of $20.

12. a. The labor fee ($25) plus the deposit ($65) plus the basic service ($15) equals $105. The difference between the total bill, $112.50, and $105 is $7.50, the cost of the news channels.

13. d. Eighty out of 100 is 80%. Eighty percent of 30,000 is 24,000.

14. d. 27.5% of 400 is 110.

15. b. Rock is 45.5%; when we add 4.5% for classical we arrive at 50%.

16. c. If 60% of the people were satisfied with their new car, 40% were unsatisfied; 40% of 220 is 88.

17. c. Divide 135 Spanish-speaking students by 1,125 total number of students to arrive at .12 or 12%.

18. a. The first step in solving the problem is to subtract 86 from 148. The remainder, 62, is then divided by 2.

19. c. Three feet 4 inches equals 40 inches; 40 divided by 5 is 8.

20. a. It will cost $3 for a sandwich and a cookie. To get two additional sandwiches, it would cost another $4. Therefore, it would cost $7 to get three sandwiches and a cookie. Since she only has $6 to spend, this combination is not possible.

21. d. Area is width times length, in this case, 5 times 7, or 35 square feet.

22. b. Use the formula beginning with the operation in parentheses: $98 - 32 = 66$. Then multiply 66 by $\frac{5}{9}$, first multiplying 66 by 5 to get 330; 330 divided by 9 is 36.66667, which is rounded up to 36.7.

23. c. Each 9-foot wall has an area of 9×8 or 72 square feet. There are two such walls, so those two walls combined have an area of 72×2 or 144 square feet. Each 11-foot wall has an area of 11×8 or 88 square feet, and again there are two such walls: $88 \times 2 = 176$. To find the total surface area, add 144 and 176 to get 320 square feet.

24. b. $1\frac{1}{2}$ cups equals $\frac{3}{2}$ cups. The ratio is 6 people to 4 people, which is equal to the ratio of x to $\frac{3}{2}$. By cross multiplying, we get $6(\frac{3}{2})$ equals $4x$, or 9 equals $4x$. Dividing both sides by 4, we get $\frac{9}{4}$, or $2\frac{1}{4}$ cups.

25. a. The distance between Plattville and Quincy is the hypotenuse of a right triangle with sides of length 80 and 60. The length of the hypotenuse equals the square root of $(80^2 + 60^2)$, which equals the square root of $(6{,}400 + 3{,}600)$, which equals the square root of 10,000, which equals 100 miles.

26. d. The volume of concrete is 27 cubic feet. Volume is length times width times depth, or $(L)(W)(D)$, so $(L)(W)(D) = 27$. We're told that the length L is 6 times the width W, so L equals $6W$. We're also told that the depth is 6 inches, or 0.5 feet. Substituting what we know about the length and depth into the original equation and solving for W, we get $(L)(W)(D) = (6W)(W)(0.5) =$

$27. 3W^2 = 27$; $W^2 = 9$, so $W = 3$. To get the length, we remember that L equals $6W$, so L equals $(6)(3)$, or 18 feet.

27. c. Find the price per ounce of each brand, as follows: Brand W is $\frac{21}{6}$ or 3.5 cents per ounce; Brand X is $\frac{48}{15}$ or 3.2 cents per ounce; Brand Y is $\frac{56}{20}$ or 2.8 cents per ounce; Brand Z is $\frac{96}{32}$ or 3.0 cents per ounce. It is then easy to see that Brand Y, at 2.8 cents per ounce, is the least expensive.

28. a. 2,052 miles divided by 6 days is 342 miles per day; 342 miles divided by 2 stops is 171 miles.

29. b. $K + F + S = 540$. Also, $K = 2F$ and $S = 2F$, which changes the original equation to $2F + F + 2F = 540$, so $5F = 540$ and $F = 108$. Since there is one fork per place setting, the cook can buy 108 place settings.

30. c. First find the total price of the pencils: (24 pencils)($0.05) = $1.20. Then find the total price of the paper: (3.5 reams)($7.50 per ream) = $26.25. Next, add the two totals together: $1.20 + 26.25 = $27.45.

Part 3: Word Knowledge

1. e. To *mediate* is to settle disputes; to *reconcile* is to bring into agreement.

2. a. To *expedite* a process is to hurry it up or *accelerate* it.

3. b. If something is plausible, it is believable or *credible*.

4. b. *Concurrent* means happening at the same time; *simultaneous* means the same thing.

5. d. *Impromptu* means without preparation; *spontaneous* means unpremeditated.

6. a. To *induce* is to bring about; to *prompt* is to provoke or induce to action.

7. c. To *infer* something is to *surmise* it or deduce it from the evidence.

8. c. To *saturate* is to fill or to load to capacity; to *soak* is to penetrate or permeate.

9. a. A *synopsis* is an abbreviated version; a *summary* is a brief statement of facts or points.

10. b. A *hyperbole* is an extravagant statement; an *exaggeration* is an overstatement.

11. d. One of the meanings of to *proscribe* is to prohibit; to *forbid* is to command (someone) not to do something. *Proscribe* should not be confused with *prescribe,* which is what a doctor does with a medication.

12. a. A *proponent* is a supporter of something; an *advocate* is someone who supports something—for instance, a cause.

13. d. An *intrepid* person approaches a challenge without fear; a *fearless* person behaves the same way.

14. b. A *statute* is a law; an *ordinance* is a rule or law.

15. b. To be *apathetic* is to show little or no interest or to be *indifferent.*

16. a. To be *fortified* is to be strengthened or *reinforced.*

17. a. To *refrain* is to hold back from doing something; to *desist* is to cease doing something.

18. d. To *delegate* a task is to *assign* it or to appoint another to do it.

19. b. Something that is *spurious* is not genuine; something that is *false* is also not genuine.

20. d. To *articulate* something is to give words to it or *express* it.

21. d. To *disparage* is to talk about something or someone in a negative manner; to *criticize* is to find fault with.

22. c. If something is *expansive,* it is broad, open, or *spacious.*

23. c. To be *urbane* is to show the refined manners of high society; to be *sophisticated* is to show worldly knowledge or refinement.

24. a. A *rationale* is a reason for something; an *explanation* is a clarification or definition or something.

25. b. If a thing is *detrimental,* it is injurious or *harmful.*

Part 4: Paragraph Comprehension

1. d. Although the last sentence expands on the main point, the rest of the passage explains why hearsay evidence is only admissible when it doesn't matter whether or not the statement is true.

2. a. This statement may be true, but it isn't in the passage.

3. b. See the last sentence of the passage.

4. c. The passage mentions the truthfulness of testimony several times.

5. d. The first two sentences of the passage state that bus operators must have twenty hours of training on a simulator.

6. a. The second sentence in the second paragraph states that the simulator reinforces safe driving habits. Although choices **b, c,** and **d** are possible benefits of the program, these are not the main purpose of the refresher course.

7. c. The directions indicate that the city prefers, but does not require, use of the new container. In addition, it appears the city only charges residents for additional containers.

8. d. The directions state the city would like households to use the new containers as their primary containers; this means other containers are allowed.

9. d. The directions mention nothing about main or secondary roads.

10. a. The other choices are not mentioned in the directions.

11. a. The passage states that the events it described happened in 1956; this rules out choice **c.** The purpose of the passage is to explain a historical event, so choices **b** and **d** are clearly wrong.

12. b. See the first paragraph. Choice **a** is contradicted in the first paragraph, and the passage does not discuss Lucy's later profession (choice **c**) or major (choice **d**).

13. c. Choice **a** is incorrect because the first sentence suggests that becoming hardened is unavoidable. Choices **b** and **d** are implied in the passage but neither is the main idea.

14. b. See the first two sentences of the passage.

15. c. The passage claims that becoming jaded is inevitable.

Part 5: Auto and Shop Information

1. d. The crankshaft is rotated by the up and down movement of the piston and transfers the energy from the internal combustion engine to the drive train (transmission). The spark plugs provide fuel ignition. The radiator provides engine cooling. The oil provides lubrication.

2. b. Vernier calipers are used to determine precise internal or external measurement.

3. a. A lever is the correct choice. A protractor is used to measure angles. A spring is used for many purposes but not to gain a mechanical advantage. A gear is used to change rotational speeds of shafts.

4. d. All of these wrenches can be used on different size objects.

5. a. A speed gauge is the correct answer. A depth gauge would use units of length such as feet or meters. A pressure gauge would use units of pressure such as psi (pounds per square inch) or bar. A temperature gauge would use units of temperature such as degrees Celsius or degrees Fahrenheit.

6. c. The muffler is placed at the end of the exhaust system of an automobile to reduce engine noise. It is a chamber that dampens the noise coming from the internal combustion engine.

7. b. Hinges are found on car doors, as well as on other parts such as the trunk lid, the hood, and the gas cap lid.

8. b. Preventive maintenance is periodically making small changes and adjustments on a device to prevent failure. Examples include changing the oil in a car engine, adjusting the brakes on a car, lubricating the moving parts on a pump, and changing the fan belts and hoses on a truck.

9. c. A hacksaw is the correct answer. This type of saw is similar to a saw for cutting wood except that the teeth are very small and close together.

10. d. The flow meter gauge measures liquid flow rate, which is typically measured in units of volume per unit time, such as gallons per minute or cubic meters per second.

11. d. The transmission uses different size gears in order to adjust for different speeds. With a manual transmission, the driver changes these gears with the gear shift. An automatic transmission changes the gears at preset speeds.

12. b. Kilometers per hour is the correct answer. A kilometer is a unit of distance in the metric system that is roughly equivalent to 0.6 miles.

13. d. This tool carves wood. Hammers are used to drive nails; welders or torches are used to weld metal; wrenches are used to tighten bolts.

14. b. The suspension of an automobile is typically composed of springs, shocks, wheels, and tires.

15. d. All these are names applied to various kinds of wrenches.

16. a. The correct answer is a crescent wrench.

17. c. The foundation is the base upon which the building is constructed. Therefore, it must be constructed before the framing, the walls, or the flooring.

18. a. Wood is typically used to build the walls of houses or pedestrian bridges. The other materials listed are used in buildings for purposes other than structural support.

19. d. The saw could be used to cut the wood used for the forms for a concrete bridge foundation. It could be used for cutting the studs for the apartment building wall. It could also be used for cutting the wood for a cedar deck railing.

20. b. Surveying is the practice of determining locations and elevations of structures and roadways. This is accomplished through the use of many instruments and tools, including levels for measuring elevations or heights, tape measures for measuring distances, and transits for measuring angles.

21. b. The sub-floor of a residential house consists of joists to support the structural load and decking for the surface. The joists are usually made of 2-inch by 10-inch lumber, and the decking is usually made of $\frac{3}{4}$-inch plywood.

22. a. A Phillips screwdriver is a very common type used on screws that have an indented cross on the head. You may find this type of screw on objects such as door hinges, television sets, and bicycles.

23. b. The internal combustion engine in an automobile generates heat and must be cooled. The typical cooling system is based on pumping water around the hot engine block. The heated water is then pumped into the radiator, where it is cooled and then re-circulated back to the engine block. The thermostat is used to regulate the flow of water to keep the engine warm but not let it overheat.

24. a. *Diamond point* is a kind of chisel. *Dovetail* and *coping* describe kinds of saws. *Duck bill* describes a kind of pliers.

25. c. Use jumper cables to get a charge from another battery. Installing a new starter will not help; the battery will still be dead. Adding fuel and changing fuses also will not recharge the battery. Jumper cables can be used to connect your dead battery to another live car battery to start the car.

Part 6: Mathematics Knowledge

1. b. *PQ* and *RS* are intersecting lines. The fact that angle *POS* is a 90-degree angle means that *PQ* and *RS* are perpendicular, indicating that all the angles formed by their intersection, including *ROQ*, measure 90 degrees.

2. a. Incorrect answers include adding both the numerator and the denominator and not converting fifths to tenths properly.

3. c. To convert a fraction to a decimal, divide the numerator, 3, by the denominator, 4. $3.00 \div 4 = 0.75$

4. b. The correct answer is $88\frac{1}{3}$.

5. b. Divide the numerator by the denominator; $1.000 \div 3 = 0.33\overline{3}$. Round the answer to the hundredths place (two decimal places) to get the answer 0.33.

6. d. You have to convert all three fractions to twelfths before adding them.

7. d. Choice **a** reads 276; choice **b** reads 2,706; choice **c** reads 20,076.

8. a. The first box is one greater than –5; the second is one greater than 0.

9. d. $1\frac{1}{2}$ is a mixed number. To convert this into a decimal, first take the whole number (in this case, 1) and place it to the left of the decimal point. Then, take the fraction (in this case, $\frac{1}{2}$) and convert it to a decimal by dividing the numerator by the denominator. Putting these two steps together gives the answer, 1.50.

10. a. Raise the fraction $\frac{2}{9}$ to 54ths by multiplying both numerator and denominator by 6.

11. d. $6(7)(2) = 84$.

12. d. Divide 3 by 8 in order to convert the fraction into a decimal. $3.000 \div 8 = 0.375$.

13. c. The meaning of 4^3 is 4 times itself 3 times.

14. a. The total on the right is 35. On the left, you need an operation you can do on 5 to get 35. Multiplying by 7—5 + 2—does the trick.

15. b. Use 35 for C; $F = (\frac{9}{5} \times 35) + 32$. Therefore $F = 63 + 32$, or 95.

16. c. $5(3)(8) = 120; 120 ÷ 3 = 40$

17. c. $10(10)(10) = 1,000; 1,000(7.25) = 7,250$

18. b. To solve this problem, you must first convert yards to inches. There are 36 inches in a yard; $36(3\frac{1}{3}) = 120$.

19. a. Divide 3 by 5 to convert from a fraction into a decimal; $3 ÷ 5 = 0.60$.

20. a. 0.97 multiplied by 100 is 97; therefore, the correct answer is 97%.

21. c. The sum of the measure of the angles in a triangle is 180 degrees; 70 degrees + 30 degrees = 100 degrees; 180 degrees − 100 degrees = 80 degrees. Therefore, angle C is 80 degrees.

22. a. Since the solution to the problem $x + 25 = 13$ is $x = -12$, choices **b**, **c**, and **d** are all too large to be correct.

23. c. Divide 1 by 10 to convert the fraction into a decimal. $1.00 ÷ 10 = 0.10$.

24. b. A cube has 4 sides, a top, and a bottom, which means that it has 6 faces.

25. a. Divide 1 by 2 in order to convert the fraction into a decimal; $1.00 ÷ 2 = 0.50$. Finally, add the negative sign to get −0.50.

26. d. To solve this problem you should use the formula $A = lw$, or $117 = 9l$. Next, you must divide 117 by 9 to find the answer.

27. d. A square is a special case of all of these figures except the trapezoid. A square is a parallelogram, because its opposite sides are parallel. A square is a rectangle because it is a quadrilateral with 90-degree angles. A square is a rhombus because it is a parallelogram with all sides equal in length. However, a square is not a trapezoid because a trapezoid has only two sides parallel.

28. b. The Pythagorean theorem states that the square of the length of the hypotenuse of a right triangle is equal to the sum of the squares of the other two sides, so we know that $1^2 + x^2 = (\sqrt{10})^2$, so $1 + x^2 = 10$, so $x^2 = 10 - 1 = 9$, so $x = 3$.

29. d. Separate the mixed number into the whole number plus the fraction; $3\frac{1}{4} = 3.0 + \frac{1}{4}$; divide 1 by 4 to convert the fraction to a decimal; $1.00 ÷ 4 = 0.25; 3.0 + 0.25 = 3.25$.

30. d. If the figure is a regular decagon, it can be divided into ten equal sections by lines passing through the center. Two such lines form the indicated angle, which includes three of the ten sections; $\frac{3}{10}$ of 360 degrees = 108 degrees.

31. c. The easiest way to calculate the area is to realize that the shaded figure is made up of half a circle of diameter 4 (radius = $\frac{4}{2} = 2$) on top of a rectangle that is 4 units wide and 6 units tall. The area of a half circle is $(\frac{1}{2})\pi r^2$, and the area of a rectangle is length times width. So the shaded area equals $(\frac{1}{2})\pi(2)^2 + (4)(6) = 24 + 2\pi$.

32. d. Since there is a number, 1, to the left of the decimal, this will be the whole number. The fraction is found by using the number to the right of the decimal. The 5 is in the tenths place, so the fraction $\frac{5}{10}$ which can be reduced to $\frac{1}{2}$ (divide both the numerator and the denominator by 5). The final mixed number is the whole number (1), plus the fraction ($\frac{1}{2}$). Adding the negative, the answer is $-1\frac{1}{2}$.

33. b. 62.5% is $\frac{62.5}{100}$. You should multiply both the numerator and denominator by 10 to move the decimal point, resulting in $\frac{625}{1,000}$, and then factor both the numerator and denominator to find out how far you can reduce the fraction; $\frac{625}{1,000}$ equals $\frac{(5)(5)(5)(5)}{(5)(5)(5)(8)}$. If you cancel the three 5s that are in both the numerator and denominator, you will get $\frac{5}{8}$.

34. d. A line that intersects two parallel lines forms complementary angles on either side of it. Complementary angles are angles whose measures add up to 180 degrees; $180 - 40 = 140$.

35. a. In the decimal, 0.05, the 5 falls in the hundredths place (two places to the right of the decimal). To convert this to a fraction, the 5 is placed over 100 and then reduced; $\frac{5 ÷ 5}{100 ÷ 5} = \frac{1}{20}$.

Part 7: Mechanical Comprehension

1. b. (200 pounds)(10 feet) = f(16 feet). Solving for f gives 125 pounds.

2. d. All the choices are true. Velocity is measured in units of distance in a certain amount of time. All of the answers use these units.

3. b. The blocks are tied together with a cable, which keeps the distance between the blocks constant. Therefore, if block B is to be lowered 10 feet to the floor, then block A must be raised the same amount.

4. d. Of all the items, only a pogo stick uses springs.

5. a. The bar on which the seesaw pivots is the fulcrum of the lever. Also, the seesaw raises and lowers a load (person) on one end when a force (pushing off the ground) is applied on the other end.

6. d. All of the choices are correct. A motor is used to wind a cable around a pulley in order to raise and lower the car.

7. c. The two people at the poles will just spin around the axis of rotation and have no tangential velocity. The person at the equator will travel much faster since he or she is rotating at the same rate as the people at the poles and is located far away—half the diameter of the Earth—from the axis of rotation.

8. b. Lori's acceleration rate is twice Steve's rate. Since they both started at the same time and accelerated for the same amount of time, Lori will travel twice as far as Steve.

9. a. The equation used to solve this problem is: distance equals rate multiplied by time ($d = r \times t$). The distance is 350 miles; the time is 7 hours (from 1:00 P.M. to 8:00 P.M.). Solving for the rate gives 50.

10. c. Both balls hit the ground at the same time, because gravity affects all objects in the same manner.

11. d. Friction is the force that must be overcome in order to slide one object across another.

12. c. Pumps are used to move liquids through piping systems.

13. a. Gear C is 4 times the diameter of gear A. Since the gears are all connected by a chain, the tip velocity of all the gears must be the same; otherwise, the chain would come off the gears. Therefore, if the tip velocity is to be the same for all gears and gear C is 4 times larger than gear A, then gear C must be turning 4 times slower than gear A. 20 RPM divided by 4 equals 5 RPM.

14. a. Since mercury is more dense (one cubic foot of mercury weighs more than one cubic foot of water), it will sink to the bottom of the glass.

15. d. The bar will get longer. Metallic objects such as this steel bar have a positive coefficient of thermal expansion, which means that, as their temperature increases, their volume or length will increase. Moving the bar from the freezer to the room causes the bar's temperature to increase.

16. c. The truck is supported equally by Pier A and Pier B. Since the truck is exactly in the center of the bridge, half of its weight is transferred to each pier.

17. a. As the object goes deeper, there is more weight of water pressing on it; therefore, the pressure increases.

18. c. This is the Archimedes Principle. If you fill a glass to the top with water and then place a ball in the glass, some water will spill over the top. If the weight of this displaced water is more than the weight of the ball, it will float. If not, it will sink. The same is true for the ship.

19. a. The truck travels for 1 hour and 30 minutes, which is 1.5 hours. According to the formula, then, the distance traveled is 1.5 hours times 50 mph, or 75 miles.

20. c. A compression coil spring is typically placed behind the button. When the button is pressed, the spring is compressed and then springs back to return the button to its original position.

21. b. A wire cutter whose handles are longer than its blades provides the mechanical advantage of a lever.

22. a. The circumference is the distance around the outer edge of the wheel. Two revolutions of a wheel 6 feet in diameter would result in a distance traveled of 12 feet.

23. a. A pressure gauge is measured in psi. The other gauges are read in the following units: A depth gauge uses a unit of length such as feet or meters; a speed gauge uses a unit of velocity such as miles per hour (mph) or kilometers per hour (kph); the RPM gauge measures revolutions per minute.

24. d. Newton's First Law mandates that a vehicle will move "at the same speed" unless an outside force is applied. Both the brakes and the gas pedal could be used to apply such a force. Newton's Second Law also mandates that the vehicle will travel "along the same straight line" unless an outside force—the action of the steering wheel, for instance—is applied. The radiator has nothing to do with the speed or direction of the vehicle.

25. b. All three springs must be stretched 2 inches. The question tells you that it takes 5 pounds to stretch spring A one inch. Therefore, it takes 10 pounds to stretch it 2 inches. Apply this to the other two springs and add up the total to get 44 pounds.

Part 8: Electronics Information

1. c. The prefix "kilo" is a multiplier of 1000; $200 \times + 1000$ is 200,000.

2. b. A static charge does not move. It has the potential to do work; it does not do work. It is not a force.

3. d. Voltage is defined to be the potential of electric charge to do work.

4. a. $I = \frac{Q}{T} = \frac{300\,C}{60\,seconds} = 5\,A$.

5. d. Gold is a metal and a good conductor.

6. b. Resistance is defined as the opposition to the flow of current.

7. c. The three elements of an electric circuit are a potential voltage source, resistance, and a closed path for current to flow.

8. b. Power is measured in watts. Voltage is measured in volts. Resistance is measured in ohms.

9. a. Current is defined as electric charge in motion.

10. d. Silicon is a semiconductor material.

11. b. A good conductor has electrons which are free to move, and metal is a good conductor. Metals are low in resistance. Metals can be expensive and easily formed into wires; however, that is not why they are good conductors.

12. a. An insulator has very large resistance. A conductor has a small resistance. A semiconductor has a medium resistance. A transformer is a coil of wire and has a small resistance.

13. d. The voltage across the meter will equal the sum of the voltages across the series resistors R1 and R2. So: $V = (I \times R_1) + (I \times R_2) = (2\,A \times 10\,\Omega) + (2\,A \times 5\,\Omega) = 20\,V + 10\,V = 30\,V$.

14. b. In a series circuit, the current is the same everywhere in the circuit.

15. c. The total resistance of series resistors is the sum of the resistance. $RT = R1 + R2 = 5\,\Omega + 5\,\Omega = 10\,\Omega$.

16. a. The meter will read zero because the meter is not connected across a resistance.

17. c. Because the resistances are equal, they will each have one-half of the applied voltage across them.

18. d. The total current supplied is equal to the sum of the currents through each of the three toasters.

19. c. Transformers are used to scale the value of an AC voltage. The ratio of the number of coils determines the voltage.

20. a. The resistance that results from combining two parallel resistances is always less than either of the original resistances.

Write your raw score (the number you got right) for each test in the blanks below. Then turn to Chapter 3 to find out how to convert these raw scores into the scores the armed services use.

1. General Science: _____ right out of 25
2. Arithmetic Reasoning: _____ right out of 30
3. Word Knowledge: _____ right out of 25
4. Paragraph Comprehension: _____ right out of 15
5. Auto and Shop Information: _____ right out of 25
6. Mathematics Knowledge: _____ right out of 35
7. Mechanical Comprehension: _____ right out of 25
8. Electronics Information: _____ right out of 20

CHAPTER

6 General Science
Review

CHAPTER SUMMARY

This chapter presents an outline and review of the important general science concepts that are tested by the ASVAB.

This chapter helps you prepare for the ASVAB's General Science subtest by reviewing some of the important science topics you're likely to encounter on the test. Use it as an aid to help you recall what you learned in high school and to identify what you have forgotten and need to review further.

The General Science subtest of the ASVAB deals with basic concepts and terms covered in most high school science curricula. It is a survey of important topics in life science, physical science, and earth science, with the first two being the most important.

Each of these three major areas covers more specific fields:

- **Life science** includes biology, ecology, human anatomy, and nutrition
- **Physical science** includes chemistry, measurements, and physics
- **Earth science** includes astronomy, geology, and meteorology

▶ Life Science

Biology is the study of living things. We share the planet with over a million plants and animals. A Swedish scientist named Carl Linné, also known as Linnaeus, devised the classification system used in modern biological science. Every organism is grouped according to seven basic levels of classification, which are, from broadest to most specific: kingdom, phylum, class, order, family, genus, species.

Classification

Linnaeus's system describes organisms that have shared physical traits with a two-word, or **binomial**, name. The scientific name of an organism consists of a **genus** name and a **species** name. A genus name, always capitalized, precedes the species name, which is in lowercase. Both genus and species names are underlined or italicized.

- A human belongs to genus *Homo*, species *sapiens*, so it is *Homo sapiens*.
- A common frog belongs to genus *Rana*, species *temporaria*, so it is *Rana temporaria*.
- An African violet belongs to genus *Saintpaulia*, species *ionantha*, so it is *Saintpaulia ionantha*.

Most biologists divide all living things into five major types, each forming a kingdom: animals, plants, fungi, protists, and monerans. This chapter focuses on animals and plants because those kingdoms contain the majority of life. It is useful, however, to know a little about the other three kingdoms.

Monerans, such as blue-green algae and bacteria, are single-celled organisms containing no nuclei. Blue-green algae produce their own food through photosynthesis (defined later in this chapter). Many bacteria are parasites that cause diseases, or they are decomposers, meaning that they absorb food from decaying material.

Protists, such as protozoa and algae, are single-celled organisms that contain cell nuclei. **Fungi,** such as molds and mushrooms, are multiple-celled organisms that form spores and decompose other organic matter. Yeasts are unicellular fungi that form colonies.

Kingdom	Number of Cells	Type
Monera	one-celled organisms	"simple," no cell nucleus
Protista	one-celled organisms	"complex," contain cell nucleus
Fungi	multiple-celled organisms	"complex," contain organized cell nucleus, decomposers, form spores

Plants

Plants contain many cells and make their own food through photosynthesis. The two phyla, or large groupings within the plant kingdom, are the **Bryophyta,** such as mosses and hornworts, and the **Tracheophyta,** including flowering plants and pine trees. Bryophytes are tiny, grow on surfaces, and reproduce by spores. They are simply organized and lack the structural support of true roots, stems and woody tissue. Tracheophytes, or vascular plants, are the plants that we encounter every day. Almost all have roots, stems of woody tissue—which allow them to grow to great heights and in soil with a dry surface—and leaves.

The largest class of the Tracheophyta is composed of the following divisions:

- **Filicophytes,** or ferns
- **Angiosperms (Magnoliophyta),** flowering plants that produce seeds with protective coverings
- **Gymnosperms (encompassing four divisions),** which produce seeds without protective covering, though some produce seed cones, such as the pine cone

Angiosperms are further divided into monocots and dicots. **Monocots** bear seeds with only one **cotyledon,** a leaf within the embryo. Monocots, such as onions, tulips, and palms, are characterized by parallel leaf veins and flowers in groups of threes. **Dicots** bear two cotyledons. Dicots, such as potatoes, roses, and oaks, are characterized by net-like leaf veins and flower parts in fours, fives, or multiples of either four or five.

Animals

Animals are many-celled, mobile organisms that cannot produce their own food. The animal kingdom is divided into approximately 26 phyla. Some of the major animal phyla are shown in the table on this page.

Vertebrates

The vertebrates are a subphlylum in the chordate phylum and include birds, fish, mammals, and reptiles. (All other animals are invertebrates.) Vertebrates have a spinal cord enclosed in a flexible, bony column that extends down the long axis of the body, providing skeletal support. There are eight classes of vertebrates. Four of the vertebrate classes are fish: agnatha (lamprey), chondrichthyes (shark), osteichthyes (trout), and the extinct placodermi. The other four classes of vertebrates and some of their characteristics are listed in the table on the next page.

ANIMAL PHYLA		
Phylum	**Characteristics**	**Example**
Porifera	aquatic; pores in body allow flow of water to bring in nutrients and take out waste products	sponges
Coelenterata	aquatic; have stinging cells to capture prey; may be free-swimming or sedentary	jellyfish, coral
Platyhelminthes	flat body; one opening to digestive system; often live as parasites in humans	flukes, tapeworms
Aschelminthes	smooth, round body tapered at both ends; two openings to digestive system; often parasitic	nematodes
Annelida	segmented worms; closed circulatory system	earthworms
Mollusca	most have unsegmented bodies, hard shells	clams, snails
Echinodermata	marine; usually having five radial arms	starfish
Arthropoda	jointed exoskeletons and at least three pairs of jointed legs	insects, crabs, spiders
Chordata	inner skeleton; gills at some point in development; hollow, dorsal nerve cord	humans, horses, geckos, trout

VERTEBRATES		
Class	**Characteristics**	**Example**
Amphibia	aquatic as both eggs and larvae; land-dwelling as adults	frogs
Aves	have feathers; external development of eggs	birds
Mammalia	have fur and are milk-producing; internal development of eggs	humans
Reptilia	eggs laid on land, land-dwelling adults, scaly skin	turtles

Only the aves and mammalia are **warm-blooded**. Birds and humans generate and regulate their own body heat. Feathers on birds and fur on mammals help them retain body heat, and sweating (yes, birds sweat) helps them cool down. All of the other vertebrates are **cold-blooded**. This means that their body temperature is determined by the temperature of their surrounding environment.

Mammals

All mammals share certain characteristics. They are warm-blooded, have a hair or fur covering for insulation, have a four-chambered heart, and breathe with lungs. In addition, females produce milk for their young. Mammals are divided further by body structures into 17 orders containing a total of only approximately 4,250 species. Some of the more important mammal orders are shown on the table at the bottom of this page.

Viruses

Viruses are difficult to classify because scientists do not agree on the definition of a virus. Some scientists believe that a virus is nonliving because, alone, a virus is incapable of reproducing. However, viruses consist of a DNA or RNA core encapsulated in a protein coat (a capsid), which causes many to argure for its status as a life form. A virus has no true cell structure, and it is incapable of independent metabolism and reproduction without the aid of a host cell. Once inside another cell, a virus takes over and uses the host cell's resources to replicate viral DNA. Eventually the host cell dies and the (many) replicated viruses are released to infect new cells. Viral diseases in animals include the common cold, influenza, herpes, measles, polio, and rabies.

Basic Life Principles

All living organisms perform certain biochemical and biophysical activities to achieve homeostasis—

MAMMALS		
Order	**Characteristics**	**Example**
Cetaceans	marine; forelimbs are flippers	whales, dolphins
Marsupials	carry young in a pouch	kangaroos, possums
Primates	highly developed brain; stand erect	humans, apes
Rodents	teeth specialized for gnawing	mice, beavers
Ungulates	hoofed, teeth specialized for grinding	horses, deer

a balanced internal environment. The life functions are as follows:

- **Circulation:** the transport of materials such as oxygen and nutrients throughout an organism
- **Excretion:** the elimination of metabolic waste products from an organism
- **Growth:** cell division and/or enlargement
- **Nutrition:** getting nutrients, or food molecules, from the environment via eating, absorption, or photosynthesis
- **Regulation:** the chemical control and coordination of life activities
- **Reproduction:** the production of new individuals
- **Respiration:** organic substances are broken down to simpler products with the release of energy, which is used to fuel other metabolic processes (in animals and plants)

The Cell

Cells are the basic structural and functional unit of living things. One cell, alone, is the smallest unit of matter that is considered living. In general, plant and animal cells are similar, except that plant cells contain chloroplasts and cell walls. Chloroplasts contain chlorophyll, a food-generating substance. Cell walls, containing cellulose and other compounds, give plant cells a rigid structure and prevent desiccation, or drying out.

The size of cells varies, but most are microscopic (an average of 0.01–0.1 mm in diameter). They may exist independently, or they may form colonies or tissues—like those in plants and animals. Each cell contains a mass of protein, called protoplasm, that consists of jelly-like cytoplasm and a nucleus. The nucleus, in turn, contains deoxyribonucleic acid, or DNA, which is the genetic material of most organisms. The protoplasm is bound by a cell or plasma membrane, which controls the materials that pass in and out of the cell.

There are two types of cells, distinguished from one another by a number of characteristics, one being the way in which they reproduce. Bacteria are one example of **prokaryotic cells.** The nuclear material in prokaryotic cells is not bound by a membrane, and cell reproduction occurs by fission—asexual cell cleavage—the cell breaks apart to form another, identical cell. The other type of cell, found in most plants and animals, is a **eukaryotic cell,** in which the nucleus is separated from the cytoplasm by the nuclear membrane and there are separate organelles. In

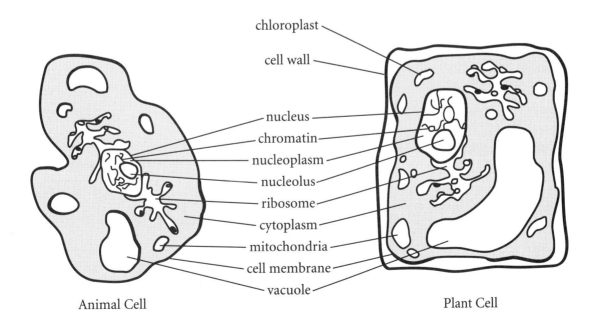

chloroplast

cell wall

nucleus

chromatin

nucleoplasm

nucleolus

ribosome

cytoplasm

mitochondria

cell membrane

vacuole

Animal Cell

Plant Cell

eukaryotic plant and animal cells, the major cell organelles are as follows:

- **Cell membrane:** partially permeable membrane that regulates flow of materials in and out of the cell and holds the structure of the cell together
- **Cytoplasm:** jelly-like material that encompasses the other cell structures
- **Endoplasmic reticulum:** a network of membranes extending from the nucleus into the cytoplasm, responsible for making lipids, proteins (in association with ribosomes), and transporting these products throughout the cell
- **Golgi body/apparatus:** stores and transports secretory products within the cell
- **Lysosome:** contains and releases enzymes within the cell
- **Mitochondrion:** the largest organelle and site of energy production, known as cellular respiration, in the cell (there are several mitochondria in each cell)
- **Nucleus:** contains genetic material and functions as the control center of the cell
- **Ribosome:** site of protein synthesis (there are many ribosomes in each cell)

Plant cells additionally have chloropoasts, where photosynthesis takes place, and a cell wall.

Genetics

Genetics is the study of heredity and variation. **Heredity** is the transmission of characteristics from parents to offspring via chromosomes. Gregor Mendel, a European monk in the late 18th century, developed some of the basic laws of heredity which have been updated, but are still applicable today:

- **Law of Segregation:** each hereditary characteristic is controlled by alleles that separate in the reproductive cells
- **Law of Independent Assortment:** each characteristic is inherited independent of other characteristics

- **Law of Dominance:** when two different alleles for the same characteristic are present in one cell, only one allele will be expressed, or **dominant**, and the other will be masked, or **recessive**.

The structure and function of every cell in the human body is predetermined by units of heredity called **genes**, located in specific positions on the chromosomes in a cell nucleus. Genes are made up of DNA. Genes give the cell instructions about how to function, when to reproduce, and even when to die. The process of cell reproduction through cell division is called *mitosis*. During mitosis, the genes of the parent cell are copied. Then, when the parent cell divides, it becomes two identical daughter cells.

Most cells in the human body have 46 chromosomes—23 chromosomcs from the mother (female, egg cell) and 23 chromosomes from the father (male, sperm cell). However, human sex cells (egg or sperm) have 23 chromosomes each. When the sex cells, or **gametes**, undergo the process of **fertilization**—the union of female and male sex cells—the resulting fertilized cell has 46 chromosomes. This fertilized cell will multiply to form a new individual consisting of a combination of chromosomes from the mother and the father. This fusion of two gametes during fertilization to produce offspring is referred to as sexual reproduction.

The sex of a human embryo is determined by the 23rd chromosome in the sperm. Human females have the chromosome pair XX. Males have the pair XY. Females, therefore, always give offspring an X chromosome, whereas males give either an X or a Y chromosome to the offspring.

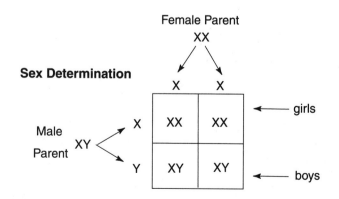

Sex Determination

Structure and Function of Human Systems

The human body can be divided into 11 systems, each of which is discussed below.

Integumentary System

The integument—the skin—is the outermost covering of the body. It consists of the epidermis (the thinner outermost layer) and the dermis (the thicker innermost layer). It also includes the hair and nails. Beneath the skin is the subcutaneous tissue.

The integumentary system has the following functions:

- Protecting the body from injury, dehydration, and invasion by harmful agents such as bacteria
- Providing sensitivity to pain, temperature, and pressure
- Regulating body temperature

Skeletal System

The skeleton provides the structure of the body. Comprised of 206 bones, along with cartilage and ligament, the skeletal system is rigid yet flexible. Joints are points where bones meet and may or may not move against each other. The cartilage is the flexible but strong substance found in joints, nose, and ears. The ligaments, made of softer, flexible tissue, attach bones to each other.

The skeletal system has the following functions:

- Providing mechanical support
- Protecting body organs
- Making body movement possible (along with the muscles)
- Storing calcium in the bones, which contain marrow for production of red and white blood cells and platelets

Muscular System

Muscles are made of sheets or bundles of cells. Muscles can do work only by contracting; expansion is passive. Therefore, skeletal muscles are usually attached to a bone in opposing pairs—one to contract while the other expands. There are three major types of muscles:

- **Voluntary** (or striated) muscles can be controlled by conscious thought.
- **Involuntary** (or smooth) muscles cannot be controlled by the will.
- **Cardiac** (or heart) muscles exist only in the heart. They contract spontaneously without needing nervous stimulation.

Tendons attach muscles to the skeleton.

Circulatory System

The circulatory system consists of the cardiovascular and lymphatic systems, including:

- the heart
- blood components such as red blood cells and platelets
- blood vessels, including arteries, veins, and capillaries
- lymphatic vessels and nodes
- lymph

The circulatory system circulates blood throughout the body, making the body's other functions possible by bringing oxygen and other materials to the cells and carrying away waste products and other secretions.

Immune System

The immune system is the body's protective mechanism. It consists of the lymphatic system; the white cells of the blood and bone marrow; antibodies; the thymus gland; and the skin.

The basic characteristics of the immune system include the concepts of:

- **Specificity:** the capacity to recognize and get rid of **antigens** by producing lymphocytes and antibodies. An antigen (literally meaning "antibody-generating") can include anything "foreign" to the body, such as viruses, bacteria, pollen, and, unfortunately, tissue that has been transplanted.
- **Diversity:** the capacity to respond to millions of kinds of invaders.
- **Self/nonself recognition:** the ability to distinguish the body's own molecules ("self") from antigens ("nonself").
- **Memory:** the capacity to "remember" previously encountered antigens and react more quickly when exposed again. This process is called acquired immunity.

The immune system's basic function is to protect the body from disease and injury.

Respiratory System

The respiratory system is responsible for taking oxygen into the body and eliminating carbon dioxide. It includes the lungs, nose, pharynx, larynx, trachea, bronchi, and diaphragm.

Digestive (or Gastrointestinal) System (GI)

The digestive system includes the gastrointestinal (GI) tract (also called the alimentary canal). This is basically a tube with two openings—the mouth and anus—for intake of food and elimination of waste. The parts of the GI tract are the mouth, the esophagus, the stomach, the small intestine, and the large intestine. Also included in this system are structures such as teeth, tongue, liver, pancreas, and gallbladder.

The digestive system breaks down food for energy, reabsorbs water and nutrients, and eliminates waste.

Urinary or Excretory System

The urinary system consists of:

- **Kidneys:** two compact, bean-shaped organs through which blood is cycled for removal of waste
- **Nephrons:** excretory tubes in the kidneys
- **Blood vessels** that serve the kidneys
- **Urinary structures** that carry waste out of the body—the ureters, bladder, and urethra

The kidneys remove waste or toxic byproducts from the blood and maintain homeostasis of blood and body fluids.

Nervous System

The nervous system is made up of the nerves, brain, spinal cord, and sense organs for sight, sound, smell, and taste. The brain is the nervous system's main control center and consists of three parts:

- The **cerebral hemispheres** are responsible for the higher functions, such as speech and hearing.
- The **cerebellum** is responsible for subconscious activities and some balance functions.
- The **brain stem** is responsible for basic functions such as breathing and circulation

The nervous system controls the flow of information between the sensory and motor cells and organs.

Endocrine System

The endocrine system controls communication between systems in the body. It consists of:

- **Hormones** are substances that regulate the growth or function of a specific tissue or organ. Hormones include insulin, sex hormones, adrenaline, and serotonin.

VITAMINS		
Vitamin	Sources	Results of Deficiency
A	green and yellow vegetables	night blindness, skin problems
B1 (thiamine)	cereals and yeast	beriberi
B2 (riboflavin)	green vegetables, yeast, liver, milk	sores on tongue, lips, mouth
B12	liver and meat (strictly from animals)	anemia—iron-poor blood
C (ascorbic acid)	green vegetables and citrus fruits	scurvy
D	fortified milk, fish-liver oils	rickets—deformed, weakened bones
E	cereal grains, green vegetables	muscular dystrophy, liver damage, infertility

■ **Glands** that secrete hormones include the pituitary, adrenal gland, thyroid, ovary, testis, and part of the pancreas.

Together with the nervous system, the endocrine system regulates and balances bodily fluids and chemicals. Hormones affect the body's growth, the development and functioning of reproductive organs and sexual characteristics, the development of higher nervous functions such as personality, and the ability of the body to handle stress and resist disease.

Reproductive System

Reproduction in humans involves two sets of organs, the internal reproductive organs and the external genitalia. In reproduction, the female ovum and the male spermatozoon fuse to form a zygote, which eventually develops into a fetus.

The reproductive system functions to create new individuals from existing ones and propagate the species.

Nutrition

The process by which organisms obtain energy from food for growth, maintenance, and repair is called **nutrition**. Food provides nutrients, such as carbohydrates, proteins, and fats. In humans, energy in the form of calories is gleaned chiefly from carbohydrates.

A calorie is actually a unit of heat. It is the unit of heat necessary to raise the temperature of one gram of water one degree Celsius.

Carbohydrates are starches or sugars that fuel all of the cells in the body. Common sources of carbohydrates are potatoes, beans, cereals, fruit, and milk. Both starches and sugars ultimately yield glucose. Cells convert glucose to energy or store excess glucose, called glycogen, in the liver and muscles. If the excess glucose exceeds a certain point, the excess glucose is converted to fat and stored.

Proteins are abundant in all living organisms. Structural proteins make up the fingernails, skin, bones, and teeth in humans. Other proteins regulate metabolism, produce movement, and transport oxygen and other substances in and out of body cells. Common sources of protein are meat, cheese, beans, nuts, and fish.

Fats are also essential for human nutrition. Fats function in cellular structure, composition, and transport. Containing approximately twice the caloric value of carbohydrates, fats are found in butter, cream, eggs, and most cheese.

Vitamins are other organic substances required in small amounts to maintain normal health. Most animals cannot manufacture many vitamins themselves and must have adequate amounts in the diet. The table above shows the major vitamins.

► Ecology

Ecology is the study of interrelationships between organisms and their physical environment. Ecologists consider animals and plants in terms of an ecosystem—the interaction of different populations of the same species in a shared environment. The sun fuels all of the energy in an ecosystem.

Ecosystems vary in size. Each contains air, soil, Producers, Consumers, and Decomposers; the latter three transfer energy in a process called the food chain. A food chain can be visualized as follows:

sunlight ➡ green plants (Producers) ➡ herbivores (Consumers) ➡ carnivores (Consumers) ➡ bacteria (Decomposers) ➡ soil ➡ green plants, etc.

Producers, such as green plants, use sunlight in the photosynthesis process to create their own food. The Producers are the food for Consumers, such as animals, which can't make their own food. The two main types of Consumers are herbivores and carnivores. **Herbivores** are animals that eat only vegetation. They have teeth and digestive systems adapted for processing plants. Examples of herbivores include rabbits, cows, and squirrels. **Carnivores** are animals that feed only on the flesh of other animals. They have powerful jaws and teeth. Examples of carnivores are tigers, wolves, and hyenas. Human beings are **omnivores**. Our bodies are capable of meeting nutritional needs using both plants and animal matter. All Consumers eat either Producers or other Consumers and use the energy to do work or radiate the energy back into the atmosphere.

When animals die, the dead organic matter is broken down by Decomposers, such as fungi. During this process of decay, Decomposers reintroduce minerals back into the soil in the ecosystem. Producers then recycle the minerals as they grow, and the process begins again.

Biomes are established ecological systems that extend over a large geographical area and are characterized by a dominant type of vegetation or climatic condition. Organisms in a biome are adapted to the climate associated with the region. The seven major biomes on Earth are:

- **Arctic Tundra:** treeless plains surrounding the Arctic Ocean, with permanently frozen subsoil
- **Deciduous:** leaf-shedding forests in mild climates
- **Desert:** environment with irregular or infrequent rainfall and high temperatures
- **Grassland:** areas with rainfall insufficient to support many trees; grass species dominate
- **Marine:** oceans and seas
- **Taiga:** evergreen forests that survive long winters
- **Tropical rainforest:** constant precipitation and high temperatures, with many plant species

► Earth Science

Earth scientists study the Earth or its parts including astronomy, meteorology, geology, and oceanography.

Astronomy

Astronomy, also considered a subdiscipline of physics, is the study of the universe beyond Earth's atmosphere. A solar system consists of a star and its natural satellites: asteroids, comets, meteoroids, and planets. The Sun is at the center of our solar system, which consists of the following planets (listed in order moving away from the sun, with the planet's rank in diameter in parentheses): Mercury (8), Venus (6), Earth (5), Mars (7), Jupiter (1), Saturn (2), Uranus (3), Neptune (4), and Pluto (9).

The Sun consists of approximately 75 percent hydrogen and 25 percent helium. With a diameter of 1,392,000 km, the Sun dwarfs everything in our solar system (compare: the Earth has a diameter of 12,756 km).

Other minor bodies in the solar system include:

- **Asteroids:** minor planets sometimes called planetoids
- **Comets:** small bodies of gas and dust consisting of a nucleus of ice and dust, a coma of gas and dust, and the tail (also gas and dust) that is only visible when the comet approaches the sun
- **Meteors:** any matter that collides with the Earth

The moon orbits the Earth approximately every 27 days. Its gravitational pull on the Earth causes the tides in the ocean. Moonlight is simply reflected sunlight. A lunar eclipse is caused when the Earth comes between the Sun and the moon. A solar eclipse is caused by the moon blocking sunlight from the Earth.

The Earth orbits the Sun while rotating on its axis, an imaginary line that bisects the Earth from the North to the South Pole. This rotation causes night and day. Only twice a year, on the autumnal and vernal equinoxes, are night and day of exactly equal length. The revolution of the Earth around the Sun causes the seasons. One revolution around the Sun is approximately 365 days, one year.

Meteorology

Meteorology is the study of Earth's atmosphere and its changes and interaction with the ground. The atmosphere consists of several layers:

- The troposphere (0–10 km)—where weather occurs
- The stratosphere (10–40 km)—contains the jet stream and the ozone layer
- The mesosphere (40–70 km)
- The thermosphere (70–400 km)
- The exosphere (400 km and higher)

Weather refers to the state of the atmosphere, including humidity, precipitation, temperature, cloud cover, visibility, and wind. Most sunlight is reflected by the Earth's atmosphere. Some sunlight penetrates the atmosphere and is absorbed by the Earth's crust. Wind, the motion of air relative to Earth's surface, can be measured with an anemometer and is caused (in part) by the difference in the amount of radiation received at different points on Earth.

Water on Earth is constantly turning to vapor in a process called **evaporation**. When warm air becomes saturated, or full of moisture, the water forms droplets in a process called **condensation**. Then it falls back down to Earth as precipitation: rain, sleet, snow, or hail. Humidity is the amount of moisture in the air at any time. It is measured using a hygrometer. A barometer measures air pressure, which is dependent on both temperature and humidity.

Geology

Geology is the study of the origin, structure, and composition of the Earth. Scientists calculate the age of Earth to be approximately 4,600 million years old. This time has been divided into four geologic eras:

- **Precambrian:** oldest era; a time of massive volcanic activity
- **Paleozoic:** 570 million years ago; the emergence of continents and mountains
- **Mesozoic:** 225 million years ago; more volcanic eruptions; also known as "The Age of Reptiles" (time of dinosaurs)
- **Cenozoic:** began about 65 million years ago. Giant glaciers (slow-moving sheets of ice) retreated from land masses allowing mammals and flowering plants the opportunity to diversify. We are still in the Cenozoic era today.

The Earth is a composed of three layers: the 7,000 km thick central core of solid iron and nickel, the 3,000 km thick semi-molten mantle, and the outer layer of crust. **Plate tectonics** is the study of the movement of large chunks or plates of the Earth's crust. **Faults** are cracks in the Earth's crust. Earthquakes, the sudden movement of plates, are measured according to seismic waves on the Richter Scale.

Rocks, the most familiar and tangible geologic objects, are made of one or more minerals on or just below the surface of the Earth. There are three main types of rocks:

- **Igneous:** formed by the crystallization of magma, or molten lava. An example is granite.
- **Sedimentary:** formed by the accumulation of silt or other rock fragments. Limestone is an example.
- **Metamorphic:** formed when pre-existing rock is subjected to chemical or physical alteration by high heat and pressure. An example is marble.

▶ Physical Science

Chemistry

Chemistry is the study of elements and the compounds they form. Matter can take the form of an element, a compound, or a mixture.

An **element** is the basic form of matter, incapable of being decomposed by chemical means into simpler substances. Each element has distinct chemical and physical characteristics. Hydrogen (H), oxygen (O), and carbon (C) are elements.

A **compound** is a combination of two or more elements chemically combined in a specific proportion. Compounds can be separated by chemical means, and are represented by chemical formulas that include the symbols of all the elements present. Examples of familiar compounds are water (H_2O) and table salt (NaCl). In order to be considered organic, a compound must contain carbon.

A **mixture** is a combination of two or more substances that are not chemically combined. Dissolving salt in water results in a mixture. The two compounds don't react with each other and can be separated by physical means—in this case, heating the water so it evaporates, leaving the salt behind.

All matter is made up of atoms. The following terms are used to define atomic structure:

- **Atom:** the smallest unit of an element that retains all of the element's chemical properties. An atom is composed of three primary particles: electrons, protons, and neutrons.
- **Electron:** found outside the nucleus (the center of an atom), it has a negligible mass and a charge of –1.
- **Proton:** found in the nucleus, it has a mass of 1 amu (atomic mass unit) and a charge of +1.
- **Neutron:** found in the nucleus, it has a mass of 1 amu and no charge.

An atom contains an identical number of protons and electrons, making it electrically neutral.

Atoms of the same element generally have the same properties, unless they are **isotopes**, which can behave differently. Atoms of different elements have different properties and different masses. Atoms of elements combine in simple whole number ratios.

Periodic Table

The periodic table (next page) lists all of the known elements according to their atomic numbers.

Atomic number is the number of protons in the atom. The atomic number determines the element.

Mass number is the total number of protons and neutrons in one atom of an element. Mass number can vary because the number of neutrons in an atom can change.

The horizontal rows of elements in the periodic table are called **periods**. There are seven periods in all. Moving from left to right across a period, the atomic number increases by one from one element to the next.

PERIODIC TABLE OF THE ELEMENTS

IA																	VIIIA
1 H 1.0	IIA											IIIA	IVA	VA	VIA	VIIA	2 He 4.0
3 Li 6.9	4 Be 9.0											5 B 10.8	6 C 12.0	7 N 14.0	8 O 16.0	9 F 19.0	10 Ne 20.2
11 Na 23.0	12 Mg 24.3	IIIB	IVB	VB	VIB	VIIB		VIIIB		IB	IIB	13 Al 27.0	14 Si 28.1	15 P 31.0	16 S 32.1	17 Gl 35.5	18 Ar 39.9
19 K 139.1	20 Ca 40.1	21 Sc 45.0	22 Ti 47.9	23 V 50.9	24 Cr 52.0	25 Mn 54.9	26 Fe 55.8	27 Co 58.9	28 Ni 58.7	29 Cu 63.5	30 Zn 65.4	31 Ga 69.7	32 Ge 72.6	33 As 74.9	34 Se 79.0	35 Br 79.9	36 Kr 83.8
37 Rb 85.5	38 Sr 87.6	39 Y 88.9	40 Zr 91.2	41 Nb 92.9	42 Mo 95.9	43 Tc (97)	44 Ru 101.1	45 Rh 102.9	46 Pd 106.7	47 Ag 107.9	48 Cd 112.4	49 In 114.8	50 Sn 118.7	51 Sb 121.8	52 Te 127.6	53 I 126.9	54 Xe 131.3
55 Cs 132.9	56 Ba 137.3	see below 57-71	72 Hf 178.5	73 Ta 180.9	74 W 183.9	75 Re 186.2	76 Os 190.2	77 Ir 192.2	78 Pt 195.1	79 Au 197.0	80 Hg 200.6	81 7i 204.4	82 Pb 207.2	83 Bi 209.0	84 Po 210	85 At (210)	86 Rn (222)
87 Fr (223)	88 Ra (226)	see below 89-103															

57 La 138.9	58 Ce 140.1	59 Pr 140.9	60 Nd 144.2	61 Pm (145)	62 Sm 150.4	63 Eu 152.0	64 Gd 157.3	65 Tb 158.9	66 Dy 162.5	67 Ho 164.9	68 Er 167.3	69 Tm 168.9	70 Yb 173.0	71 Lu 175.0
89 Ac 227	90 Th 232.0	91 Pa (231)	92 U 238.0	93 Np (237)	94 Pu (244)	95 Am (243)	96 Cm (247)	97 Bk (247)	98 Cf (251)	99 Es (254)	100 Fm (257)	101 Md (256)	102 No (254)	103 Lw (257)

Each successive element has one more electron in its outer shell. All elements in the same period have the same number of shells.

The vertical columns of elements in the periodic table are **groups**. Elements in the same group have the same number of electrons in their outer shell. They therefore have similar chemical properties.

Electronic Structure of Atoms

According to the periodic table, the atomic number of hydrogen (H) is 1, because it has one proton in its nucleus. The number of protons in an atom determines its atomic nucleus. The atomic number of nitrogen (N) is 7; nitrogen has seven protons in its nucleus.

Niels Bohr, a Danish physicist, proposed a model of the atom that had a nucleus surrounded by concentric orbits.

P = proton
N = neutron
e⁻ = electron

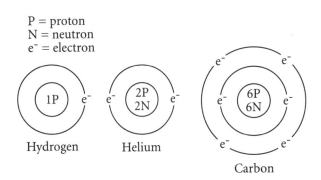

Hydrogen   Helium

Carbon

Electrons are found in the orbits. When electrons become excited, they absorb energy and move to an orbit farther from the nucleus. When they release energy, they fall to an orbit with lower energy closer to the nucleus. The energy level (also called electron **shell**) is a region of space in which electrons move around the nucleus.

Chemical Equations

Chemical equations are used to show the result of a physical or chemical change in matter. A physical change is when the shape or size of matter is changed, but the molecules remain unchanged. Steam from a boiling pot of water is an example of a physical change. A chemical change is one in which two or more molecules interact to form new molecules. Paper burning is an example of a chemical change—the paper changes to carbon.

The sum of the atomic weights of all the atoms in a formula is called the formula weight. A mole is the amount of substance containing Avogadro's number of particles, 6.02×10^{23} atoms of an element. The abbreviation is mol.

Use the following rules in balancing equations:

1. All reactants (starting materials) and products must be known, and their formulas must be correctly written.
2. The formulas are never changed in order to balance an equation.
3. The number of atoms of each element in the reactants must be equal to the number of atoms of the element in the products.
4. The numbers to the left of each formula (coefficients) must be reduced to the smallest possible whole numbers.

Types of chemical reactions include:

- **Combination or synthesis reactions:** two chemicals combine to form a new substance
- **Decomposition reactions:** one substance breaks down to create two or more substances

Concentration, Acids, Bases, and pH

Concentration is a measure of how much solute is in a solution. A **solute** is a substance that is dissolved in a medium, and a **solvent** is a medium in which a solute is dissolved. For instance: salt water is a solution—a homogenous mixture consisting of the solute (salt) and the solvent (water).

Acids are proton donors; they release hydrogen ions (protons). Acids have a sour taste. Bases are proton acceptors; they take up hydrogen ions. Bases have a bitter taste and feel slippery. Strong bases take up more hydrogen ions than weak bases.

The relative concentration of hydrogen ions is measured in concentration units called pH units. The pH scale runs from 0 to 14. A substance with a pH of 7 is neutral. Substances such as vinegar and orange juice, with a pH of less than 7, are considered acidic. Substances such as soaps and ammonia, with a pH of more than 7, are considered alkaline.

Measurement

Although you may be more familiar with the English system of measurement (inches, pounds, and so on), the metric system is the standard system of measurement in science. The metric system is a decimal system based on multiples and fractions of ten. The meter (m) is the standard unit of length in the decimal system:

1 meter = 100 centimeters (cm)
1 kilometer (km) = 1,000 meters

The gram (g) is the metric system unit of mass:

1 gram = 1,000 milligrams (mg)
1 kilogram (kg) = 1,000 grams

Volume, the amount of space occupied by a fluid or body, is usually measured using the liter. The cubic meter (cm^3) is actually the standard metric unit of volume, but it is infrequently used.

1 liter (L) = 1,000 milliliters (ml)
$1 cm^3 = 1$ ml

In science, temperature is most often measured using degrees Celsius (°C). On the Celsius scale, the freezing point for water is 0° and the boiling point for water is 100°. This makes it much easier to use than the Fahrenheit scale, which has a freezing point of 32° and a boiling point of 212°. The two equations below show how to convert a temperature measurement from one scale to the other.

$$°C = \frac{5}{9}(°F - 32)$$
$$°F = \frac{9}{5}(°C + 32)$$

Other important equations are as follows:

- **Speed** is the distance covered or traveled by an object per a certain unit or amount of time:
Speed = distance/time
- **Momentum** is the tendency of an object to continue moving in the same direction:
Momentum = mass × speed
- **Work** is a force applied to an object which, in turn, results in movement:
Work = force × distance
- **Power** is the rate at which work is done. It is measured in joules (J):
Power = work/time

Note: **Mass** should not be confused with **weight**. Mass is the measurement of the amount of matter in an object. Weight is the force by which gravity attracts a body to Earth.

Energy

Energy, the capacity to do work, is never created or destroyed—it may only be changed in form. There are many forms of energy, including light, sound, heat, chemical, mechanical, and electrical. Energy, like power, is measured in joules.

The two forms of energy are potential and kinetic energy. **Potential energy** is the energy stored in a body or system as a consequence of its position, shape, or state. **Kinetic energy** is the energy of motion, and is usually defined as the work that will be done by the body possessing the energy when it is brought to rest.

Sound and light are measured by their wavelength. A wave is a periodic disturbance in a medium or space. **Sound** is a vibration at a frequency and intensity audible to the normal human ear (20–20,000 Hertz). Vibrations that have a lower frequency are called **infrasounds**, and those with a higher frequency are called **ultrasounds**. **Light** is a form of electromagnetic radiation. Light can pass through a vacuum, but sound cannot. The electromagnetic spectrum is displayed in the diagram below.

Refraction is the bending of light, especially when it moves from one material to another. The refraction of sunlight results in a spectrum of colors, such as a rainbow. The colors in a spectrum are red, orange, yellow, green, blue, indigo, and violet.

Another form of energy—heat—may be transferred via conduction, convection, or radiation. **Conduction** is the transmission of heat from a region of high temperature to a region of lower temperature. Putting a cool kettle of water on a stove to boil is a good example. **Convection** is the process by which parts of a fluid or gas change density due to the uneven application of heat. For instance, as a stove heats a cool room, the warmer (less dense) air rises and the cold air remains lower. **Radiation** is heat transmitted via electromagnetic waves. The sun's heat warming the petals of a flower is an example of radiation.

Math Review

CHAPTER SUMMARY

This chapter gives you some important tips for dealing with math questions and reviews some of the most commonly tested concepts. If you need to learn or review important math skills, this chapter is for you.

Two subtests of the ASVAB—Arithmetic Reasoning and Mathematics Knowledge—cover math skills. Arithmetic Reasoning is basically math word problems. Mathematics Knowledge tests your knowledge of math concepts, principles, and procedures. You don't have to do a lot of calculation in the Mathematics Knowledge subtest; you need to know basic terminology (like *sum* and *perimeter)*, formulas (such as the area of a square), and computation rules. Both subtests cover the subjects you probably studied in school. This chapter reviews concepts you will need for both Arithmetic Reasoning and Mathematics Knowledge.

▶ Math Strategies

- **Don't work in your head!** Use your test book or scratch paper to take notes, draw pictures, and calculate. Although you might think that you can solve math questions more quickly in your head, that's a good way to make mistakes. Write out each step.
- **Read a math question in *chunks* rather than straight through from beginning to end.** As you read each *chunk,* stop to think about what it means and make notes or draw a picture to represent that *chunk.*

- **When you get to the actual question, circle it.** This will keep you more focused as you solve the problem.
- **Glance at the answer choices for clues.** If they are fractions, you probably should do your work in fractions; if they are decimals, you should probably work in decimals; etc.
- **Make a plan of attack to help you solve the problem.**
- **If a question stumps you, try one of the *backdoor* approaches explained in the next section.** These are particularly useful for solving word problems.
- **When you get your answer, reread the circled question to make sure you have answered it.** This helps avoid the careless mistake of answering the wrong question.
- **Check your work after you get an answer.** Test takers get a false sense of security when they get an answer that matches one of the multiple-choice answers. Here are some good ways to check your work *if you have time:*
  - Ask yourself if your answer is reasonable, if it makes sense.
  - Plug your answer back into the problem to make sure the problem holds together.
  - Do the question a second time, but use a different method.
- **Approximate when appropriate.** For example:
  - $5.98 + $8.97 is a little less than $15. (Add: $6 + $9)
  - .9876 × 5.0342 is close to 5. (Multiply: 1 × 5)
- **Skip hard questions and come back to them later.** Mark them in your test book so you can find them quickly.

Backdoor Approaches for Answering Tough Questions

Many word problems are actually easier to solve by backdoor approaches. The two techniques that follow are time-saving ways to solve multiple-choice word problems that you don't know how to solve with a straightforward approach. The first technique, *nice numbers*, is useful when there are unknowns (like x) in the text of the word problem, making the problem too abstract for you. The second technique, *working backward*, presents a quick way to substitute numeric answer choices back into the problem to see which one works.

Nice Numbers

1. When a question contains unknowns, like x, plug nice numbers in for the unknowns. A nice number is easy to calculate with and makes sense in the problem.
2. Read the question with the nice numbers in place. Then solve it.
3. If the answer choices are all numbers, the choice that matches your answer is the right one.
4. If the answer choices contain unknowns, substitute the same nice numbers into all the answer choices. The choice that matches your answer is the right one. If more than one answer matches, do the problem again with different nice numbers. You will only have to check the answer choices that have already matched.

Example: Judi went shopping with p dollars in her pocket. If the price of shirts was s shirts for d dollars, what is the maximum number of shirts Judi could buy with the money in her pocket?

a. psd

b. $\frac{ps}{d}$

c. $\frac{pd}{s}$

d. $\frac{ds}{p}$

To solve this problem, let's try these nice numbers: $p = \$100$, $s = 2$; $d = \$25$. Now reread it with the numbers in place:

> Judi went shopping with *$100* in her pocket. If the price of shirts was *2* shirts for *$25*, what is the maximum number of shirts Judi could buy with the money in her pocket?

Since 2 shirts cost $25, that means that 4 shirts cost $50, and 8 shirts cost $100. So our answer is 8. Let's substitute the nice numbers into all 4 answers:

a. $100 \times 2 \times 25 = 5,000$

b. $\frac{100 \times 2}{25} = 8$

c. $\frac{100 \times 25}{2} = 1,250$

d. $\frac{25 \times 2}{100} = \frac{1}{2}$

The answer is **b** because it is the only one that matches our answer of 8.

Working Backward

You can frequently solve a word problem by plugging the answer choices back into the text of the problem to see which one fits all the facts stated in the problem. The process is faster than you think because you will probably only have to substitute one or two answers to find the right one.

This approach works only when:

- All of the answer choices are numbers.
- You are asked to find a simple number, not a sum, product, difference, or ratio.

Here's what to do:

1. Look at all the answer choices and begin with the one in the middle of the range. For example, if the answers are 14, 8, 2, 20, and 25, begin by plugging 14 into the problem.
2. If your choice doesn't work, eliminate it. Determine if you need a bigger or smaller answer.
3. Plug in one of the remaining choices.
4. If none of the answers works, you may have made a careless error. Begin again or look for your mistake.

Example: Juan ate $\frac{1}{3}$ of the jellybeans. Maria then ate $\frac{3}{4}$ of the remaining jellybeans, which left 10 jellybeans. How many jellybeans were there to begin with?

a. 60

b. 80

c. 90

d. 120

Starting with the middle answer, let's assume there were 90 jellybeans to begin with:

Since Juan ate $\frac{1}{3}$ of them, that means he ate 30 ($\frac{1}{3} \times 90 = 30$), leaving 60 of them ($90 - 30 = 60$). Maria then ate $\frac{3}{4}$ of the 60 jellybeans, or 45 of them ($\frac{3}{4} \times 60 = 45$). That leaves 15 jellybeans ($60 - 45 = 15$).

The problem states that there were 10 jellybeans left, and we wound up with 15 of them. That indicates that we started with too big a number. Thus, 90, 120, and 140 are all incorrect! With only two choices left, let's use common sense to decide which one to try. The next lower answer is only a little smaller than 90 and may not be small enough. So, let's try 60:

Since Juan ate $\frac{1}{3}$ of them, that means he ate 20 ($\frac{1}{3} \times 60 = 20$), leaving 40 of them ($60 - 20 = 40$). Maria then ate $\frac{3}{4}$ of the 40 jellybeans, or 30 of them ($\frac{3}{4} \times 40 = 30$). That leaves 10 jellybeans ($40 - 30 = 10$).

Because this result of 10 jellybeans remaining agrees with the problem, the right answer is **a**.

Glossary of Terms

Denominator	The bottom number in a fraction. *Example:* 2 is the denominator in $\frac{1}{2}$.
Difference	Subtract. The difference of two numbers means subtract one number from the other.
Divisible by	A number is divisible by a second number if that second number divides *evenly* into the original number. *Example:* 10 is divisible by 5 ($10 \div 5 = 2$, with no remainder). However, 10 is not divisible by 3. (See *Multiple of*.)
Even Integer	Integers that are divisible by 2, like . . . –4, –2, 0, 2, 4. . . . (See *Integer*.)
Integer	Numbers along the number line, like . . . –3, –2, –1, 0, 1, 2, 3. . . . Integers include the whole numbers and their opposites. (See *Whole Number*.)
Multiple of	A number is a multiple of a second number if that second number can be multiplied by an integer to get the original number. *Example:* 10 is a multiple of 5 ($10 = 5 \times 2$); however, 10 is not a multiple of 3. (See *Divisible by*.)
Negative Number	A number that is less than zero, like . . . –1, –18.6, $-\frac{3}{4}$. . . .
Numerator	The top part of a fraction. *Example:* 1 is the numerator of $\frac{1}{2}$.
Odd Integer	Integers that aren't divisible by 2, like . . . –5, –3, –1, 1, 3. . . .
Positive Number	A number that is greater than zero, like . . . 2, 42, $\frac{1}{2}$, 4.63. . . .
Prime Number	Integers that are divisible only by 1 and themselves, like . . . 2, 3, 5, 7, 11. . . . All prime numbers are odd, except for number 2. The number 1 is not considered prime.
Product	Multiply. The product of two numbers means the numbers are multiplied together.
Quotient	The answer you get when you divide. *Example:* 10 divided by 5 is 2; the quotient is 2.
Real Number	All the numbers you can think of, like . . . 17, –5, $\frac{1}{2}$, –23.6, 3.4329, 0. . . . Real numbers include the integers, fractions, and decimals. (See *Integer*.)
Remainder	The number left over after division. *Example:* 11 divided by 2 is 5, with a remainder of 1.
Sum	Add. The sum of 2 numbers means the numbers are added together.
Whole Number	Numbers you can count on your fingers, like . . . 1, 2, 3. . . . All whole numbers are positive.

▶ Word Problems

Many of the math problems on tests are word problems. A word problem can include any kind of math, including simple arithmetic, fractions, decimals, percentages, even algebra and geometry.

The hardest part of any word problem is translating English into math. When you read a problem, you can frequently translate it *word for word* from English statements into mathematical statements. At other times, however, a key word in the word problem hints at the mathematical operation to be performed. Here are the translation rules:

EQUALS key words: *is, are, has*

English	Math
Bob is 18 years old.	$b = 18$
There are seven hats.	$h = 7$
Judi has five books.	$j = 5$

ADDITION key words: *sum; more, greater, or older than; total; altogether*

English	Math
The sum of two numbers is 10.	$x + y = 10$
Karen has $5 more than Sam.	$k = 5 + s$
The base is 3" greater than the height.	$b = 3 + h$
Judi is two years older than Tony.	$j = 2 + t$
The total of three numbers is 25.	$a + b + c = 25$
How much do Joan and Tom have altogether?	$j + t = ?$

SUBTRACTION key words: *difference, less or younger than, remain, left over*

English	Math
The difference between two numbers is 17.	$x - y = 17$
Mike has five less cats than twice the number Jan has.	$m = 2j - 5$
Jay is two years younger than Brett.	$j = b - 2$
After Carol ate three apples, r apples remained.	$r = a - 3$

MULTIPLICATION key words: *of, product, times*

English	Math
Twenty percent of Matthew's baseball caps	$0.20 \times m$
Half of the boys	$\frac{1}{2} \times b$
The product of two numbers is 12.	$a \times b = 12$

DIVISION key word: *per*

English	Math
15 drops per teaspoon	$\frac{15 \text{ drops}}{\text{teaspoon}}$
22 miles per gallon	$\frac{22 \text{ miles}}{\text{gallon}}$

Distance Formula: Distance = Rate × Time

The key words are movement words like: plane, train, boat, car, walk, run, climb, swim.

- How far did the plane travel in 4 hours if it averaged 300 miles per hour?

  $d = 300 \times 4$

  $d = 1{,}200$ miles

- Ben walked 20 miles in four hours. What was his average speed?

  $20 = r \times 4$

  5 miles per hour $= r$

Solving a Word Problem Using the Translation Table

Remember the problem at the beginning of this chapter about the jellybeans?

Example: Juan ate $\frac{1}{3}$ of the jellybeans. Maria then ate $\frac{3}{4}$ of the remaining jellybeans, which left 10 jellybeans. How many jellybeans were there to begin with?

a. 60

b. 80

c. 90

d. 120

We solved it by *working backward.* Now let's solve it using our translation rules.

Assume Juan started with J jellybeans. Eating $\frac{1}{3}$ of them means eating $\frac{1}{3} \times J$ jellybeans. Maria ate a fraction of the remaining jellybeans, which means we must subtract to find out how many are left: $J - \frac{1}{3} \times J = \frac{2}{3} \times J$. Maria then ate $\frac{3}{4}$, leaving $\frac{1}{4}$ of the $\frac{2}{3} \times J$ jellybeans, or $\frac{1}{4} \times \frac{2}{3} \times J$ jellybeans. Multiplying out $\frac{1}{4} \times \frac{2}{3} \times J$ gives $\frac{1}{6}J$ as the number of jellybeans left. The problem states that there were 10 jellybeans left, meaning that we set $\frac{1}{6} \times J$ equal to 10:

$$\tfrac{1}{6} \times J = 10.$$

Solving this equation for J gives $J = 60$. Thus, the right answer is **a** (the same answer we got when we *worked backward*). As you can see, both methods—working backward and translating from English to math—work. You should use whichever method is more comfortable for you.

Practice Word Problems

You will find word problems using fractions, decimals, and percentages in those sections of this chapter. For now, practice using the translation table on problems that just require you to work with basic arithmetic. Answers are found on page 135.

1. Joan went shopping with $100 and returned home with only $18.42. How much money did she spend?
   a. $81.58
   b. $72.68
   c. $72.58
   d. $71.68
   e. $71.58

2. Mark invited ten friends to a party. Each friend brought three guests. How many people came to the party, excluding Mark?
   a. 3
   b. 10
   c. 30
   d. 40
   e. 41

3. The office secretary can type 80 words per minute on his word processor. How many minutes will it take him to type a report containing 760 words?
   a. 8
   b. $8\frac{1}{2}$
   c. 9
   d. $9\frac{1}{2}$
   e. 10

4. Mr. Wallace is writing a budget request to upgrade his personal computer system. He wants to purchase a cable modem, which will cost $100, two new software programs at $350 each, a color printer for $249, and an additional color cartridge for $25. What is the total amount Mr. Wallace should write on his budget request?
   a. $724
   b. $974
   c. $1,049
   d. $1,064
   e. $1,074

► Fraction Review

Problems involving fractions may be straightforward calculation questions, or they may be word problems. Typically, they ask you to add, subtract, multiply, divide, or compare fractions.

Working with Fractions

A fraction is a part of something.

> *Example:* Let's say that a pizza was cut into eight equal slices and you ate three of them. The fraction $\frac{3}{8}$ tells you what part of the pizza you ate. The pizza below shows this: 3 of the 8 pieces (the ones you ate) are shaded.

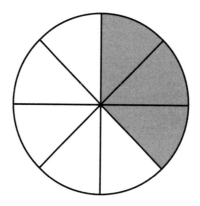

Three Kinds of Fractions

Proper fraction: The top number is less than the bottom number:

$$\frac{1}{2}, \frac{2}{3}, \frac{4}{9}, \frac{8}{13}$$

The value of a proper fraction is less than 1.

Improper fraction: The top number is greater than or equal to the bottom number:

$$\frac{3}{2}, \frac{5}{3}, \frac{14}{9}, \frac{12}{12}$$

The value of an improper fraction is 1 or more.

Mixed number: A fraction written to the right of a whole number:

$$3\frac{1}{2}; 4\frac{2}{3}; 12\frac{3}{4}; 24\frac{3}{4}$$

The value of a mixed number is more than 1; it is the sum of the whole number plus the fraction.

Changing Improper Fractions into Mixed or Whole Numbers

It's easier to add and subtract fractions that are mixed numbers rather than improper fractions. To change an improper fraction, say $\frac{13}{2}$, into a mixed number, follow these steps:

1. Divide the bottom number (2) into the top number (13) to get the whole number portion (6) of the mixed number:

$$2\overline{)13} \quad \begin{array}{r} 6 \\ \underline{12} \\ 1 \end{array}$$

2. Write the remainder of the division (1) over the old bottom number (2): $\quad 6\frac{1}{2}$
3. Check: Change the mixed number back into an improper fraction (see steps below).

Changing Mixed Numbers into Improper Fractions

It's easier multiply and divide fractions when you're working with improper fractions rather than mixed numbers. To change a mixed number, say $2\frac{3}{4}$, into an improper fraction, follow these steps:

1. Multiply the whole number (2) by the bottom number (4): $\quad\quad 2 \times 4 = 8$
2. Add the result (8) to the top number (3): $\quad\quad 8 + 3 = 11$
3. Put the total (11) over the bottom number (4): $\quad\quad \frac{11}{4}$
4. Check: Reverse the process by changing the improper fraction into a mixed number. If you get back the number you started with, your answer is right.

Reducing Fractions

Reducing a fraction means writing it in *lowest terms*, that is, with smaller numbers. For instance, 50¢ is $\frac{50}{100}$ of a dollar, or $\frac{1}{2}$ of a dollar. In fact, if you have 50¢ in your pocket, you say that you have half a dollar. Reducing a fraction does not change its value.

Follow these steps to reduce a fraction:

1. Find a whole number that divides *evenly* into both numbers that make up the fraction.
2. Divide that number into the top of the fraction, and replace the top of the fraction with the quotient (the answer you got when you divided).
3. Do the same thing to the bottom number.
4. Repeat the first 3 steps until you can't find a number that divides evenly into both numbers of the fraction.

For example, let's reduce $\frac{8}{24}$. We could do it in two steps $\frac{8 \div 4}{24 \div 4} = \frac{2}{6}$; then $\frac{2 \div 2}{6 \div 2} = \frac{1}{3}$. Or we could do it in a single step $\frac{8 \div 8}{24 \div 8} = \frac{1}{3}$.

Shortcut: When the top and bottom numbers both end in zeroes, cross out the same number of zeroes in both numbers to begin the reducing process. For example $\frac{300}{4,000}$ reduces to $\frac{3}{40}$ when you cross out two zeroes in both numbers.

Whenever you do arithmetic with fractions, reduce your answer. On a multiple-choice test, don't panic if your answer isn't listed. Try to reduce it and then compare it to the choices.

Reduce these fractions to lowest terms.

_____ **5.** $\frac{3}{12}$

_____ **6.** $\frac{14}{35}$

_____ **7.** $\frac{27}{72}$

Raising Fractions to Higher Terms

Before you can add and subtract fractions, you have to know how to raise a fraction to higher terms. This is actually the opposite of reducing a fraction.

Follow these steps to raise $\frac{2}{3}$ to 24ths:

1. Divide the old bottom number (3) into the new one (24): $3\overline{)24} = 8$

2. Multiply the answer (8) by the old top number (2): $2 \times 8 = 16$

3. Put the answer (16) over the new bottom number (24): $\frac{16}{24}$

4. Check: Reduce the new fraction to see if you get back the original one: $\frac{16 \div 8}{24 \div 8} = \frac{2}{3}$

Raise these fractions to higher terms.

_____ **8.** $\frac{5}{12} = \frac{}{24}$

_____ **9.** $\frac{2}{9} = \frac{}{27}$

_____ **10.** $\frac{2}{5} = \frac{}{500}$

Adding Fractions

If the fractions have the same bottom numbers, just add the top numbers together and write the total over the bottom number.

Examples: $\frac{2}{9} + \frac{4}{9} = \frac{2+4}{9} = \frac{6}{9}$ Reduce the sum: $\frac{2}{3}$.

             $\frac{5}{8} + \frac{7}{8} = \frac{12}{8}$.   Change the sum to a mixed number: $1\frac{4}{8}$; then reduce: $1\frac{1}{2}$.

There are a few extra steps to add mixed numbers with the same bottom numbers, say $2\frac{3}{5} + 1\frac{4}{5}$:

1. Add the fractions: $\frac{3}{5} + \frac{4}{5} = \frac{7}{5}$

2. Change the improper fraction into a mixed number: $\frac{7}{5} = 1\frac{2}{5}$

3. Add the whole numbers: $2 + 1 = 3$

4. Add the results of steps 2 and 3: $1\frac{2}{5} + 3 = 4\frac{2}{5}$

Finding the Least Common Denominator

If the fractions you want to add don't have the same bottom number, you will have to raise some or all of the fractions to higher terms so that they all have the same bottom number, called the common denominator. All of the original bottom numbers divide evenly into the common denominator. If it is the smallest number that they all divide evenly into, it is called the **least common denominator (LCD).**

Here are a few tips for finding the LCD, the smallest number that all the bottom numbers evenly divide into:

- See if all the bottom numbers divide evenly into the biggest bottom number.
- Check out the multiplication table of the largest bottom number until you find a number that all the other bottom numbers evenly divide into.
- When all else fails, multiply all the bottom numbers together.

Example: $\frac{2}{3} + \frac{4}{5}$

1. Find the LCD. Multiply the bottom numbers: $\qquad 3 \times 5 = 15$

2. Raise each fraction to 15ths:

$$\frac{2}{3} = \frac{10}{15}$$
$$+\frac{4}{5} = \frac{12}{15}$$

3. Add as usual:

$$\frac{22}{15}$$

Try these addition problems:

_____ **11.** $\frac{3}{4} + \frac{1}{6}$

_____ **12.** $\frac{7}{8} + \frac{2}{3} + \frac{3}{4}$

_____ **13.** $4\frac{1}{3} + 2\frac{3}{4} + \frac{1}{6}$

Subtracting Fractions

If the fractions have the same bottom numbers, just subtract the top numbers and write the difference over the bottom number.

Example: $\frac{4}{9} - \frac{3}{9} = \frac{4-3}{9} = \frac{1}{9}$

If the fractions you want to subtract don't have the same bottom number, you will have to raise some or all of the fractions to higher terms so that they all have the same bottom number, or LCD. If you forgot how to find the LCD, just read the section on adding fractions with different bottom numbers.

Example: $\frac{5}{6} - \frac{3}{4}$

1. Raise each fraction to 12ths because 12 is the LCD, the smallest number that 6 and 4 both divide into evenly:

2. Subtract as usual:

$$\begin{array}{r} \frac{5}{6} = \frac{10}{12} \\ -\frac{3}{4} = \frac{9}{12} \\ \hline \frac{1}{12} \end{array}$$

Subtracting mixed numbers with the same bottom number is similar to adding mixed numbers.

Example: $4\frac{3}{5} - 1\frac{2}{5}$

1. Subtract the fractions: $\qquad \frac{3}{5} - \frac{2}{5} = \frac{1}{5}$

2. Subtract the whole numbers: $\qquad 4 - 1 = 3$

3. Add the results of steps 1 and 2: $\qquad \frac{1}{5} + 3 = 3\frac{1}{5}$

Sometimes there is an extra "borrowing" step when you subtract mixed numbers with the same bottom numbers, say $7\frac{3}{5} - 2\frac{4}{5}$:

1. You can't subtract the fractions the way they are because $\frac{4}{5}$ is bigger than $\frac{3}{5}$. So you borrow 1 from the 7, making it 6, and change that 1 to $\frac{5}{5}$ because 5 is the bottom number: $\qquad 7\frac{3}{5} = 6\frac{5}{5} + \frac{3}{5}$

2. Add the numbers from step 1: $\qquad 6\frac{5}{5} + \frac{3}{5} = 6\frac{8}{5}$

3. Now you have a different version of the original problem: $\qquad 6\frac{8}{5} - 2\frac{4}{5}$

4. Subtract the fractional parts of the two mixed numbers: $\qquad \frac{8}{5} - \frac{4}{5} = \frac{4}{5}$

5. Subtract the whole number parts of the two mixed numbers: $\qquad 6 - 2 = 4$

6. Add the results of the last 2 steps together: $\qquad 4 + \frac{4}{5} = 4\frac{4}{5}$

Try these subtraction problems:

_____ **14.** $\frac{4}{5} - \frac{2}{3}$

_____ **15.** $\frac{7}{8} - \frac{1}{4} - \frac{1}{2}$

_____ **16.** $4\frac{1}{3} - 2\frac{3}{4}$

Now let's put what you have learned about adding and subtracting fractions to work in some real-life problems.

_____ **17.** Manuel drove $3\frac{1}{2}$ miles to work. Then he drove $4\frac{3}{4}$ miles to the store. When he left there, he drove 2 miles to the dry cleaners. Then he drove $3\frac{2}{3}$ miles back to work for a meeting. Finally, he drove $3\frac{1}{2}$ miles home. How many miles did he travel in total?

    a. $17\frac{5}{12}$
    b. $16\frac{5}{12}$
    c. $15\frac{7}{12}$
    d. $15\frac{5}{12}$
    e. $13\frac{11}{12}$

_____ **18.** Before leaving the warehouse, a truck driver noted that the mileage gauge registered $4{,}357\frac{4}{10}$ miles. When he arrived at the delivery site, the mileage gauge then registered $4{,}400\frac{1}{10}$ miles. How many miles did he drive from the warehouse to the delivery site?

    a. $42\frac{3}{10}$
    b. $42\frac{7}{10}$
    c. $43\frac{7}{10}$
    d. $47\frac{2}{10}$
    e. $57\frac{3}{10}$

Multiplying Fractions

Multiplying fractions is actually easier than adding them. All you do is multiply the top numbers and then multiply the bottom numbers.

Examples: $\frac{2}{3} \times \frac{5}{7} = \frac{2\times5}{3\times7} = \frac{10}{21}$

            $\frac{1}{2} \times \frac{3}{5} \times \frac{7}{4} = \frac{1\times3\times7}{2\times5\times4} = \frac{21}{40}$

Sometimes you can *cancel* before multiplying. Canceling is a shortcut that makes the multiplication go faster because you're multiplying with smaller numbers. It's very similar to reducing: if there is a number that divides evenly into a top number and bottom number, do that division before multiplying. If you forget to cancel, you will still get the right answer, but you will have to reduce it.

Example: $\frac{5}{6} \times \frac{9}{20}$

1. Cancel the 6 and the 9 by dividing 3 into both of them: $6 \div 3 = 2$ and $9 \div 3 = 3$. Cross out the 6 and the 9.
2. Cancel the 5 and the 20 by dividing 5 into both of them: $5 \div 5 = 1$ and $20 \div 5 = 4$. Cross out the 5 and the 20.
3. Multiply across the new top numbers and the new bottom numbers: $\frac{1\times3}{2\times4} = \frac{3}{8}$.

Try these multiplication problems.

———— **19.** $\frac{1}{5} \times \frac{2}{3}$

———— **20.** $\frac{2}{3} \times \frac{4}{7} \times \frac{3}{5}$

———— **21.** $\frac{3}{4} \times \frac{8}{9}$

To multiply a fraction by a whole number, first rewrite the whole number as a fraction with a bottom number of 1.

Example: $5 \times \frac{2}{3} = \frac{5}{1} \times \frac{2}{3} = \frac{10}{3}$

(Optional: convert $\frac{10}{3}$ to a mixed number: $3\frac{1}{3}$)

To multiply with mixed numbers, it's easier to change them to improper fractions before multiplying.

Example: $4\frac{2}{3} \times 5\frac{1}{2}$

1. Convert $4\frac{2}{3}$ to an improper fraction: $\qquad$ $4\frac{2}{3} = \frac{(4 \times 3 + 2)}{3} = \frac{14}{3}$

2. Convert $5\frac{1}{2}$ to an improper fraction: $\qquad$ $5\frac{1}{2} = \frac{(5 \times 2 + 1)}{2} = \frac{11}{2}$

3. Cancel and multiply the fractions: $\qquad$ $\frac{\overset{7}{\cancel{14}}}{3} \cdot \frac{11}{\underset{1}{\cancel{2}}} = \frac{77}{3}$

4. Optional: convert the improper fraction to a mixed number: $\qquad$ $\frac{77}{3} = 25\frac{2}{3}$

Now try these multiplication problems with mixed numbers and whole numbers:

———— **22.** $4\frac{1}{3} \times \frac{2}{5}$

———— **23.** $2\frac{1}{2} \times 6$

———— **24.** $3\frac{3}{4} \times 4\frac{4}{5}$

Here are a few more real-life problems to test your skills:

———— **25.** After driving $\frac{2}{3}$ of the 15 miles to work, Mr. Stone stopped to make a phone call. How many miles had he driven when he made his call?

    a. 5

    b. $7\frac{1}{2}$

    c. 10

    d. 12

    e. $15\frac{2}{3}$

_____ **26.** If Henry worked $\frac{3}{4}$ of a 40-hour week, how many hours did he work?

    a. $7\frac{1}{2}$

    b. 10

    c. 20

    d. 25

    e. 30

_____ **27.** Technician Chin makes \$14.00 an hour. When she works more than 8 hours a day, she gets overtime pay of $1\frac{1}{2}$ times her regular hourly wage for the extra hours. How much did she earn for working 11 hours in one day?

    a. \$77

    b. \$154

    c. \$175

    d. \$210

    e. \$231

Dividing Fractions

To divide one fraction by a second fraction, invert the second fraction (that is, flip the top and bottom numbers) and then multiply.

Example: $\frac{1}{2} \div \frac{3}{5}$

1. Invert the second fraction $(\frac{3}{5})$: $\frac{5}{3}$
2. Change the division sign ($\div$) to a multiplication sign ($\times$)
3. Multiply the first fraction by the new second fraction: $\frac{1}{2} \times \frac{5}{3} = \frac{1 \times 5}{2 \times 3} = \frac{5}{6}$

To divide a fraction by a whole number, first change the whole number to a fraction by putting it over 1. Then follow the division steps above.

Example: $\frac{3}{5} \div 2 = \frac{3}{5} \div \frac{2}{1} = \frac{3}{5} \times \frac{1}{2} = \frac{3 \times 1}{5 \times 2} = \frac{3}{10}$

When the division problem has a mixed number, convert it to an improper fraction and then divide as usual.

Example: $2\frac{3}{4} \div \frac{1}{6}$

1. Convert $2\frac{3}{4}$ to an improper fraction: $2\frac{3}{4} = \frac{2 \times 4 + 3}{4} = \frac{11}{4}$

2. Divide $\frac{11}{4}$ by $\frac{1}{6}$; flip $\frac{1}{6}$ to $\frac{6}{1}$; change $\div$ to $\times$ $\frac{11}{4} \div \frac{1}{6} = \frac{11}{4} \times \frac{6}{1}$

3. Cancel and multiply: $\frac{11}{\underset{2}{4}} \times \frac{\overset{3}{6}}{1} = \frac{11 \times 3}{2 \times 1} = \frac{33}{2}$

Here are a few division problems to try.

_____ **28.** $\frac{1}{3} \div \frac{2}{3}$

_____ **29.** $2\frac{3}{4} \div \frac{1}{2}$

_____ **30.** $\frac{3}{5} \div 3$

_____ **31.** $3\frac{3}{4} \div 2\frac{1}{3}$

Let's wrap this up with some real-life problems.

_____ **32.** If four friends evenly split $6\frac{1}{2}$ pounds of candy, how many pounds of candy does each friend get?

    a. $\frac{8}{13}$

    b. $1\frac{5}{8}$

    c. $1\frac{1}{2}$

    d. $1\frac{5}{13}$

    e. 4

_____ **33.** How many $2\frac{1}{2}$-pound chunks of cheese can be cut from a single 20-pound piece of cheese?

    a. 2

    b. 4

    c. 6

    d. 8

    e. 10

_____ **34.** Ms. Goldbaum earned $36.75 for working $3\frac{1}{2}$ hours. What was her hourly wage?

    a. $10.00

    b. $10.50

    c. $10.75

    d. $12.00

    e. $12.25

▶ Decimals

A decimal is a special kind of fraction. You use decimals every day when you deal with money—$10.35 is a decimal that represents 10 dollars and 35 cents. The decimal point separates the dollars from the cents. Because there are 100 cents in one dollar, 1¢ is $\frac{1}{100}$ of a dollar, or $.01.

Each decimal digit to the right of the decimal point has a name:

Examples: $.1 = 1 \text{ tenth} = \frac{1}{10}$
$.02 = 2 \text{ hundredths} = \frac{2}{100}$
$.003 = 3 \text{ thousandths} = \frac{3}{1,000}$
$.0004 = 4 \text{ ten-thousandths} = \frac{4}{10,000}$

When you add zeroes after the rightmost decimal place, you don't change the value of the decimal. For example, 6.17 is the same as all of these:

6.170
6.1700
6.17000000000000000

If there are digits on both sides of the decimal point (like 10.35), the number is called a mixed decimal. If there are digits only to the right of the decimal point (like .53), the number is called a decimal. A whole number (like 15) is understood to have a decimal point at its right (15.). Thus, 15 is the same as 15.0, 15.00, 15.000, and so on.

Changing Fractions to Decimals

To change a fraction to a decimal, divide the bottom number into the top number after you put a decimal point and a few zeroes on the right of the top number. When you divide, bring the decimal point up into your answer.

Example: Change $\frac{3}{4}$ to a decimal.

1. Add a decimal point and 2 zeroes to the top number (3):   3.00
2. Divide the bottom number (4) into 3.00:
   Bring the decimal point up into the answer:

$$4\overline{)3.00} \quad \begin{array}{r} .75 \\ \hline 3.00 \\ 2\,8 \\ \hline 20 \\ 20 \\ \hline 0 \end{array}$$

3. The quotient (result of the division) is the answer: .75

Some fractions may require you to add many decimal zeroes in order for the division to come out evenly. In fact, when you convert a fraction like $\frac{2}{3}$ to a decimal, you can keep adding decimal zeroes to the top number forever because the division will never come out evenly. As you divide 3 into 2, you will keep getting 6's:

$$2 \div 3 = .6666666666 \text{ etc.}$$

This is called a *repeating decimal* and it can be written as $.66\overline{6}$ or as $.66\frac{2}{3}$. You can approximate it as .67, .667, .6667, and so on.

Changing Decimals to Fractions

To change a decimal to a fraction, write the digits of the decimal as the top number of a fraction and write the decimal's name as the bottom number of the fraction. Then reduce the fraction, if possible.

Example: .018

1. Write 18 as the top of the fraction: $\underline{18}$
2. Three places to the right of the decimal means *thousandths,* so write 1,000 as the bottom number: $\frac{18}{1,000}$
3. Reduce by dividing 2 into the top and bottom numbers: $\frac{18 \div 2}{1,000 \div 2} = \frac{9}{500}$

Change these decimals or mixed decimals to fractions.

35. .005

36. 3.48

37. 123.456

Comparing Decimals

Because decimals are easier to compare when they have the same number of digits after the decimal point, tack zeroes onto the end of the shorter decimals. Then all you have to do is compare the numbers as if the decimal points weren't there:

Example: Compare .08 and .1

1. Tack one zero at the end of .1: .10
2. To compare .10 to .08, just compare 10 to 8.
3. Since 10 is larger than 8, .1 is larger than .08.

Adding and Subtracting Decimals

To add or subtract decimals, line them up so their decimal points are even. You may want to tack on zeroes at the end of shorter decimals so you can keep all your digits lined up evenly. Remember, if a number doesn't have a decimal point, then put one at the right end of the number.

Example: 1.23 + 57 + .038

1. Line up the numbers like this:
2. Add.

$$\begin{array}{r} 1.230 \\ 57.000 \\ + \ .038 \\ \hline 58.268 \end{array}$$

Example: 1.23 − .038

1. Line up the numbers like this:
2. Subtract.

$$\begin{array}{r} 1.230 \\ - \ .038 \\ \hline 1.192 \end{array}$$

Try these addition and subtraction problems.

_____ **38.** .905 + .02 + 3.075

_____ **39.** .005 + 8 + .3

_____ **40.** 3.48 − 2.573

_____ **41.** 123.456 − 122

_____ **42.** A park ranger drove 3.7 miles to the state park. He then walked 1.6 miles around the park to make sure everything was all right. He got back into the car, drove 2.75 miles to check on a broken light and then drove 2 miles back to the ranger station. How many miles did he drive in total?
   a. 8.05
   b. 8.45
   c. 8.8
   d. 10
   e. 10.05

_____ **43.** The average number of customers at a diner fell from 486.4 per week to 402.5 per week. By how many customers per week did the average fall?
   a. 73.9
   b. 83
   c. 83.1
   d. 83.9
   e. 84.9

Multiplying Decimals

To multiply decimals, ignore the decimal points and just multiply the numbers. Then count the total number of decimal digits (the digits to the *right* of the decimal point) in the numbers you are multiplying. Count off that number of digits in your answer beginning at the right side and put the decimal point to the *left* of those digits.

Example: 215.7×2.4

1. Multiply 2,157 times 24:

$$
\begin{array}{r}
2{,}157 \\
\times\,24 \\
\hline
8{,}628 \\
4{,}314 \\
\hline
51{,}768
\end{array}
$$

2. Because there are a total of two decimal digits in 215.7 and 2.4, count off two places from the right in 51,768, placing the decimal point to the *left* of the last two digits:

517.68

If your answer doesn't have enough digits, tack zeroes on to the left of the answer.

Example: $.03 \times .006$

1. Multiply 3 times 6: $3 \times 6 = 18$
2. You need five decimal digits in your answer, so tack on three zeroes: 00018
3. Put the decimal point at the front of the number (which is
   five digits in from the right):   .00018

You can practice multiplying decimals with these.

_____ **44.** $.05 \times .6$

_____ **45.** $.053 \times 6.4$

_____ **46.** $38.1 \times .0184$

_____ **47.** Joe earns $14.50 per hour. Last week he worked 37.5 hours. How much money did he earn that week?
   a. $518.00
   b. $518.50
   c. $525.00
   d. $536.50
   e. $543.75

_____ **48.** Nuts cost $3.50 per pound. Approximately how much will 4.25 pounds of nuts cost?
   a. $12.25
   b. $12.50
   c. $12.88
   d. $14.50
   e. $14.88

Dividing Decimals

To divide a decimal by a whole number, set up the division $(8\overline{).256})$ and immediately bring the decimal point straight up into the answer $(8\overline{).256})$. Then divide as you would normally divide whole numbers:

Example:

```
   .032
8)1.256
   0
   25
   24
   16
   16
    0
```

To divide any number by a decimal, there is an extra step to perform before you can divide. Move the decimal point to the very right of the number you are dividing by, counting the number of places you are moving it. Then move the decimal point the same number of places to the right in the number you are dividing into. In other words, first change the problem to one in which you are dividing by a whole number.

Example: $.06\overline{).218}$

1. Because there are 2 decimal digits in .06, move the decimal point two places to the right in both numbers and move the decimal point straight up into the answer:

   $.06.\overline{)1.21.8}$

2. Divide using the new numbers:

```
     20.3
6)121.8
   12
   01
   00
    18
    18
     0
```

Under certain conditions, you have to tack on zeroes to the right of the last decimal digit in the number you are dividing into:

- if there aren't enough digits for you to move the decimal point to the right
- if the answer doesn't come out evenly when you do the division
- if you are dividing a whole number by a decimal. Then you will have to tack on the decimal point as well as some zeroes.

Try your skills on these division problems:

_____ **49.** 7)9.8

_____ **50.** .0004).0512

_____ **51.** .5)28.6

_____ **52.** .14)196

_____ **53.** If James Worthington drove his truck 92.4 miles in 2.1 hours, what was his average speed in miles per hour?
   a. 41
   b. 44
   c. 90.3
   d. 94.5
   e. 194.04

_____ **54.** Mary Sanders walked a total of 18.6 miles in 4 days. On average, how many miles did she walk each day?
   a. 4.15
   b. 4.60
   c. 4.65
   d. 22.60
   e. 74.40

▶ Percents

A percent is a special kind of fraction or part of something. The bottom number (the *denominator*) is always 100. For example, 17% is the same as $\frac{17}{100}$. Literally, the word *percent* means *per 100 parts*. The root *cent* means 100: a *century* is 100 years; there are 100 *cents* in a dollar, etc. Thus, 17% means 17 parts out of 100. Because fractions can also be expressed as decimals, 17% is also equivalent to .17, which is 17 hundredths.

You come into contact with percents every day. Sales tax, interest, and discounts are just a few common examples.

If you're shaky on fractions, you may want to review the fraction section before reading further.

Changing a Decimal to a Percent and Vice Versa

To change a decimal to a percent, move the decimal point two places to the right and tack on a percent sign (%) at the end. If the decimal point moves to the very right of the number, you don't have to write the decimal point. If there aren't enough places to move the decimal point, add zeroes on the right before moving the decimal point.

To change a percent to a decimal, drop off the percent sign and move the decimal point two places to the left. If there aren't enough places to move the decimal point, add zeroes on the left before moving the decimal point.

Try changing these decimals to percents.

_____ **55.** .45

_____ **56.** .008

_____ **57.** .16$\frac{2}{3}$

Now, change these percents to decimals.

_____ **58.** 12%

_____ **59.** 87$\frac{1}{2}$%

_____ **60.** 250%

Changing a Fraction to a Percent and Vice Versa

To change a fraction to a percent, there are two techniques. Each is illustrated by changing the fraction $\frac{1}{4}$ to a percent:

Technique 1: Multiply the fraction by 100%.

Multiply $\frac{1}{4}$ by 100%: $\frac{1}{\overset{}{\underset{1}{4}}} \times \frac{\overset{25}{100\%}}{1} = 25\%$.

Technique 2: Divide the fraction's bottom number into the top number; then move the decimal point two places to the right and tack on a percent sign (%).

Divide 4 into 1 and move the decimal point 2 places to the right:

$\begin{array}{r} .25 \\ 4\overline{)1.00} \end{array}$ .25 = 25%

To change a percent to a fraction, remove the percent sign and write the number over 100. Then reduce if possible.

Example: Change 4% to a fraction.

1. Remove the % and write the fraction 4 over 100: $\frac{4}{100}$
2. Reduce: $\frac{4 \div 4}{100 \div 4} = \frac{1}{25}$

Here's a more complicated example: Change 16$\frac{2}{3}$% to a fraction

1. Remove the % and write the fraction 16$\frac{2}{3}$ over 100: $\frac{16\frac{2}{3}}{100}$
2. Since a fraction means "top number divided by bottom number," rewrite the fraction as a division problem: 16$\frac{2}{3}$ ÷ 100
3. Change the mixed number (16$\frac{2}{3}$) to an improper fraction ($\frac{50}{3}$): $\frac{50}{3} \div \frac{100}{1}$
4. Flip the second fraction ($\frac{100}{1}$) and multiply: $\frac{\overset{1}{50}}{3} \times \frac{1}{\underset{2}{100}} = \frac{1}{6}$

Try changing these fractions to percents.

_____ **61.** $\frac{1}{8}$

_____ **62.** $\frac{13}{25}$

_____ **63.** $\frac{7}{12}$

Now change these percents to fractions.

_____ **64.** 95%

_____ **65.** $37\frac{1}{2}\%$

_____ **66.** 125%

Sometimes it is more convenient to work with a percentage as a fraction or a decimal. Rather than have to _calculate_ the equivalent fraction or decimal, consider memorizing the equivalence table below. Not only will this increase your efficiency on the math test, but it will also be practical for real life situations.

CONVERSION TABLE		
Decimal	**%**	**Fraction**
.25	25%	$\frac{1}{4}$
.50	50%	$\frac{1}{2}$
.75	75%	$\frac{3}{4}$
.10	10%	$\frac{1}{10}$
.20	20%	$\frac{1}{5}$
.40	40%	$\frac{2}{5}$
.60	60%	$\frac{3}{5}$
.80	80%	$\frac{4}{5}$
$.33\overline{3}$	$33\frac{1}{3}\%$	$\frac{1}{3}$
$.66\overline{6}$	$66\frac{2}{3}\%$	$\frac{2}{3}$

Percent Word Problems

Word problems involving percents come in three main varieties:

- Find a percent of a whole.
  Example: What is 30% of 40?
- Find what percent one number is of another number.
  Example: 12 is what percent of 40?
- Find the whole when the percent of it is given.
  Example: 12 is 30% of what number?

While each variety has its own approach, there is a single shortcut formula you can use to solve each of these:

$$\frac{is}{of} = \frac{\%}{100}$$

The *is* is the number that usually follows or is just before the word *is* in the question.
The *of* is the number that usually follows the word *of* in the question.
The % is the number that is in front of the % or *percent* in the question.

Or you may think of the shortcut formula as:

$$\frac{part}{whole} = \frac{\%}{100}$$
$$part \times 100 = whole \times \%$$

To solve each of the three varieties, let's use the fact that the cross-products are equal. The cross-products are the products of the numbers diagonally across from each other. Remembering that *product* means *multiply,* here's how to create the cross-products for the percent shortcut:

$$\frac{part}{whole} = \frac{\%}{100}$$
$$part \times 100 = whole \times \%$$

Here's how to use the shortcut with cross-products:

- Find a percent of a whole.
  What is 30% of 40?
  30 is the % and 40 is the *of* number: $\frac{is}{40} = \frac{30}{100}$
  Cross multiply and solve for *is*: $is \times 100 = 40 \times 30$
  $$is \times 100 = 1{,}200$$
  $$12 \times 100 = 1{,}200$$

  Thus, 12 *is* 30% of 40.
- Find what percent one number is of another number.
  12 is what percent of 40?
  12 is the *is* number and 40 is the *of* number: $\frac{12}{40} = \frac{\%}{100}$
  Cross multiply and solve for %: $12 \times 100 = 40 \times \%$
  $$1{,}200 = 40 \times \%$$
  $$1{,}200 = 40 \times 30$$

  Thus, 12 is 30% of 40.

- Find the whole when the percent of it is given.

    12 is 30% of what number?

    12 is the *is* number and 30 is the %: $\quad\quad\quad\quad\quad \frac{12}{of} = \frac{30}{100}$

    Cross-multiply and solve for the *of* number: $\quad 12 \times 100 = of \times 30$

    $$1,200 = of \times 30$$

    $$1,200 = 40 \times 30$$

Thus 12 is 30% of 40.

You can use the same technique to find the percent increase or decrease. The *is* number is the actual increase or decrease, and the *of* number is the original amount.

> *Example:* If a merchant puts his $20 hats on sale for $15, by what percent does he decrease the selling price?

1. Calculate the decrease, the *is* number: $\quad\quad\quad\quad\quad\quad$ $20 - $15 = $5

2. The *of* number is the original amount, $20.

3. Set up the equation and solve for *of* by cross multiplying: $\quad \frac{5}{20} = \frac{\%}{100}$

$$5 \times 100 = 20 \times \%$$

$$500 = 20 \times \%$$

$$500 = 20 \times 25$$

4. Thus, the selling price is decreased by 25%.

If the merchant later raises the price of the hats from $15 $\quad \frac{5}{15} = \frac{\%}{100}$

back to $20, don't be fooled into thinking that the percent $\quad 5 \times 100 = 15 \times \%$

increase is also 25%! It's actually more, because the $\quad\quad 500 = 15 \times \%$

increase amount of $5 is now based on a lower original $\quad\quad 500 = 15 \times 33\frac{1}{3}$

price of only $15:

Thus, the selling price is increased by 33%.

Find a percent of a whole:

———— **67.** 1% of 25

———— **68.** 18.2% of 50

———— **69.** $37\frac{1}{2}$ of 100

———— **70.** 125% of 60

Find what percent one number is of another number.

_____ **71.** 10 is what % of 20?

_____ **72.** 4 is what % of 12?

_____ **73.** 12 is what % of 4?

Find the whole when the percent of it is given.

_____ **74.** 15% of what number is 15?

_____ **75.** $37\frac{1}{2}$% of what number is 3?

_____ **76.** 200% of what number is 20?

Now try your percent skills on some real life problems.

_____ **77.** Last Monday, 20% of 140 staff members was absent. How many employees were absent that day?
- **a.** 14
- **b.** 20
- **c.** 28
- **d.** 112
- **e.** 126

_____ **78.** 40% of Vero's postal service employees are women. If there are 80 women in Vero's postal service, how many men are employed there?
- **a.** 32
- **b.** 112
- **c.** 120
- **d.** 160
- **e.** 200

_____ **79.** Of the 840 shirts sold at a retail store last month, 42 had short sleeves. What percent of the shirts were short sleeved?
- **a.** .5%
- **b.** 2%
- **c.** 5%
- **d.** 20%
- **e.** 50%

_____ **80.** Sam's Shoe Store put all of its merchandise on sale for 20% off. If Jason saved $10 by purchasing one pair of shoes during the sale, what was the original price of the shoes before the sale?

    a. $12

    b. $20

    c. $40

    d. $50

    e. $70

▶ Averages

An average, also called an arithmetic mean, is a number that *typifies* a group of numbers, a measure of central tendency. You come into contact with averages on a regular basis: your bowling average, the average grade on a test, the average number of hours you work per week.

To calculate an average, add up the number of items being averaged and divide by the number of items.

Example: What is the average of 6, 10, and 20?

Solution: Add the three numbers together and divide by 3: $\frac{6 + 10 + 20}{3} = 12$

Shortcut

Here's a shortcut for some average problems.

- Look at the numbers being averaged. If they are equally spaced, like 5, 10, 15, 20, and 25, then the average is the number in the middle, or 15 in this case.
- If there is an even number of such numbers, say 10, 20, 30, and 40, then there is no middle number. In this case, the average is half-way between the two middle numbers. In this case, the average is half-way between 20 and 30, or 25.
- If the numbers are almost evenly spaced, you can probably estimate the average without going to the trouble of actually computing it. For example, the average of 10, 20, and 32 is just a little more than 20, the middle number.

Try these average questions.

_____ **81.** Bob's bowling scores for the last five games were 180, 182, 184, 186, and 188. What was his average bowling score?

    a. 182

    b. 183

    c. 184

    d. 185

    e. 186

_____ **82.** Conroy averaged 30 miles an hour for the two hours he drove in town and 60 miles an hour for the two hours he drove on the highway. What was his average speed in miles per hour?

    a. 18

    b. $22\frac{1}{2}$

    c. 45

    d. 60

    e. 90

_____ **83.** There are 10 females and 20 males in a history class. If the females achieved an average score of 85 and the males achieved an average score of 95, what was the class average? (Hint: don't fall for the trap of taking the average of 85 and 95; there are more 95s being averaged than 85s, so the average is closer to 95.)

    a. $90\frac{2}{3}$

    b. $91\frac{2}{3}$

    c. 92

    d. $92\frac{2}{3}$

    e. 95

▶ Geometry

Typically, there are very few geometry problems on the math test. The problems that are included tend to cover the basics: lines, angles, triangles, rectangles, squares, and circles. You may be asked to find the area or perimeter of a particular shape or the size of an angle. The arithmetic involved is pretty simple, so all you really need are a few definitions and formulas.

Glossary of Geometry Terms

Angle	Two rays with a common endpoint called a vertex. There are four types of angles:
	    Acute: less than 90°
	    Obtuse: more than 90°
	    Right: 90°
	    Straight: 180°

Circle	Set of all points that are the same distance from the center.
	    Area $= \pi r^2$
	    Circumference $= 2\pi r$
	    ($\pi = 3.14$; r = radius)

Circumference	Distance around a circle. (See _Circle._)

radius

Diameter   A line through the center of a circle. The diameter is twice the length of the radius. (See *Circle, Radius.*)

Line   A line extends endlessly in both directions. It is referred to by a letter at the end of it or by two points on it. Thus, the line below may be referred to as line *l* or as $\overline{AB}$.

$$l \longleftrightarrow \overset{A \qquad B}{\bullet \qquad \bullet}$$

Parallel Lines   Two lines in the same plane that do not intersect::   *l*

l ∥ *m*   *m*

Perimeter   Distance around a figure, such as a triangle or a rectangle. The perimeter of a circle is called its *circumference.*

Perimeter = sum of length of all sides

Perpendicular Lines Two lines in the same plane that intersect to form four right angles. (See *Right Angle.*)

Point   A point has a location but no size or dimension. It is referred to by a letter close to it, like this: • *A*

Radius   Line segment from the center to any point on a circle. The radius is half the diameter. (See *Circle, Diameter.*)

Rectangle   Four-sided figure with a right angle and both pairs of opposite sides parallel (which implies that all four sides are right angles and that opposite sides are equal in length).

Area = *length* × *width*
Perimeter = 2 × *length* + 2 × *width*

Square   Rectangle with four equal sides (see *Rectangle*):
Area = (*side*)²
Perimeter = 4 × *side*

Triangle   Three-sided figure:
Area = $\frac{1}{2}$(*base* × *height*)
Perimeter = sum of the lengths of all three sides
Angles: The sum of the three angles of a triangle is always 180°.

height

base

Practice Problems

Try your hand at these sample problems.

84. What is the area in inches of a triangle with base 10" and height 8"?
   a. 80
   b. 40
   c. 20
   d. 10
   e. 8

85. Find the perimeter of a triangle with sides of length 3, 4, and 5 units.
   a. 60 units
   b. 20 units
   c. 12 units
   d. 9 units
   e. 7 units

86. If the area of a square field measures 256 square feet, how many feet of fencing are needed to completely surround the field?
   a. 256
   b. 128
   c. 64
   d. 32
   e. It cannot be determined.

87. The length of a rectangle is twice its width. If the perimeter of the rectangle is 30 units, what is the width of the rectangle?
   a. 30
   b. 20
   c. 15
   d. 10
   e. 5

88. A circular opening has a diameter of $8\frac{1}{2}$ inches. What is the radius in inches of a circular disk that will exactly fit into the opening?
   a. 17
   b. 8.5
   c. 8
   d. 4.25
   e. 4

_____ **89.** The radius of a hoop is 10". If you roll the hoop along a straight path through 6 complete revolutions, approximately how far will it roll, in inches? (Use a value of 3.14 for π.)
- **a.** 31.4
- **b.** 62.8
- **c.** 188.4
- **d.** 376.8
- **e.** 1,884

▶ Algebra

Algebra questions do not appear on every test. However, when they do, they typically cover the material you learned in pre-algebra or in the first few months of your high school algebra course. Popular topics for algebra questions include:

- solving equations
- positive and negative numbers
- algebraic expressions

What Is Algebra?

Algebra is a way to express and solve problems using numbers and symbols. These symbols, called *unknowns* or *variables,* are letters of the alphabet that are used to represent numbers.

For example, let's say you are asked to find out what number, when added to 3, gives you a total of 5. Using algebra, you could express the problem as $x + 3 = 5$. The variable x represents the number you are trying to find.

Here's another example, but this one uses only variables. To find the distance traveled, multiply the rate of travel (speed) by the amount of time traveled: $d = r \times t$. The variable d stands for *distance,* r stands for *rate,* and t stands for *time.*

In algebra, the variables may take on different values. In other words, they *vary,* and that's why they're called *variables.*

Operations

Algebra uses the same operations as arithmetic: addition, subtraction, multiplication, and division. In arithmetic, we might say $3 + 4 = 7$, while in algebra we would talk about two numbers whose values we don't know that add up to 7, or $x + y = 7$. Here's how each operation translates to algebra:

ALGEBRAIC OPERATIONS	
The sum of two numbers	$x + y$
The difference of two numbers	$x - y$
The product of two numbers	$x \times y$ or $x \bullet y$ or xy
The quotient of two numbers	$\frac{x}{y}$

Equations

An equation is a mathematical sentence stating that two quantities are equal. For example:

$$2x = 10$$
$$x + 5 = 8$$

The idea is to find a replacement for the unknown that will make the sentence true. That's called *solving* the equation. Thus, in the first example, $x = 5$ because $2 \times 5 = 10$. In the second example, $x = 3$ because $3 + 5 = 8$.

Sometimes you can solve an equation by inspection, as with the above examples. Other equations may be more complicated and require a step-by-step solution, for example:

$$\frac{n+2}{4+1} = 3$$

The general approach is to consider an equation like a balance scale, with both sides equally balanced. Essentially, whatever you do to one side, you must also do to the other side to maintain the balance. Thus, if you were to add 2 to the left side, you would also have to add 2 to the right side.

Let's apply this *balance* concept to our complicated equation above. Remembering that we want to solve it for n, we must somehow rearrange it so the n is isolated on one side of the equation. Its value will then be on the other side. Looking at the equation, you can see that n has been increased by 2 and then divided by 4 and ultimately added to 1. Therefore, we will undo these operations to isolate n.

Begin by subtracting 1 from both sides of the equation:

$$\frac{n+2}{4} + 1 = 3$$
$$\underline{-1 \quad -1}$$
$$\frac{n+2}{4} = 2$$

Next, multiply both sides by 4:

$$4 \times \frac{n+2}{4} = 2 \times 4$$
$$n + 2 = 8$$

Finally, subtract 2 from both sides:

$$\underline{-2 \quad -2}$$
$$n = 6$$

Which isolates n and solves the equation: $n = 6$.

Notice that each operation in the original equation was undone by using the inverse operation. That is, addition was undone by subtraction, and division was undone by multiplication. In general, each operation can be undone by its *inverse*.

ALGEBRAIC INVERSES	
Operation	**Inverse**
Addition	Subtraction
Subtraction	Addition
Multiplication	Division
Division	Multiplication

After you solve an equation, check your work by plugging the answer back into the original equation to make sure it balances. Let's see what happens when we plug 6 in for *n*:

$$\frac{6+2}{4} + 1 = 3?$$
$$\frac{8}{4} + 1 = 3?$$
$$2 + 1 = 3?$$
$$3 = 3\checkmark$$

Solve each equation:

_____ **90.** $x + 5 = 12$

_____ **91.** $3x + 6 = 18$

_____ **92.** $\frac{1}{4}x = 7$

Positive and Negative Numbers

Positive and negative numbers, also known as *signed* numbers, are best shown as points along the number line:

Numbers to the left of 0 are *negative* and those to the right are *positive*. Zero is neither negative nor positive. If a number is written without a sign, it is assumed to be *positive*. Notice that when you are on the negative side of the number line, numbers with bigger values are actually smaller. For example, –5 is *less than* –2. You come into contact with negative numbers more often than you might think; for example, very cold temperatures are recorded as negative numbers.

As you move to the right along the number line, the numbers get larger. Mathematically, to indicate that one number, say 4, is *greater than* another number, say –2, the *greater than* sign (>) is used:

$$4 > -2$$

On the other hand, to say that –2 is *less than* 4, we use the *less than* sign, (<):

$$-2 < 4$$

Arithmetic with Positive and Negative Numbers

The table below illustrates the rules for doing arithmetic with signed numbers. Notice that when a negative number follows an operation (as it does in the second example below), it is enclosed in parentheses to avoid confusion.

RULE	EXAMPLE
Addition	
If both numbers have the same sign, just add them. The answer has the same sign as the numbers being added. If both numbers have different signs, subtract the smaller number from the larger. The answer has the same sign as the larger number. If both numbers are the same but have opposite signs, the sum is zero.	$3 + 5 = 8$ $-3 + (-5) = -8$ $-3 + 5 = 2$ $3 + (-5) = -2$ $3 + (-3) = 0$
Subtraction	
Change the sign of the number to be subtracted and then add as above.	$3 - 5 = 3 + (-5) = -2$ $-3 - 5 = -3 + (-5) = -8$ $-3 - (-5) = -3 + 5 = 2$
Multiplication	
Multiply the numbers together. If both numbers have the same sign, the answer is positive; otherwise, it is negative.	$3 \times 5 = 15$ $-3 \times (-5) = 15$ $-3 \times 5 = -15$ $3 \times (-5) = -15$
If one number is zero, the answer is zero.	$3 \times 0 = 0$
Division	
Divide the numbers. If both numbers have the same sign, the answer is positive; otherwise, it is negative.	$15 \div 3 = 5$ $-15 \div (-3) = 5$ $15 \div (-3) = -5$ $-15 \div 3 = -5$
If the top number is zero, the answer is zero.	$0 \div 3 = 0$

When more than one arithmetic operation appears, you must know the correct sequence in which to perform the operations. For example, do you know what to do first to calculate $2 + 3 \times 4$? You're right if you said, "multiply first." The correct answer is 14. If you add first, you will get the wrong answer of 20. The correct sequence of operations is:

1. parentheses
2. exponents
3. multiplication
4. division
5. addition
6. subtraction

If you remember this saying, you will know the order of operations: **P**lease **e**xcuse **m**y **d**ear **A**unt **S**ally.

Even when signed numbers appear in an equation, the step-by-step solution works exactly as it does for positive numbers. You just have to remember the arithmetic rules for negative numbers. For example, let's solve $14x + 2 = 5$.

1. Subtract 2 from both sides:

$$-14x + 2 = -5$$
$$\underline{\quad -2 \quad -2 \quad}$$
$$-14x = -7$$

2. Divide both sides by -14: $\quad -14x \div -14 = -7 \div -14$
$$x = \tfrac{1}{2}$$

Now try these problems with signed numbers.

_____ **93.** $1 - 3 \times (-4) = x$

_____ **94.** $-3x + 6 = -18$

_____ **95.** $\frac{x}{-4} + 3 = -7$

Algebraic Expressions

An algebraic expression is a group of numbers, unknowns, and arithmetic operations, like: $3x - 2y$. This one may be translated as, "3 times some number minus 2 times another number." To *evaluate* an algebraic expression, replace each variable with its value. For example, if $x = 5$ and $y = 4$, we would evaluate $3x - 2y$ as follows:

$$3(5) - 2(4) = 15 - 8 = 7$$

Evaluate these expressions.

_____ **96.** $4a + 3b$; $a = 2$ and $b = -1$

_____ **97.** $3mn - 4m + 2n$; $m = 3$ and $n = -3$

_____ **98.** $-2x - \frac{1}{2}y + 4z$; $x = 5$, $y = -4$, and $z = 6$

_____ **99.** The volume of a cylinder is given by the formula $V = \pi r^2 h$, where r is the radius of the base and h is the height of the cylinder. What is the volume of a cylinder with a base radius of 3 and height of 4? (Leave π in your answer.)

_____ **100.** If $x = 3$, what is the value of $3x - x$?

▶ Answers

Word Problems

1. a.

2. d.

3. d.

4. e.

Fractions

5. $\frac{1}{4}$

6. $\frac{2}{5}$

7. $\frac{3}{8}$

8. 10

9. 6

10. 200

11. $\frac{11}{12}$

12. $\frac{55}{24}$ or $2\frac{7}{24}$

13. $7\frac{1}{4}$

14. $\frac{2}{15}$

15. $\frac{1}{8}$

16. $\frac{19}{12}$ or $1\frac{7}{12}$

17. a.

18. b.

19. $\frac{2}{15}$

20. $\frac{8}{35}$

21. $\frac{2}{3}$

22. $\frac{26}{15}$ or $1\frac{11}{15}$

23. 15

24. $\frac{33}{2}$ or $16\frac{1}{2}$

25. c.

26. e.

27. c.

28. $\frac{1}{2}$

29. $5\frac{1}{2}$

30. $\frac{1}{5}$

31. $\frac{45}{28}$ or $1\frac{17}{28}$

32. b.

33. d.

34. b.

Decimals

35. $\frac{5}{1,000}$ or $\frac{1}{200}$

36. $3\frac{12}{25}$

37. $123\frac{456}{1,000}$ or $123\frac{57}{125}$

38. 4

39. 8.305

40. 0.907

41. 1.456

42. b.

43. d.

44. 0.03

45. 0.3392

46. 0.70104

47. e.

48. e.

49. 1.4

50. 128

51. 572

52. 1,400

53. b.

54. c.

Percents

55. 45%

56. 0.8%

57. 16.67% or $16\frac{2}{3}$%

58. 0.12

59. 0.875

60. 2.5

61. 12.5% or $12\frac{1}{2}$%

62. 52%

63. 58.33% or $58\frac{1}{3}$%

64. $\frac{19}{20}$

65. $\frac{3}{8}$

66. $\frac{5}{4}$ or $1\frac{1}{4}$

67. $\frac{1}{4}$ or .25

68. 9.1

69. $37\frac{1}{2}$ or 37.5

70. 75

71. 50%

72. $33\frac{1}{3}$%

73. 300%

74. 100

75. 8

76. 10

77. c.

78. c.

79. c.

80. d.

Averages

81. c.

82. c.

83. b.

Geometry

84. b.

85. c.

86. c.

87. e.

88. d.

89. d.

Algebra

90. 7

91. 4

92. 28

93. 13

94. 8

95. 40

96. 5

97. −45

98. 16

99. 36π

100. 6

CHAPTER

8 ▶ Word Knowledge Review

CHAPTER SUMMARY
This chapter will help you improve your vocabulary skills so that you can score higher on the Word Knowledge section of the ASVAB.

The Word Knowledge subtest of the ASVAB is basically a vocabulary test.
Combined with the Paragraph Comprehension score, Word Knowledge helps make up your Verbal Equivalent score—it is one of the four subtests that determine whether you will be allowed to enlist. Your ability to understand your training materials depends in part on your reading comprehension and vocabulary skills.
There are two different kinds of questions on the Word Knowledge subtest:

- **Synonyms**: identifying words that mean the same as the given words
- **Context**: determining the meaning of a word or phrase by noting how it is used in a sentence or paragraph

▶ Synonyms

A word is a **synonym** of another word if it has the same or nearly the same meaning as the other word. Test questions often ask you to find the synonym or antonym of a word. If you're lucky, the word will be surrounded by a sentence that helps you guess what the word means. If you're less lucky, you will just get the word, and then you have to figure out what the word means without any context.

Questions that ask for synonyms can be tricky because they require you to recognize the meaning of several words that may be unfamiliar—not only the words in the questions but also the answer choices. Usually the best strategy is to *look* at the structure of the word and to *listen* for its sound. See if a part of a word looks familiar. Think of other words you know that have similar key elements. How could those words be related?

Synonym Practice

Try identifying the word parts and related words in these sample synonym questions. Circle the word that means the same or about the same as the italicized word. Answers and explanations appear right after the questions.

1. *incoherent* answer
   a. not understandable
   b. not likely
   c. undeniable
   d. challenging

2. *ambiguous* questions
   a. meaningless
   b. difficult
   c. simple
   d. vague

3. covered with *debris*
   a. good excuses
   b. transparent material
   c. scattered rubble
   d. protective material

4. *inadvertently* left
   a. mistakenly
   b. purposely
   c. cautiously
   d. carefully

5. *exorbitant* prices
   a. expensive
   b. unexpected
   c. reasonable
   d. outrageous

6. *compatible* workers
   a. gifted
   b. competitive
   c. harmonious
   d. experienced

7. *belligerent* attitude
   a. hostile
   b. reasonable
   c. instinctive
   d. friendly

Answers

The explanations are important because they show you how to go about choosing a synonym if you don't know the word.

1. **a.** *Incoherent* means *not understandable*. To *cohere* means to *connect*. A coherent answer connects or makes sense. The prefix *in-* means *not*.

2. **d.** *Ambiguous* questions are *vague* or uncertain. The key part of this word is *ambi-*, which means *two* or *both*. An ambiguous question can be taken two ways.

3. **c.** *Debris* is scattered fragments and trash.

4. **a.** *Inadvertently* means *by mistake*. The key element in this word is the prefix *in-*, which usually means *not*, or *the opposite of.*

5. **d.** The key element here is *ex-*, which means *out of* or *away from*. Exorbitant literally means "out of orbit." An *exorbitant* price would be an *outrageous* one.

6. c. *Compatible* means *harmonious.*

7. a. The key element in this word is the root *belli-*, which means *warlike.* The synonym choice, then, is *hostile.*

▶ Context Questions

Context is the surrounding text in which a word is used. Most people use context to help them determine the meaning of an unknown word. A vocabulary question that gives you a sentence around the vocabulary word is usually easier to answer than one with little or no context. The surrounding text can help you as you look for synonyms for the specified words in the sentences.

The best way to take meaning from context is to look for key words in sentences or paragraphs that convey the meaning of the text. If nothing else, the context will give you a means to eliminate wrong answer choices that clearly don't fit. The process of elimination will often leave you with the correct answer.

Context Practice

Try these sample questions. Circle the word that best describes the meaning of the italicized word in the sentence.

8. The maintenance workers were *appalled* by the filthy, cluttered condition of the building.
   a. horrified
   b. amused
   c. surprised
   d. dismayed

9. Even though she seemed rich, the defendant claimed to be *destitute.*
   a. wealthy
   b. ambitious
   c. solvent
   d. poor

10. Though she was *distraught* over losing her keys, the woman was calm enough to remember she had a spare set.
   a. punished
   b. distracted
   c. composed
   d. anguished

11. The evil criminal expressed no *remorse* for his actions.
   a. sympathy
   b. regret
   c. reward
   d. complacency

Answers

Check to see whether you were able to pick out the key words that help you define the target word, as well as whether you got the right answer.

8. a. The key words *filthy* and *cluttered* signify horror rather than the milder emotions described by the other choices.

9. d. The key word here is *rich*, but this is a clue by contrast. The introductory *even though* signals that you should look for the opposite of the idea of having financial resources.

10. d. The key words here are *though* and *losing her keys*, signaling that you are looking for an opposite of *calm* in describing the woman. The only word strong enough to match the situation is *anguish.*

11. b. *Remorse* means *regret* for one's actions. The part of the word here to beware of is the prefix *re-*. It doesn't signify anything in this word, though it often means again or back. Don't be confused by the two choices that also contain the prefix *re-*. The strategy here is to see which word sounds better in the sentence. The key words are *evil* and *no*, indicating that you are looking for something that shows no repentance.

Be very careful not to be confused by the sound of words that may mislead you. Be sure to look at the word carefully, and pay attention to the structure and appearance of the word as well as its sound. You may be used to hearing English words spoken with an accent. The sounds of those words may be misleading in choosing a correct answer.

► Word Parts

The best way to improve your vocabulary is to learn word parts: roots, which are the main part of the word; prefixes, which go before the root word; or suffixes, which go after. Any of these elements can carry meaning or change the use of a word in a sentence. For instance, the suffix -s or -es can change the meaning of a noun from singular to plural: *boy, boys.* The prefix *un-* can change the meaning of a root word to its opposite: *necessary, unnecessary.*

In the sections on **prefixes** and **suffixes** are some of the word elements seen most often in vocabulary tests. Simply reading them and their examples for five to ten minutes a day will give you the quick recognition you need to make a good association with the meaning of an unfamiliar word.

Prefixes

In order to be able to unlock the meaning of many words in our language, it is useful for you to understand what a prefix is. A prefix is a word part at the beginning of a word that changes or adds to the meaning of the root word in some way. By learning some common prefixes, you will learn to recognize many unfamiliar words. After you have completed the exercises in this chapter, you will become acquainted with the meanings suggested by some of the more common prefixes, which will improve your reading, speaking, and listening vocabularies.

antecedent   (an·ti·ˈsēd·ənt)
prefix: **ante** means before
(*adj.*)
going before in time
The event was   to the Civil War.

antipathy   (an·ˈtip·ə·thē)
prefix: anti **means against**
(*noun*)
revulsion; any object of strong dislike
The child had an   toward snakes.

circumvent   (sər·kəm·ˈvent)
prefix: **circum and circ** mean around
(*verb*)
to go around; to catch in a trap; to gain superiority
      over; to prevent from happening
Police tried to   the riot by moving the
      crowd along.

consensus   (kən·ˈsen·səs)
prefix: **con** means with, together
(*noun*)
agreement, especially in opinion
The committee reached   about gun control.

controversy   (ˈkon·trə·ver·sē)
prefix: **contr** means against
(*noun*)
a discussion of a question in which opposing views
      clash
There is a   about building nuclear power
      plants.

decimate   ('des·i·māt)
prefix: **dec** means ten
(*verb*)
to destroy or kill a large portion of something; to take
    or destroy a tenth part of something
Caterpillars can   trees.

demote   (di·mōt)
prefix: **de** means down, away from
(*verb*)
to lower in grade or position
Upper ranked officers can   a lower ranked
    person.

disinterested   (dis·'in·tər·est·ed)
prefix: **dis** means not, opposite of
(*adj.*)
not motivated by personal interest or selfish motives
A loyal citizen is   .

euphemism   ('u·fə·mizm)
prefix: **eu** means good, well
(*noun*)
the use of a word or phrase that is considered less dis-
    tasteful or offensive than another
"She is at rest" is a   for "she is dead."

exorbitant   (ek·'zor·bi·tənt)
prefix: **ex** means out of, away from
(*adj.*)
going beyond what is reasonable and proper
The colonists rebelled against   taxes.

illegible   (i·'lej·ə·bəl)
prefix: **il** means not, opposite
(*adj.*)
not able to be read
The student had to rewrite the   paper.

intermittent   (in·tər·'mit·ənt)
prefix: **inter** means between
(*adj.*)
stopping and starting again at intervals
The weather forecaster predicted _____ showers.

malevolent   (mə·'lev·ə·lent)
prefix: **mal** means bad
(*adj.*)
having an evil disposition toward others
A _____ person rejoices in the misfortune of
    others.

precursor   (pre·'kər·sər)
prefix: **pre** means before
(*noun*)
a forerunner, a harbinger; one who or that which
    goes before
Calmness is usually a _____ to a storm.

prognosis   (prog·'nō·sis)
prefix: **pro** means before
(*noun*)
a forecast; especially in medicine
The injured animal's _____ for recovery is good.

retrospect   ('ret·rō·spekt)
prefix: **retro** means back, again
(*verb*)
to think about the past
(*noun*)
looking back on or thinking about things past
In _____, the world leader wished he had acted
    differently.

subordinate   (sub·'or·din·it)
prefix: **sub** means under
(*adj.*)
inferior to or placed below another in rank, power,
　　or importance
(*noun*)
a person or thing of lesser power or importance
　　than another
(*verb*)   (sub·'or·din·āt)
to treat as inferior or less important
The wise president treated her _____ with
　　respect.

synthesis   ('sin·thə·sis)
prefix: **syn**, or **sym** means with or together
(*noun*)
putting of two or more things to together to form a
　　whole
In chemistry, the process of making a compound by
　　joining elements together is called _____.

transcend   (tran·'send)
prefix: **trans** means across
(*verb*)
to go beyond the limits of; to overstep; to exceed
A seeing eye dog enables blind people to _____
　　their disability.

trivial   ('triv·ē·əl)
prefix: **tri** means three
(*adj.*)
of little worth or importance
The research scientist did not have time for
　　_____ pursuits because he was so busy
　　conducting important experiments.

Words in Context

The following exercise will help you figure out the
meaning of some words from the previous list. Circle
any context clues that help you figure out the meaning
of the bold words.

In our country, the use of nuclear power as a viable
source of energy has been an ongoing **controversy.**
During the gas and oil shortages of the 1970s, energy
prices were **exorbitant.** The federal government supported nuclear power as a new energy source that
would be cost effective. Now, the President's
National Energy Policy Report lists nuclear power as
a safe and affordable alternative. Today, as in the
past, many people have voiced their **antipathy**
toward nuclear power plants, especially in the wake
of the 1979 partial meltdown of the Three Mile
Island nuclear power plant. At that time, scientists
scrambled to **circumvent** a total meltdown in a facility that was designed to be fail-safe. There was great
fear that the meltdown would be complete and **decimate** the area. Now, the federal government is once
again promoting this alternative energy source.

Suffixes

Word endings that are added to the main part or root
of words are called **suffixes.** Suffixes are word parts
that signal how a word is being used in a sentence. You
will note that each word in the list is a particular part
of speech (*noun, verb, adjective,* or *adverb*). Suffixes
often change the part of speech of a word.

For example, take the word *deferment* from the
list below. A *deferment* is a noun that means a postponement. If the suffix (*-ment*) is removed, the word
becomes *defer,* and it is used as a verb meaning to post-
pone.

As a *verb* it appears as *defer*:
I will *defer* the payment until next month.

As a *noun* it appears as it is:
The bank gave him a *deferment.*

As an *adjective* it appears as *deferred*:
The *deferred* payment is due in one month.

The following table shows a list of common suffixes. They are divided into the parts of speech, or the "jobs" they suggest for words. In the last column, add at least one other word that uses the suffix, besides the examples in the word list.

NOUN ENDINGS			
Suffix	**Meaning**	**Examples**	**Your Word**
-tion	act or state of	retraction, contraction	
-ment	quality	deportment, impediment	
-ist	one who	anarchist, feminist	
-ism	state or doctrine of	barbarism, materialism	
-ity	state of being	futility, civility	
-ology	study of	biology	
-esence	state of	adolescence	
-y, -ry	state of	mimicry, trickery	

ADJECTIVE ENDINGS			
Suffix	**Meaning**	**Examples**	**Your Word**
-able	capable	perishable, flammable	
-ic	causing, making	nostalgic, fatalistic	
-ian	one who is or does	tactician, patrician	
-ile	pertaining to	senile, servile	
-ious	having the quality of	religious, glorious	
-ive	having the nature of	sensitive, divisive	
-less	without	guileless, reckless	

VERB ENDINGS			
Suffix	**Meaning**	**Examples**	**Your Word**
-ize	to bring about	colonize, plagiarize	
-ate	to make	decimate, tolerate	
-ify	to make	beautify, electrify	

agrarian   (ə·'grer·ē·ən)
suffix: **-ian** means one who is or does
(*adj.*)
having to do with agriculture or farming
The farmer loved his   life.

antagonist   (an·'ta·gə·nist)
suffix: **-ist** means one who
(*noun*)
one that contends with or opposes another
In the movie *Batman*, the Joker is Batman's   .

bigotry   ('big·ə·trē)
suffix: **-ry** means state of
(*noun*)
unreasonable zeal in favor of a party, sect, or opinion; excessive prejudice
          can lead to malevolent actions.

consummate   ('kon·səm·māt)
suffix: **-ate** means to make
(*verb*)
to complete; to carry to the utmost degree
The business woman needed to   the
    deal quickly.

copious   ('cōp·ē·əs)
suffix: **-ious** means having the quality of
(*adj.*)
abundant; plentiful; in great quantities
A   amount of sunshine is predicted for
    the summer.

cryptic   ('krip·tik)
suffix: **-ic** means causing
(*adj.*)
hidden; secret; having a hidden or ambiguous
    meaning
The detective uncovered the meaning of the
            message.

deferment   (di·'fər·mənt)
suffix: **-ment** means quality of
(*noun*)
the act of putting off or delaying; postponement
The bank offered the struggling college graduate a
            on his student loan payment.

furtive   ('fər·tiv)
suffix: **-ive** means having the nature of
(*adj.*)
done in a stealthy manner; sly and underhanded
The two criminals who were in cahoots gave
    each other   looks behind the
    detective's back.

laudable   ('law·də·bəl)
suffix: **-able** means capable of
(*adj.*)
praiseworthy
Her dedication and ability to rehabilitate the injured
    is   .

geology   (jē·'ä·lə·jē)
suffix: **-ology** means study of
(*noun*)
the study of the history of the Earth and its life,
    especially as recorded in rocks
The   major traveled to Mt. Etna to
    examine the effects of the volcano's most
    recent eruption.

minimize   ('mi·nə·mīz)
suffix: **-ize** means to subject to an action
(*verb*)
to play down; to keep to a minimum
The President tried to   his involvement in
    the trial so that he would not be implicated in
    the scandal.

mutation   (mū·'tā·shən)
suffix: **-tion** means action of, state of
(*noun*)
the act or process of changing
Scientists research gene   in fruit flies to
    see how genes change from one generation to
    the next.

obsolescence   (äb·sə·'les·ens)
suffix: **-escence** means state of
(*noun*)
the state of being outdated
With the advent of the personal computer, the type-
    writer has been in   for many years.

parity   ('par·i·tē)
suffix: **-ity** means state of being
(*noun*)
the state or condition of being the same in power,
    value, or rank; equality
Women and minorities continue to fight for
              in the workplace.

pragmatism   (′prag·mə·tizm)

suffix: **-ism** means state or doctrine of

(*noun*)

faith in the practical approach

The man's _____ enabled him to run a
    successful business.

provocative   (prō·′vok·ə·tiv)

suffix: **-ive** means having the nature of

(*adj.*)

something that stirs up an action

The _____ words of the environmental activist
    inspired many to go volunteer for the commu-
    nity clean-up day.

puerile   (′pyoor·əl)

suffix: **-ile** means pertaining to

(*adj.*)

childish, silly, immature

The teen's _____ actions at the party couldn't
    be ignored.

rectify   (′rek·ti·fī)

suffix: **-ify** means to make

(*verb*)

to make right; to correct

The newspaper tried to _____ the mistake by
    correcting the misprint.

relentless   (re·′lənt·les)

suffix: **-less** means without

(*adj.*)

harsh; unmoved by pity; unstoppable

She was _____ in her search for knowledge; she
    read everything she could get her hands on.

venerate   (′ven·ə·rāt)

suffix: **-ate** means to make

(*verb*)

to look upon with deep respect and reverence

Some cultures _____ their elders.

Words in Context

The following exercise will help you figure out the
meaning of some words from the previous list by looking at context clues. Circle any context clues that help
you figure out the meaning of the bold word.

The latest remake of *Planet of the Apes* develops the
theme of **bigotry** in a world where apes are the
dominant culture and humans are enslaved. **Parity**
between the two species is unthinkable because the
simians regard humans as inferior creatures. Leo,
the central character, is the story's protagonist. He
is a human astronaut who lands on a strange
planet where apes **venerate** their own kind by
offering praise and promotions for negative
actions taken against humans. Leo's **antagonist**,
General Thade is the leader of the apes in this
bizarre culture, and encourages the mistreatment
of humans by apes. In General Thade's opinion,
extermination of the humans is a **laudable** cause
and he mounts a full-scale campaign to extermi-
nate humans from the planet.

More Vocabulary Practice

Here is another set of practice exercises with samples of
each kind of question covered in this chapter. Answers
are at the end of the exercise.

Select the word that means the same or nearly the
same as the italicized word.

12. *congenial* company
    a. friendly
    b. dull
    c. tiresome
    d. angry

13. *conspicuous* mess
    a. secret
    b. notable
    c. visible
    d. boorish

- The key to answering vocabulary questions is to **notice and connect** what you do know to what you may not recognize.
- **Know your word parts.** You can recognize or make a good guess at the meanings of words when you see some suggested meaning in a root word, prefix, or suffix.
- **Use a process of elimination.** Think of how the word makes sense in the sentence.
- **Don't be confused by words that sound like other words**, but may have no relation to the word you need.

---

14. *meticulous* record-keeping
   a. dishonest
   b. casual
   c. painstaking
   d. careless

15. *superficial* wounds
   a. life-threatening
   b. bloody
   c. severe
   d. surface

16. *impulsive* actions
   a. cautious
   b. sudden
   c. courageous
   d. cowardly

17. *tactful* comments
   a. polite
   b. rude
   c. angry
   d. confused

Using the context, choose the word that means the same or nearly the same as the italicized word.

18. Though flexible about homework, the teacher was *adamant* that papers be in on time.
   a. liberal
   b. casual
   c. strict
   d. pliable

19. The condition of the room after the party was *deplorable.*
   a. regrettable
   b. pristine
   c. festive
   d. tidy

20. Though normally very *gregarious*, Martin was uncharacteristically shy and reserved when he attended the party.
   a. generous
   b. sociable
   c. stingy
   d. happy

Answers
12. a.
13. c.
14. c.
15. d.
16. b.
17. a.
18. c.
19. a.
20. b.

CHAPTER

Paragraph Comprehension Review

CHAPTER SUMMARY

Because reading is such a vital skill, the Armed Services Vocational Aptitude Battery includes a reading comprehension section that tests your ability to understand what you read. The tips and exercises in this chapter will help you improve your comprehension of written passages so that you can increase your score in this area.

Memos, policies, procedures, reports—these are all things you will be expected to understand if you enlist in the armed services. Understanding written materials is part of almost any job. That's why the ASVAB attempts to measure how well applicants understand what they read.

The Paragraph Comprehension subtest of the ASVAB is in multiple-choice format and asks questions based on brief passages, much like the standardized tests that are offered in schools. For that matter, almost all standardized test questions test your reading skills. After all, you can't answer the question if you can't read it. Similarly, you can't study your training materials or learn new procedures once you are on the job if you can't read well. So, reading comprehension is vital not only on the test but also for the rest of your career.

▶ Types of Reading Comprehension Questions

You have probably encountered reading comprehension questions before, where you are given a passage to read and then have to answer multiple-choice questions about it. This kind of question has advantages for you as a test taker: You don't have to know anything about the topic of the passage because you are being tested only on the information the passage provides.

But the disadvantage is that you have to know where and how to find that information quickly in an unfamiliar text. This makes it easy to fall for one of the wrong answer choices, especially since they are designed to mislead you.

The best way to do your best on this passage/ question format is to be very familiar with the kinds of questions that are typically asked on the test. Questions most frequently ask you to:

1. identify a specific **fact or detail** in the passage
2. note the **main idea** of the passage
3. make an **inference** based on the passage
4. define a **vocabulary** word from the passage

In order for you to do well on a reading comprehension test, you need to know exactly what each of these questions is asking. **Facts and details** are the specific pieces of information that support the passage's main idea. The **main idea** is the thought, opinion, or attitude that governs the whole passage. Generally speaking, facts and details are indisputable—things that don't need to be proven, like statistics (18 million people) or descriptions (a green overcoat). Let's say, for example, you read a sentence that says *"After the department's reorganization, workers were 50% more productive."* A sentence like this, which gives you the fact that workers were 50% more productive, might support a main idea that says, *"Every department should be reorganized."* Notice that this main idea is not something indisputable; it is an opinion. The writer thinks all departments should be reorganized, and because this is his opinion (and not everyone shares it), he needs to support his opinion with facts and details.

An **inference**, on the other hand, is a conclusion that can be drawn based on fact or evidence. For example, you can infer—based on the fact that workers became 50% more productive after the reorganization, which is a dramatic change—that the department had not been efficiently organized. The fact sentence, *"After the department's reorganization, workers were 50% more productive,"* also implies that the reorganization of the department was the reason

workers became more productive. There may, of course, have been other reasons, but we can infer only one from this sentence.

As you might expect, **vocabulary** questions ask you to determine the meaning of particular words. Often, if you've read carefully, you can determine the meaning of such words from their context, that is, how the word is used in the sentence or paragraph.

Practice Passage 1: Using the Four Question Types

The following is a sample test passage, followed by four questions. Read the passage carefully, and then answer the questions, based on your reading of the text, by selecting your choice. Then refer to the previous list and note under your answer which type of question has been asked. Correct answers appear immediately after the questions.

In the last decade, community policing has been frequently touted as the best way to reform urban law enforcement. The idea of putting more officers on foot patrol in high crime areas, where relations with police have frequently been strained, was initiated in Houston in 1983 under the leadership of then-Commissioner Lee Brown. He believed that officers should be accessible to the community at the street level. If officers were assigned to the same area over a period of time, those officers would eventually build a network of trust with neighborhood residents. That trust would mean that merchants and residents in the community would let officers know about criminal activities in the area and would support police intervention. Since then, many large cities have experimented with Community-Oriented Policing (COP) with mixed results. Some have found that police and citizens are grateful for the opportunity to work together. Others have found that unrealistic expectations by citizens and resistance from officers have combined to hinder the effectiveness of COP. It seems possible, therefore, that a good idea may need improvement before it can truly be considered a reform.

1. Community policing has been used in law enforcement since

   a. the late 1970s.

   b. the early 1980s.

   c. the Carter administration.

   d. Lee Brown was New York City Police Commissioner.

   Question type _____

2. The phrase "a network of trust" in this passage suggests that

   a. police officers can rely only on each other for support.

   b. community members rely on the police to protect them.

   c. police and community members rely on each other.

   d. community members trust only each other.

   Question type _____

3. The best title for this passage would be:

   a. "Community Policing: The Solution to the Drug Problem"

   b. "Houston Sets the Pace in Community Policing"

   c. "Communities and Cops: Partners for Peace"

   d. "Community Policing: An Uncertain Future?"

   Question type _____

4. The word "touted" in the first sentence of the passage most nearly means

   a. praised.

   b. denied.

   c. exposed.

   d. criticized.

   Question type _____

Answers and Explanations

Don't just look at the right answers and move on. The explanations are the most important part, so read them carefully. Use these explanations to help you understand how to tackle each kind of question the next time you come across it.

1. b. Question type: **1,** fact or detail. The passage identifies 1983 as the first large-scale use of community policing in Houston. Don't be misled by trying to figure out when Carter was president. Also, if you happen to know that Lee Brown was New York City's police commissioner, don't let that information lead you away from the information contained in the passage alone. Brown was commissioner in Houston when he initiated community policing.

2. c. Question type: **3,** inference. The "network of trust" referred to in this passage is between the community and the police, as you can see from the sentence where the phrase appears. The key phrase in the question is *in this passage.* You may think that police can rely only on each other, or one of the other answer choices may appear equally plausible to you. But, your choice of answers must be limited to the one suggested *in this passage.* Another tip for questions like this: Beware of absolutes! Be suspicious of any answer containing words like *only, always,* or *never.*

3. d. Question type: **2,** main idea. The title always expresses the main idea. In this passage, the main idea comes at the end. The sum of all the details in the passage suggests that community policing is not without its critics and that therefore its future is uncertain. Another key phrase is *mixed results,* which means that some communities haven't had full success with community policing.

4. **a.** Question type: 4, vocabulary. The word *touted* is linked in this passage with the phrase *the best way to reform*. Most people would think that a good way to reform something is praiseworthy. In addition, the next few sentences in the passage describe the benefits of community policing. Criticism or a negative response to the subject doesn't come until later in the passage.

▶ Detail and Main Idea Questions

Main idea questions and fact or detail questions are both asking you for information that's right there in the passage. All you have to do is find it.

Detail or Fact Questions

In detail or fact questions, you have to identify a specific item of information from the text. This is usually the simplest kind of question. You just have to be able to separate important information from less important information. However, the choices may often be very similar, so you must be careful not to get confused.

Be sure you read the passage and questions carefully. In fact, it is usually a good idea to read the questions first, *before* you even read the passage, so you will know what details to look out for.

Main Idea Questions

The main idea of a passage, like that of a paragraph or a book, is what it is *mostly* about. The main idea is like an umbrella that covers all of the ideas and details in the passage, so it is usually something general, not specific. For example, in Practice Passage 1, question 3 asked you what title would be best for the passage, and the correct answer was "Community Policing: An Uncertain Future?" This is the best answer because it's the only one that includes both the positive and negative sides of community policing, both of which are discussed in the passage.

Sometimes the main idea is stated clearly, often in the first or last sentence of the passage. The main idea is expressed in the *last* sentence of Practice Passage 1, for example. The sentence that expresses the main idea is often referred to as the **topic sentence**.

At other times, the main idea is not stated in a topic sentence but is *implied* in the overall passage, and you will need to determine the main idea by inference. Because there may be much information in the passage, the trick is to understand what all that information adds up to—the gist of what the author wants you to know. Often some of the wrong answers on main idea questions are specific facts or details from the passage. A good way to test yourself is to ask, "Can this answer serve as a *net* to hold the whole passage together?" If not, chances are you have chosen a fact or detail, not a main idea.

Practice Passage 2: Detail and Main Idea Questions

Practice answering main idea and detail questions by working on the questions that follow this passage. Circle the answers to the questions, and then check your answers against the key that appears immediately after the questions.

There are three different kinds of burns: first degree, second degree, and third degree. It is important for firefighters to be able to recognize each of these types of burns so that they can be sure burn victims are given proper medical treatment. The least serious burn is the first-degree burn, which causes the skin to turn red but does not cause blistering. A mild sunburn is a good example of a first-degree burn, and, like a mild sunburn, first-degree burns generally do not require medical treatment other than a gentle cooling of the burned skin with ice or cold tap water. Second-degree burns, on the other hand, do cause blistering of the skin and should be treated immediately. These burns should be immersed in warm water and then wrapped in a sterile dressing or bandage. (Do not apply butter or grease to these burns; despite the old wives' tale, butter does *not* help burns heal and actually increases chances of infection.) If second-degree burns cover a large part of the body, then the victim should be taken to the hospital immediately for medical care. Third-degree burns are those that char the skin and turn it black, or burn so deeply that the skin shows white. These burns usually result from direct contact with flames and have a great chance of becoming infected. All third-degree burns should receive immediate hospital care. They should not be immersed in water, and charred clothing should not be removed from the victim. If possible, a sterile dressing or bandage should be applied to burns before the victim is transported to the hospital.

1. Which of the following would be the best title for this passage?
   a. Dealing with Third-Degree Burns
   b. How to Recognize and Treat Different Burns
   c. Burn Categories
   d. Preventing Infection in Burns

2. Second-degree burns should be treated with
   a. butter.
   b. nothing.
   c. cold water.
   d. warm water.

3. First-degree burns turn the skin
   a. red.
   b. blue.
   c. black.
   d. white.

4. Which of the following best expresses the main idea of the passage?
   a. There are three different types of burns.
   b. Firefighters should always have cold compresses on hand.
   c. Different burns require different types of treatment.
   d. Butter is not good for healing burns.

Answers and Explanations

1. **b.** A question that asks you to choose a title for a passage is a main idea question. This main idea is expressed in the second sentence, the topic sentence: *It is important for firefighters to be able to recognize each of these types of burns so that they can be sure burn victims are given proper treatment.* Choice **b** expresses this idea and is the only title that encompasses all of the ideas expressed in the passage. Choice **a** is too limited; it deals only with one of the kinds of burns discussed in the passage. Likewise, choices **c** and **d** are also too limited. Choice **c** covers types of burns but not their treatment, and **d** deals only with preventing infection, which is only a secondary part of the discussion of treatment.

2. **d.** The answer to this fact question is clearly expressed in the sentence, "These burns should be immersed in warm water and then wrapped in a sterile dressing or bandage." The hard part is keeping track of whether "These burns" refers to the kind of burns in the question, which is second-degree burns. It's easy to choose a wrong answer here because all of the answer choices are mentioned in the passage. You need to read carefully to be sure you match the right burn to the right treatment.

3. a. This is another fact or detail question. The passage says that a first-degree burn "causes the skin to turn red." Again, it's important to read carefully because all of the answer choices (except **b**, which can be eliminated immediately) are listed elsewhere in the passage.

4. c. Clearly this is a main idea question, and **c** is the only answer that encompasses the whole passage. Choices **b** and **d** are limited to *particular* burns or treatments, and answer a discusses only burns and not their treatment. In addition, the second sentence tells us that "It is important for firefighters to be able to *recognize each of these types of burns so that they can be sure burn victims are given proper medical treatment.*"

▶ Inference and Vocabulary Questions

Questions that ask you about the meaning of vocabulary words in the passage and those that ask what the passage *suggests* or *implies* (inference questions) are different from detail or main idea questions. In vocabulary and inference questions, you usually have to pull ideas from the passage, sometimes from more than one place.

Inference Questions
Inference questions can be the most difficult to answer because they require you to draw meaning from the text when that meaning is implied rather than directly stated. Inferences are conclusions that you draw based on the clues the writer has given you. When you draw inferences, you have to look for such clues as word choice, tone, and specific details that suggest a certain conclusion, attitude, or point of view. You have to read between the lines in order to make a judgment about what an author was implying in the passage.

A good way to test whether you have drawn an acceptable inference is to ask, "What evidence do I have for this inference?" If you can't find any, you probably have the wrong answer. You need to be sure that your inference is logical and that it is based on something that is suggested or implied in the passage itself—not by what you or others might think. You need to base your conclusions on evidence—facts, details, and other information—not on random hunches or guesses.

Vocabulary Questions
Questions designed to test vocabulary are really trying to measure how well you can figure out the meaning of an unfamiliar word from its context. *Context* refers to the words and ideas surrounding a vocabulary word. If the context is clear enough, you should be able to substitute a nonsense word for the one being sought, and you would still make the right choice because you could determine meaning strictly from the sense of the sentence.

For example, you should be able to determine the meaning of the italicized nonsense word below based on its context:

The speaker noted that it gave him great *terivinix* to announce the winner of the Outstanding Leadership Award.

In this sentence, *terivinix* most likely means
a. pain.
b. sympathy.
c. pleasure.
d. anxiety.

Clearly, the context of an award makes **c**, *pleasure,* the best choice. Awards don't usually bring pain, sympathy, or anxiety.

When confronted with an unfamiliar word, try substituting a nonsense word and see if the context gives you the clue. If you are familiar with prefixes, suffixes, and word roots, you can also use this knowledge to help you determine the meaning of an unfamiliar word.

You should be careful not to guess at the answer to vocabulary questions based on how you may have seen the word used before or what you *think* it means. Many words have more than one possible meaning, depending on the context in which they are used, and a word you have seen used one way may mean something else in a test passage. Also, if you don't look at the context carefully, you may make the mistake of confusing the vocabulary word with a similar word. For example, the vocabulary word may be *taut (meaning tight),* but if you read too quickly or don't check the context, you might think the word is *tout (meaning publicize* or *praise)* or *taunt (meaning tease).* Always read carefully and be sure that what you think the word means fits into the context of the passage you are being tested on.

Practice Passage 3: Inference and Vocabulary Questions

The questions that follow this passage are strictly vocabulary and inference questions. Select the answers to the questions, and then check your answers against the key that appears immediately after the questions.

Dealing with irritable patients is a great challenge for healthcare workers on every level. It is critical that you do not lose your patience when confronted by such a patient. When handling irate patients, be sure to remember that they are not angry at you; they are simply projecting their anger at something else *onto* you. Remember that if you respond to these patients as irritably as they act with you, you will only increase their hostility, making it much more difficult to give them proper treatment. The best thing to do is to remain calm and ignore any

imprecations patients may hurl your way. Such patients may be irrational and may not realize what they are saying. Often these patients will purposely try to anger you just to get some reaction out of you. If you react to this behavior with anger, they win by getting your attention, but you both lose because the patient is less likely to get proper care.

1. The word "irate" as it is used in the passage most nearly means
   a. irregular, odd.
   b. happy, cheerful.
   c. ill-tempered, angry.
   d. sloppy, lazy.

2. The passage suggests that healthcare workers
   a. easily lose control of their emotions.
   b. are better off not talking to their patients.
   c. must be careful in dealing with irate patients because the patients may sue the hospital.
   d. may provide inadequate treatment if they become angry at patients.

3. An "imprecation" is most likely
   a. an object.
   b. a curse.
   c. a joke.
   d. a medication.

4. Which of the following best expresses the writer's views about irate patients?
   a. Some irate patients just want attention.
   b. Irate patients are always miserable.
   c. Irate patients should be made to wait for treatment.
   d. Managing irate patients is the key to a successful career.

Answers and Explanations

1. c. This is a vocabulary question. *Irate* means *ill-tempered, angry.* It should be clear that **b,** *happy, cheerful,* is not the answer; dealing with happy patients is normally not *a great challenge.* Patients that are **a,** *irregular, odd,* or **d,** *sloppy, lazy,* may be a challenge in their own way, but they aren't likely to rouse a healthcare worker to anger. In addition, the passage explains that irate patients are not "*angry* at you," and *irate* is used as a synonym for *irritable,* which describes the patients under discussion in the very first sentence.

2. d. This is an inference question, as the phrase "The passage *suggests*" might have told you. The idea that angry healthcare workers might give inadequate treatment is implied by the passage as a whole, which seems to be an attempt to prevent angry reactions to irate patients. Furthermore, the last sentence in particular makes this inference possible: *If you react to this behavior with anger . . . you both lose because the patient is less likely to get proper care.* Choice **c** is not correct, because while it maybe true that some irate patients have sued the hospital in the past, there is no mention of suits anywhere in this passage. Likewise, choice **b** is incorrect; the passage does suggest ignoring patients' insults, but nowhere does it recommend not talking to patients—it simply recommends not talking angrily. And while it may be true that some healthcare workers may lose control of their emotions, the passage does not provide any facts or details to support answer **a,** that they "*easily* lose control." Watch out for key words like *easily* that may distort the intent of the passage.

3. b. If you didn't know what an *imprecation* is, the context should reveal that it's something you can ignore, so neither choice **a,** an *object,* nor choice **d,** a *medication,* is a likely answer. Furthermore, choice **c** is not likely either, since an irate patient is not likely to be making jokes.

4. a. The writer seems to believe that some irate patients just want attention, as is suggested by, "Often these patients will purposely try to anger you just to get some reaction out of you. If you react to this behavior with anger, they win *by getting your attention.*" It should be clear that choice **b** cannot be the answer, because it includes an absolute: "Irate patients are *always* miserable." Perhaps *some* of the patients are *often* miserable, but an absolute like *always* is almost always wrong. Besides, this passage refers to patients who maybe irate in the hospital, but we have no indication of what these patients are like at other times, and *miserable* and *irate* are not exactly the same thing, either. Choice **c** is also incorrect because the purpose of the passage is to ensure that patients receive *proper treatment* and that irate patients are not discriminated against because of their behavior. Thus, *irate patients should be made to wait for treatment* is not a logical answer. Finally, **d** cannot be correct because though it may be true, there is no discussion of career advancement in the passage.

▶ Review: Putting It All Together

A good way to solidify what you have learned about reading comprehension questions is for *you* to write the questions. Here's a passage, followed by space for you to write your own questions. Write one question for each of the four types: fact or detail, main idea, inference, and vocabulary.

The "broken window" theory was originally developed to explain how minor acts of vandalism or disrespect can quickly escalate to crimes and attitudes that break down the entire social fabric of an area. It is a theory that can easily be applied to any situation in society. The theory contends that if a broken window in an abandoned building is not replaced quickly, soon all the windows will be broken. In other words, a small violation, if condoned, leads others to commit similar or greater violations. Thus, after all the windows have been broken, the building is likely to be looted and perhaps even burned down. According to this theory, violations increase exponentially. Thus, if disrespect to a superior is tolerated, others will be tempted to be disrespectful as well. A management crisis could erupt literally overnight. For example, if one firefighter begins to disregard proper housewatch procedure by neglecting to keep up the housewatch administrative journal, and this firefighter is not reprimanded, others will follow suit by committing similar violations of procedure, thinking, "If he can get away with it, why can't I?" So what starts out as a small thing, a violation that may seem not to warrant disciplinary action, may actually ruin the efficiency of the entire firehouse, putting the people the firehouse serves at risk.

1. Detail question: _____

_____

   a.
   b.
   c.
   d.

2. Main idea question: _____

   a.
   b.
   c.
   d.

3. Inference question: _____

_____

   a.
   b.
   c.
   d.

4. Vocabulary question: _____

_____

   a.
   b.
   c.
   d.

Possible Questions

Here is one question of each type based on the passage above. Your questions may be very different, but these will give you an idea of the kinds of questions that could be asked.

1. Detail question: According to the passage, which of the following could happen "overnight"?
   a. The building will be burned down.
   b. The firehouse may become unmanageable.
   c. A management crisis might erupt.
   d. The windows will all be broken.

2. Main idea question: Which of the following best expresses the main idea of the passage?
   a. Even minor infractions warrant disciplinary action.
   b. Broken windows must be repaired immediately.
   c. People shouldn't be disrespectful to their superiors.
   d. Housewatch must be taken seriously.

3. Inference question: The passage suggests that
 a. the broken window theory is inadequate.
 b. managers need to know how to handle a crisis.
 c. firefighters are lazy.
 d. people will get away with as much as they can.

4. Vocabulary question: In this passage, *condoned* most nearly means
 a. punished.
 b. overlooked.
 c. condemned.
 d. applauded.

If English Isn't Your First Language

When non-native speakers of English have trouble with reading comprehension tests, it's often because they lack the cultural, linguistic, and historical frame of reference that native speakers enjoy. People who have not lived in or been educated in the United States often don't have the background information that comes from growing up reading American newspapers, magazines, and textbooks.

A second problem for non-native English speakers is the difficulty in recognizing vocabulary and idioms (expressions like "chewing the fat") that assist comprehension. In order to read with good understanding, it's important to have an immediate grasp of as many words as possible in the text. Test takers need to be able to recognize vocabulary and idioms immediately so that the ideas those words express are clear.

The Long View

Read newspapers, magazines, and other periodicals that deal with current events and matters of local, state, and national importance. Pay special attention to articles related to the career you want to pursue

Be alert to new or unfamiliar vocabulary or terms that occur frequently in the popular press. Use a highlighter pen to mark new or unfamiliar words as you read. Keep a list of those words and their definitions. Review them for 15 minutes each day. Though at first you may find yourself looking up a lot of words, don't be frustrated—you'll look up fewer and fewer as your vocabulary expands.

During the Test

When you are taking the test, make a picture in your mind of the situation being described in the passage. Ask yourself, "What did the writer mostly want me to think about this subject?"

Locate and underline the topic sentence that carries the main idea of the passage. Remember that the topic sentence—if there is one—may not always be the first sentence. If there doesn't seem to be one, try to determine what idea summarizes the whole passage.

Answers
1. c.
2. a.
3. d.
4. b.

▶ Additional Resources

Here are some other ways you can build the vocabulary and knowledge that will help you do well on reading comprehension questions.

- Practice asking the four sample question types about passages you read for information or pleasure.
- Use your library. Many public libraries have sections that contain materials for adult learners. In these sections you can find books with exercises in reading and study skills. It's also a good idea to enlarge your base of information by reading related books and articles. Most libraries have computer systems that allow you to access information quickly and easily. Library personnel will show you how to use the computers and other equipment.

10▶ Auto and Shop Information Review

CHAPTER SUMMARY

This chapter tells you how to prepare for the Auto and Shop Information subtest of the ASVAB. You'll learn about commonly tested concepts, including basic automotive components and systems, shop tools, and basic construction materials and procedures. As a bonus, you'll find sample questions for practice at the end of the chapter.

Repairing a vehicle, constructing a temporary shelter, pouring a foundation for a permanent structure—these are skills that many armed services personnel use regularly. If you choose a Military Occupational Specialty that focuses on automotive or shop concepts, you'll be preparing for a civilian career as well, as skilled workers in these fields are always in demand.

The Auto and Shop Information subtest on the ASVAB is used to help determine whether you can enter a specialty that requires this kind of knowledge. You'll do best on this subtest if you already have a fair amount of background in this area, whether from high school shop classes, jobs you've held, or just puttering around with cars and carpentry.

This chapter can help you review what you already know about how machines work. If you're relatively new to this area, you'll find this chapter makes a good basic introduction to Auto and Shop Information. You'll learn some of the most commonly tested tools, concepts, materials, and procedures. There are suggestions for ways to improve your knowledge by gaining hands-on experience. At the end of the chapter, you can test your knowledge with sample questions similar to those found on the ASVAB.

▶ What Auto and Shop Information Questions Are Like

The Auto and Shop Information subtest covers a wide range of topics. The questions are multiple choice, with four possible answers. You will have 11 minutes to answer 25 questions, many of which are accompanied by pictures. Most people find that they can answer all 25 questions in the time allowed. Though some questions include all the information you need to find the correct answer, most will rely on your previous knowledge of auto and shop concepts.

A typical Auto and Shop Information question will look something like this:

1. Which of the following is NOT part of a typical automotive cooling system?
   a. the radiator
   b. the oil filter
   c. the water pump
   d. the thermostat

The correct answer is b, the oil filter. You'll find that a few questions are like this one, using the word NOT to signal the correct answer. The oil filter is the part of the internal combustion engine that cleans the lubrication oil, so it is not part of the cooling system.

▶ Auto Information

Much of the Auto and Shop Information subtest, as you might expect, covers automobiles and other vehicles that use an internal combustion engine. Concepts you can expect to find on the ASVAB include the various systems of an automobile and their functions, as well as how to maintain and repair a vehicle.

Automotive Systems

Cars, trucks, buses, and other vehicles all use literally thousands of **components**, or parts. A combination of several components that work together to perform a specific function is called a **system**. There are several main systems that perform key functions in the automobile: providing power, transferring energy from the engine to the wheels, keeping the engine cool, smoothing out the bumps in the road, and more. You'll learn about the most important systems and components in this section.

The Internal Combustion Engine

Internal combustion engines power many kinds of machines, not just cars and trucks. In general, an internal combustion engine operates by burning fuel to produce kinetic energy. This energy causes the internal workings of the engine to rotate. Ultimately, this energy is transferred to the wheels of the car via gears and other linkages—and the car moves.

Kinetic energy: the energy of motion

Internal combustion engines can be fueled by gasoline, diesel fuel, natural gas, or other combustible fossil fuels. A **fuel pump** moves fuel from the fuel tank into the engine. Inside the engines are typically four, six, or eight **cylinders**, each with one **piston** that moves up and down.

The fuel is injected into the cylinders by the **carburetor** or **fuel injectors.** Each cylinder has one **spark plug** that fires at regular intervals. (The energy for the spark is provided by the electrical system; see page 162.) The spark causes a mini-explosion in the cylinder, driving the piston downward. The **tie rod** to which the piston is fastened is therefore also driven downward. The tie rod is attached to the **crankshaft,** which converts the up-and-down motion of the pistons and tie rod into rotational movement. The gears attached to the crankshaft are connected to other gears on the transmission system (see page 161). Through the transmission, eventually the power is transferred to the wheels of the vehicle, the inner workings of the pump, or whatever machine the engine is driving.

The Transmission System

The **transmission** is the link that transfers power from the engine to the tires and wheels. It typically consists of several shafts, gears, and joints. When the power from the engine rotates the transmission shafts, the car begins to move. The **driveshaft** between the transmission and the axles is typically made of steel so it can withstand the high torque of operation.

Torque: twisting force

As the speed of the car increases, the transmission rotates faster and faster. In order to keep the transmission's rotation speed at acceptable levels, several gears are used. That is why you must shift a car as your speed increases and decreases. Some vehicles have transmissions that shift automatically between the necessary gear sizes. Others, including the heavy vehicles used in the armed forces, have a manual transmission that requires the driver to change the gears using the **clutch** and the **gear shift.** The transmission is disengaged when you press the clutch pedal to the floor. After you move the gear shift into the gear you want, you slowly release the clutch pedal. The transmission gears touch and once again transfer the energy from the engine to the wheels. An automatic transmission does all this work for you.

The Cooling System

An internal combustion engine has many moving parts. As these parts slide past each other, the friction of their movement against each other generates heat. The cooling system dissipates this heat in order to prevent the engine from becoming too hot. The cooling system consists of a **pump** that moves cooling fluid, or **coolant,**

from the **radiator** through piping to the engine block. As the coolant passes over the engine block, some of the heat from the engine is transferred into the coolant. The fluid then flows back to the radiator, where it is cooled by the flow of air across the radiator. The reason a vehicle is more likely to overheat on a hot day than on a cold one is that the air moving over the radiator can't cool the fluid effectively.

The Exhaust System

The exhaust system includes a system of piping connected to the engine with welded joints. Several brackets suspend the piping beneath the automobile. The engine's exhaust gases pass from the engine through the piping to the **muffler,** which is an acoustical chamber that reduces the engine noise and removes some of the pollutants created when the fuel burns.

The Suspension System

The suspension is the system that attaches the wheels of the automobile to its body. The wheels cannot be directly attached with a hard connection because the high forces of hitting bumps in the road would cause structural failure—the connections would break. Instead, a combination of **springs** and dampeners are used to "soften" this connection. The springs are typically either leaf springs or coil compression springs. They provide a flexible link between the wheels and the body of the car.

The **shock absorbers** serve to dampen the bumps in the road. Without shock absorbers, when a car hit a bump, it would continue to bounce up and down on the suspension springs for a long time. The shock absorbers are movable but very stiff, so they quickly reduce the movement of the springs. Shock absorbers are typically oil-filled cylinders approximately 12 to 18 inches long. One end is bolted to the body of the automobile, and the other is attached to the axle of the wheels. A vehicle typically has one set of springs and shocks for each wheel.

The Electrical System

The electrical system in an automobile is incredibly complex. It provides the energy for the initial spark from the spark plug that makes the engine run, so without electricity you couldn't go anywhere. It also operates other systems and accessories, including headlights and other lights as well as power windows and door locks. The electrical system is similar to your body's cardiovascular system. The heart of the system is the **battery**. The wiring that runs throughout the automobile is similar to your veins and arteries. The wires transfer energy from the battery to the spark plugs and other devices that use electricity. There are literally hundreds of feet of electrical wiring in modern automobiles.

The battery would quickly lose its charge without a method of recharging. The component of the electrical system that charges the battery is the **alternator**. The alternator rotates to generate electrical energy, which then recharges the battery.

The Braking System

Automobile brakes are activated by pressing the brake pedal. This action compresses a piston to force hydraulic fluid through the **brake line** piping. In disc brakes, the brake fluid presses against a set of mechanical **calipers,** or levers, that squeeze the **brake pads** against the **rotors.** The friction of the pads rubbing against the rotors slows the rotation of the wheels. Springs are used to return the brake pedal and the calipers to their neutral position when the brake pedal is released.

Miscellaneous Components

Many other minor systems and components are used in internal combustion vehicles besides the major systems just listed. Gauges and pumps are used not only on automobiles but also in other kinds of machines you may encounter on the ASVAB.

Gauges

Gauges help operators monitor the condition and performance of machines such as pumps and internal combustion engines, as well as the surrounding atmospheric conditions that can indirectly affect a machine's function.

Gauges are usually marked with the *units* they are measuring. A few examples of different types of units are:

- degrees Celsius or Fahrenheit for temperature gauges (usually called *thermometers*)
- pounds per square inch (psi) for pressure gauges
- gallons or liters for fuel gauges
- amperage for battery gauges

You must be very careful to recognize and understand the units of a gauge that appears in a test question. For instance, a temperature gauge could use either degrees Fahrenheit or degrees Celsius. Mistakes on units can cause major problems, so be careful. The table on this page shows some common automotive types of gauges, what they measure, and the kind of units they use.

AUTOMOTIVE PERFORMANCE GAUGES

Gauge	What It Measures	Units
Speedometer	velocity (speed)	miles per hour (mph) or kilometers per hour (kph)
Tachometer	speed of rotation for pumps, engines, fans, etc.	revolutions per minute (rpm)
Pressure gauge	internal pressure, such as oil pressure or water pressure	pounds per square inch (psi) or inches of water
Ammeter	electrical charge	amps
Fuel gauge	remaining volume of fuel	gallons or liters

OTHER GAUGES		
Gauge	**What It Measures**	**Units**
Thermometer	temperature	degrees Fahrenheit or Celsius
Barometer	atmospheric pressure	inches or millimeters of mercury
Hygrometer	relative humidity	percentage of water in air
Flow meter	volume of flow in a piping system	cubic feet per minute (cfm) or gallons per minute (gpm)

Gauges are sometimes marked with warnings about limits of safe operation. For instance, an oil pressure gauge on an internal combustion engine may show a maximum safe working pressure of 15 psi. If you're asked about the safe operation of a device with a gauge on it, you should pay careful attention to any markings that show such a limit.

Gauges are also used for non-automotive machines as well as to monitor conditions of various mechanical and electrical systems. The table "Other Gauges" shows three atmospheric gauges and one kind of gauge used for monitoring mechanical systems not found on an automobile.

Pumps

A pump is a device used to transfer a liquid or a gas from one location, through a piping system, to another location. There are many different types of pumps, including centrifugal pumps, positive displacement pumps, metering pumps, diaphragm pumps, and progressive cavity pumps.

Generally speaking, a working pump consists of the pump itself—case, bearings, impeller, seals, shaft, base, and other components—and an outside energy source. The outside energy source may be an electric motor, an internal combustion engine, or a battery and motor. The energy from this source causes the inner workings of the pump to propel the liquid or gas through the piping system. The flow rate at which the liquid or gas is pushed through the piping system is typically measured by a flow meter in units of gallons per minute (gpm) or cubic feet per minute (cfm).

Some automotive pumps include the fuel pumps used to pump the fuel from a holding tank into your car and the pumps that transfer coolant through the engine's cooling system.

Pumps have many other uses besides automotive ones. They can be used to move drinking water from a reservoir to your house or business. Industrial pumps are also used to move industrial fluids such as chemicals or waste products from one tank to another inside a plant.

Automotive Tools

Car maintenance and repair may require specialized tools as well as some with which you are already familiar. Some of these tools are:

- **Wrenches** to tighten and loosen nuts and bolts. Examples include vice grips and box end wrenches, socket wrenches, crescent wrenches, and pipe wrenches.
- **Screwdrivers** to tighten and loosen the thousands of screws in a car. Both regular head and Phillips head screwdrivers are used. There are also screwdrivers unique to particular vehicles.
- **A spark plug wrench** to change the spark plugs. Typically a spark plug wrench is actually an adapter that connects to a socket wrench.
- **A jack** to lift a car so that you can change a tire.
- **A hoist** to lift heavy objects such as engines and transmission components in order to repair them.

There are lots specialized tools used for repair work, but you're not likely to find them on the ASVAB.

Automotive Maintenance and Troubleshooting

Today's automobiles are such complex machines that explaining how to maintain and repair them can take thousands of pages for each model of car or truck. Most automobiles are sold with a manual for that model, and if you are assigned a specific kind of vehicle in the armed forces, you'll be trained on the specific procedures for that vehicle. Some kinds of maintenance and troubleshooting, however, are common to almost all vehicles.

Preventative Maintenance

Any vehicle requires regular maintenance in order to keep it operating properly and to insure a long, reliable life. Some automotive components wear out and have to be replaced. Also, an automobile has many moving parts that require regular lubrication so they don't wear out before their time.

Obviously tires wear out with use. Tires on a typical car last 30,000 to 80,000 miles, depending on use. Car tires have wear bars that indicate when they should be replaced. Worn tires can be unsafe, so replacing them is a must.

Tires also have to be rotated. The tires in the front will wear more on the outside of the tread because of extra wear from turning. Tires should be rotated, or moved from the front to the back, every 3,000 to 5,000 miles. Tire pressure should also be checked regularly in order to insure proper handling of the car and prevent abnormal wear.

Another part of regular maintenance is keeping the engine and transmission lubricated. The engine uses petroleum-based oil to reduce the friction between moving parts such as the pistons and the cylinder wall. Over time, this oil becomes dirty and must be replaced. Most engine manufacturers recommend three months or 3,000 miles between oil changes. Also, the rotating joints in the transmission have to be lubricated with grease in order to keep operating properly.

Some automotive components that usually need to be replaced during the life of an automobile include the battery, belts and hoses, air filter, shock absorbers, and spark plugs. Also, some automotive systems use fluids that have to be replaced regularly. These include the transmission, brakes, power steering, and cooling system. The replacement intervals vary from vehicle to vehicle. Again, if you are required to do this kind of maintenance as part of your military assignment, you will be trained on the procedures for the vehicles you are responsible for.

Troubleshooting

A few questions on the ASVAB may cover basic troubleshooting—if the vehicle won't start or won't move, what might be the problem? Kinds of repair that only a trained mechanic could attempt will *not* be covered on the exam; only basic diagnosis of a problem is likely to be tested.

An internal combustion engine requires three basic items in order to operate properly: fire, fuel, and oxygen. When an engine will not start, one or more of these items is missing.

Fire—a spark, actually—is provided by the electrical system through the spark plug. If a vehicle won't start, you should check the battery and alternator, the wires connecting the electrical system to the spark plugs, and the plugs themselves.

Fuel is pumped from the fuel tank to the engine by the fuel pump through the fuel line. A lack of fuel in the engine could be caused by a ruptured fuel line or a broken fuel pump. Another possibility is a problem with the carburetor or fuel injectors, which regulate the amount of fuel going to the engine.

Oxygen is necessary for the fuel to burn. If you light a match and then place it under a glass, the match will go out in a few seconds because the oxygen in the glass has been consumed by the burning match. Oxygen—which is provided by the air since air is 21 percent oxygen—comes into the engine through the air filter, controlled by several valves. One possible cause of lack of oxygen is a dirty air filter—a problem you can diagnose simply by looking at the filter.

Another common problem is that the engine runs but the automobile will not move. This problem typically indicates that something is wrong with the transmission. Once you've determined that the transmission is indeed in the correct gear, there wouldn't be much more you could do about this problem. Transmission repair is one of those jobs that only trained mechanics should take on, so you're not likely to find any questions about it on the ASVAB.

▶ Shop Information

Besides automotive concepts, the Auto and Shop Information subtest of the ASVAB also covers shop tools, building materials, and construction procedures.

Hand Tools

Hand tools are defined as tools operated not by motors but by human power. Hand tools likely to be covered on the ASVAB include those used in construction and metalwork, as well as some lawn and garden tools.

Carpenter's Tools

Some of the hand tools used by carpenters and other workers are listed in the table on page 166, along with their most common uses and some examples of each kind.

Gardening and Lawn Care Tools

You may be asking yourself why this chapter would cover gardening hand tools. Well, you might be surprised at how often these tools are used in the armed services: shovels for latrines, trenches, or bunkers; post hole diggers for fences; axes, hoes, and rakes for firefighting. The table on page 167 shows some gardening tools and their uses.

Building Materials

The materials used to construct residential and commercial buildings, bridges, and roads are all commonly used in the armed services and may well appear on the ASVAB. Some materials play structural roles by providing support and load-bearing functions. A few of the most important structural materials include steel, concrete, wood, brick, and cinder block. Other materials are used as decoration or insulation, including glass, fiberglass, and stucco.

Steel

Steel is commonly used in construction because it is relatively inexpensive and is available in many shapes and sizes: I-shapes, channels, circular and square tubing, and rods. Steel comes in several grades, or strengths; the grade used depends on the requirements of the particular application. Structural steel members are typically connected using bolts and/or welds.

One drawback of using steel in outdoor applications, such as bridges, is that it must be painted regularly to prevent corrosion and rust. Common uses for steel include road and pedestrian bridges and large commercial buildings. The use of steel studs in the walls of houses is also gaining popularity.

Concrete

Concrete is a versatile, low-cost building material that can be formed into any shape. Forms are constructed at the project site, and the concrete is poured into the forms. It takes several days or weeks, depending on weather conditions, for the concrete to harden, or **cure**, to full strength. Concrete is very strong for compression loads; that is, it's good at holding up things that are pressing on it. However, it has poor tensile strength; that is, it doesn't hold up well under a pulling force. So concrete is typically used in combination with steel reinforcement bars (commonly called **rebars**) placed inside a concrete beam or column to provide adequate strength.

CARPENTER'S TOOLS

Tool	Description/Function	Examples
hammer	used primarily to drive and remove nails, as well as to pound on devices such as chisels	claw hammer, rubber mallet, ball-peen hammer
saw	thin metal blade with a sharp-toothed edge used to cut wood or metal	hand saw, hacksaw, jigsaw
screwdriver	used to tighten and loosen screws and bolts	slotted (regular) head, Phillips head
level	two- to four-foot long piece of metal or plastic that contains calibrated air bubble tubes, used to ensure that things are vertically plumb or horizontally level	hand level, laser level
square	used primarily to aid in drawing a cut line on a board to insure a straight, 90-degree cut	L-square, T-square
plane	metal tool with a handle and an adjustable blade, used to shave off thin strips of wood for the purpose of smoothing or leveling	block plane, various sizes of carpenter's planes
chisel	metal tool with a sharp, beveled edge that is struck with a hammer in order to cut and shape stone, metal, or wood	scoop chisel, beveled chisel, masonry chisel, cold chisel
protractor	half circle with tick marks around the edge spaced at one-degree intervals, used to measure angles	only one type, made of metal or plastic
C-clamp	C-shaped metallic instrument with a threaded stop that can be adjusted to clamp together pieces of material of different thickness	furniture clamps, many types and sizes of metallic C-clamps
compass	V-shaped metallic instrument with a sharp point on the end of one leg and a pencil or pen on the end of the other leg, used to draw circles	only one type

Concrete offers the added benefit of low maintenance since it does not need to be painted. Common structural applications of concrete include road and bridge surfaces, building foundations, and support members on some structures.

Wood

Wood is used for both structural and decorative purposes. Structural applications include use as studs and roof trusses in houses and as beams for light bridges. The decorative uses include moldings, floor coverings, doors, and windows. Wood is also used to cover over steel or concrete beams and columns. Many types of

GARDENING AND LAWN CARE TOOLS

Tool	Description/Function	Examples
shovel	a wooden handle with a metallic blade used for digging holes in the earth or for moving material such as rock from one place to another	many types and sizes: snow, flat blade, narrow spade
rake	a wooden handle with metal tines used to uniformly spread material on the ground or to separate two different materials	leaf rake, garden rakes of several sizes
hoe	a wooden handle with a V-shaped or square metallic blade used for digging small trenches and for light excavation	many types and sizes
axe	a wooden handle with a sharp metal blade used to cut wood	double blade or single blade with hammer
post hole digger	two wooden handles with metal blades used to dig small, circular holes a foot or two deep for the placement of fence posts	only one type

wood are used as building material including pine, spruce, oak, walnut, cherry, redwood, and cedar. Wood is not as strong as steel or concrete.

Brick and Block

Brick is a decorative material typically used on the outer surface of walls. Cement mortar is used between bricks to construct a solid wall that is decorative and also protects the inner wall from the elements. Brick is also sometimes used as a paving material for roads and sidewalks.

Cinder blocks are similar to bricks but much larger. The walls of small buildings are often made of cinder block because it is a low-cost material. As with brick, cement mortar is used to connect the blocks together.

Construction Procedures

Constructing a building, road, or bridge requires coordination and planning. Standard construction procedures assure that projects are finished on schedule, within budget, and according to specifications.

However, specific procedures vary, depending on what is being built and on local conditions. Some of the common terms and procedures in building construction that may appear on the ASVAB are discussed below.

Foundations

The foundation is the base that supports a building or bridge. Most foundations are made of concrete. Surveyors stake out the locations of the corners and other key areas of the building or bridge pier. Then the earth is excavated so that the forms for the concrete can be built on solid ground. A solid foundation is key to having a long-lasting structure. The design engineer will determine the size and thickness of the foundation based on the anticipated load.

Flooring

There are many kinds of flooring materials and many ways in which floors are constructed, but there are common elements. The **subfloor** is the structural portion of the flooring system; it transfers the loads placed on the floor to the foundation. The design engineer considers the loads that will be placed on the flooring in determining what materials will be used. For instance, a warehouse floor has to be much stronger than the flooring in an office. The warehouse subfloors would be made of concrete while the office subfloor might be consist of wood joists or beams.

The **decking** is the portion of the floor that lies on top of the subfloor beams. Decking usually consists plywood nailed to the beams. The final component of the flooring system is the decorative covering such as tile, vinyl, or carpet.

Framing

The term **framing** refers to the "skeleton" of a structure. In a house, the framing usually consists of wood or steel studs and roof trusses. Larger buildings may use beams and columns made of concrete and/or steel due to the larger loads involved. The framing of a building is typically built right on top of the foundation so that the weight is transferred to the supporting soil.

After it is put up, the framing is covered, on both the inside and the outside of the building, with decorative material. The outside covering might be made of brick, wood, glass, or other weatherproof material. The inside covering might be drywall, brick, or wood. Insulation is normally placed between the inside and outside cover layers in order to keep the building at a constant temperature and to minimize noise from the outside.

Roofing

Many options exist for roofing materials and designs. Roofs can be made flat or with a **pitch**, or slope. This choice affects which materials and construction techniques are used. The structural portion of the roof is typically made of wood or steel trusses, which are simply a collection of beams fastened together using special connectors. Plywood sheeting is then attached to the trusses, and some type of weatherproof covering is placed on the plywood. Options for this covering include asphalt, wood, tile, metal, or concrete shingles.

▶ How to Learn More About Auto and Shop Topics

Auto and shop information is such an integral part of everyday life that there are many real-life sources you can investigate to learn more. A construction site is a great place to visit for a day to learn more about hand tools, cranes, pumps, and other devices. Ask the construction supervisor if you can take a tour.

Another alternative would be to visit an auto repair shop. Internal combustion engines, lifts, levers, and hand tools are only a few of the types of tools and systems you could see in use.

Yet another possibility would be to visit a local manufacturer in your town. Examples include a foundry, a sheet metal fabricator, an automotive manufacturer, or a pump manufacturer. Look in the yellow pages under "manufacturing" for possibilities.

▶ Practice Questions

Try some sample Auto and Shop Information questions to get a feel for what this subtest of the ASVAB is like.

1. Of the following mechanical devices on an automobile, which one uses friction to accomplish its purpose?
   a. the steering system
   b. the exhaust system
   c. the braking system
   d. the internal combustion engine

2. What type of mechanical device is used to aid in cooling of an internal combustion engine?
   a. a pump
   b. a lever
   c. a pulley
   d. a hammer

3. What type of gauge uses units of rpm?
   a. a pressure gauge
   b. a tachometer
   c. a speedometer
   d. a thermometer

4. Which of the following types of fuel is NOT commonly used in internal combustion engines in vehicles?
   a. natural gas
   b. gasoline
   c. kerosene
   d. diesel fuel

5. The clutch, the gears, and the drive shaft are all parts of which automotive system?
   a. the exhaust system
   b. the transmission
   c. the cooling system
   d. the electrical system

6. Which of the following components provides the "fire" that ignites the fuel in an internal combustion engine?
   a. the radiator
   b. the piston
   c. the cylinder
   d. the spark plug

7. Which automotive system helps to provide a smooth ride?
   a. the suspension system
   b. the internal combustion engine
   c. the exhaust system
   d. the cooling system

8. A compass is used to
   a. measure angles.
   b. tighten and loosen nuts and bolts.
   c. drive and remove nails.
   d. draw circles of various sizes.

9. Which of the following is NOT a carpenter's hand tool?
   a. a winch
   b. a level
   c. a compass
   d. a chisel

10. A carpenter's square is used to
    a. measure a distance.
    b. cut wood.
    c. draw straight lines.
    d. draw circular arcs.

11. Which of the following building materials can be formed into any shape?
    a. brick
    b. wood
    c. steel
    d. concrete

12. Which of the following is typically used for the construction of a building foundation?
   a. glass
   b. concrete
   c. wood
   d. brick

13. A protractor is used to
   a. measure angles.
   b. check flatness.
   c. weld metal.
   d. draw circular arcs.

14. What is the term used to describe the supporting structural portion of a building?
   a. the roof
   b. the framing
   c. the foundation
   d. the atrium

▶ Answers

1. c. The braking system uses friction to slow or stop the rotation of the wheels.

2. a. The water pump moves water through the engine to help dissipate heat and keep the engine cool.

3. b. A tachometer measures rotation rate in units of revolutions per minute or rpm. Typical units of measurement for the other types of gauges listed are: pounds per square inch (psi) for a pressure gauge, miles per hour (mph) for a speedometer, and degrees Fahrenheit or Celsius for a thermometer.

4. c. Kerosene is not usually used to fuel vehicles. Gasoline and diesel fuel, of course, are the most common fuels, but natural gas is also used.

5. b. The transmission includes the clutch, gears, and driveshaft.

6. d. The spark plug provides the spark that ignites the fuel.

7. a. The suspension system, including shock absorbers and springs, keeps the bumps the tires experience from being transferred to the body of the vehicle.

8. d. A compass is used to draw circles. The other tasks listed would be accomplished using: a protractor (choice **a**), a wrench (choice **b**), and a hammer (choice **c**).

9. a. A level, a compass, and a chisel are all carpenter's hand tools. A winch is used to pull a car out of a ditch.

10. c. A carpenter's square is used to draw a straight cut line on a piece of wood or metal. One leg of the square is placed on the edge of the object to be cut. This places the other leg across the object at a 90-degree angle so that the cut will be straight.

11. d. Liquid concrete is poured into a form and cures, or hardens, into the shape of the form. Almost any shape of form can be used.

12. b. Because of its compression strength, concrete is usually used for foundations.

13. a. A protractor measures angles. A level is used to check flatness, a soldering iron to weld metal, and a compass to draw arcs.

14. c. The foundation provides the structural support for a building.

11 ▶ Mechanical Comprehension Review

CHAPTER SUMMARY
This chapter will help you prepare for the Mechanical Comprehension subtest of the ASVAB. It presents the most commonly tested concepts: basic and compound mechanical machines and devices, mechanical motion, fluid dynamics, properties of materials, and structural support.

Every day, often without even thinking about it, you use mechanical devices. These could be simple machines such as levers and pulleys, or more complex compound machines such as linkages and gears. The ability to understand and use mechanical concepts is important both for many tasks required in the armed services and in everyday life.

The Mechanical Comprehension subtest of ASVAB may cover topics you are familiar with, as well as some that are new. Understanding the concepts in this chapter will benefit you both for the exam and in your career in the armed services. After an introduction to the Mechanical Comprehension subtest, this chapter summarizes definitions and the most commonly tested mechanical concepts. It also suggests how you can add to your knowledge of mechanical concepts and related scientific and mathematical knowledge. At the end of the chapter, you get an opportunity to review what you've learned by answering sample Mechanical Comprehension questions like those found on the ASVAB.

► What Mechanical Comprehension Questions Are Like

The Mechanical Comprehension subtest covers a wide range of topics. It consists of 25 multiple-choice questions, which you will have 19 minutes to answer. Most questions require previous knowledge of the topic, while some questions will themselves provide all of the information you need to figure out the answer.

Some questions require you to identify various mechanical machines or devices. Some of the mechanical devices that may appear on the exam—and are covered in this chapter—include gears, pulleys, levers, fasteners, springs, gauges, hinges, and linkages.

Other questions require knowledge of mechanical motion such as velocity, acceleration, direction, and friction for both solid bodies and fluids. These questions test concepts such as the motion and acceleration of automobiles or the buoyancy and pressure of fluids.

The Mechanical Comprehension subtest also covers the properties of materials and the concept of structural support. The material properties include weight, strength, density, thermal properties, and center of gravity. Structural support includes concepts such as weight distribution.

A typical mechanical comprehension question will look something like this:

1. What is the main function of a pulley?
   a. to increase the strength of a construction crane
   b. to override the power of an electric motor
   c. to add energy to a system
   d. to change the direction of a pulling force

The correct answer is **d**, to change the direction of a pulling force. Pulleys are used to change not the strength of a force but its direction.

► Review of Mechanical Comprehension Concepts

As aforementioned, some of the mechanical concepts most likely to appear on the ASVAB include basic and compound machines, mechanical motion, the behavior of fluids, the properties of materials, and structual support.

Basic and Compound Machines

Most mechanical machines and devices were invented in a similar manner: people were looking for easier ways to perform their everyday jobs. Some mechanical devices are thousands of years old, such as the lever, the wheel, and many hand tools. Other more complex devices, such as pumps and valves, were invented more recently. Often the idea of a new mechanical device exists, but the technology to actually make it does not. For example, many years before the pump was invented, people probably discussed the need for an easier way to move water from the river to the town on the hill. However, the technologies of the electric motor and metal casting had not yet been discovered, so the modern pump could not be invented.

In general, a mechanical device is a tool that does physical work and is governed by mechanical forces and movements. In other words, you can usually *see* what a mechanical device does and how it works—as opposed to, say, electrical devices such as light switches or batteries. Some tools are used to directly accomplish a specific task, as when you use a hand saw to cut a piece of wood. Others, such as pulleys and gears, may be used indirectly to accomplish tasks that would be possible without the device but are easier with it. Still others, such as gauges, provide feedback on how well other mechanical devices are working. You see and use mechanical devices many times each day, so there's little reason to be intimidated by an exam question on a mechanical device.

Gears

A gear is a toothed wheel or cylinder that meshes with another gear to transmit motion or to change speed or direction. Gears are usually attached to a rotating shaft that is turned by an energy source such as an electric motor or an internal combustion engine. Mechanical devices that use gears include automotive transmissions, carpenter's hand drills, elevator lifting mechanisms, bicycles, and carnival rides such as Ferris wheels and merry-go-rounds.

Gears are used in different configurations. In an automotive transmission, for instance, two gears may directly touch each other. As one gear spins clockwise, the other rotates counterclockwise. Another possible configuration is to have two gears connected by a loop of chain, as on a bicycle. In this arrangement, the first gear rotates in one direction, causing the chain to move. Since the chain is directly connected to the second gear, the second gear will rotate in the same direction as the first gear.

Often a system will use two gears of different sizes, as on a ten-speed bicycle. This allows changes in speed of the bicycle or machine.

Test questions about gears will always involve rotation, or spinning. The easiest way to approach questions about gears is to use the picture given or to draw one, if it's not already provided. Draw an arrow next to each gear to indicate which direction (clockwise or counterclockwise) it is rotating.

Pulleys

A pulley consists of a wheel with a grooved rim through which a rope or cable is run.

Pulleys are often used to change the direction of a pulling force. For instance, a pulley could be attached to the ceiling of a room. A rope could be run from the floor, up through the pulley, and back down to a box sitting on the floor. The pulley would allow you to pull *down* on the rope and cause the box to go *up*.

Another common use for a pulley is to connect an electric motor to a mechanical device such as a pump. One pulley is placed on the shaft of the motor, and a second pulley is placed on the shaft of the pump. A belt connects the two pulleys. When the motor is turned on, the first pulley rotates and causes the belt to rotate, which in turn causes the second pulley to rotate and turn the pump. This arrangement is very similar to the previous example of a bicycle chain and gears.

You may have seen pulleys used in a warehouse to lift heavy loads. Another use for a pulley is on a large construction crane. The cable extends from the object being lifted up to the top of the crane boom, across a pulley, and back down to the electric winch that is used to pull on the cable. In this situation the pulley again causes a change in direction of the pulling force, from the downward force of the winch that pulls the cable to the upward movement of the object being lifted.

Levers

The lever is a very old mechanical device. A lever typically consists of a metal or wooden bar that pivots on a fixed point. The point of using a lever is to gain a **mechanical advantage**. Mechanical advantage results when you use a mechanical device in order to make a task easier; that is, you gain an advantage by using a mechanical device. A lever allows you to complete a task, typically lifting, that would be more difficult or even impossible without the lever.

The most common example of a lever is a playground seesaw. A force—a person's weight—is applied to one side of the lever and causes the weight on the other side—the other person—to be lifted. However, since the pivot point on a seesaw is in the center, each person must weigh the same or the seesaw won't work well. A seesaw is a lever with no mechanical advantage. If you push down on one side with a weight of ten pounds, you can only lift a maximum of ten pounds on the other side. This is no great advantage.

This brings us to the secret of the lever: in order to lift an object that is heavier than the force you want to apply to the other side of the lever, you must locate the pivot point closer to the object you want to lift. If two 50-pound children sit close to the center of the see-saw, one 50-pound child close to the end of the board on the other side will be able to lift them both.

Test questions about levers may require a bit of math—simple multiplication and division. Lever problems rely on one simple concept: the product of the weight to be lifted times the distance from the weight to the pivot point must be equal to the product of the lifting force times the distance from the force to the pivot point. Stated as an equation, $w \times d_1 = f \times d_2$. Here's an example of a test question using this concept:

2. Bill has a 15-foot long lever and he wants to lift a 100-pound box. If he locates the pivot point 5 feet from the box, leaving 10 feet between the pivot point and the other end of the lever where he will apply the lifting force, how hard must he press on the lever to lift the box?

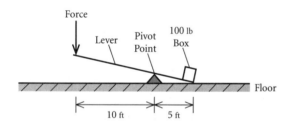

To solve this problem, use the lever formula, $w \times d_1 = f \times d_2$. The weight of 100 pounds times 5 feet must equal 10 feet times the force: $100 \times 5 = 10 \times f$. Multiply 100 by 5 to get 500, and then divide by 10 to get 50 pounds of force, which Bill must apply to the lever to raise the box.

Fasteners

A mechanical fastener is any mechanical device or process used to connect two or more items together. Typical examples of fastening **devices** are bolts, screws, nails, and rivets. **Processes** used to join items together mechanically include gluing and welding. The "hook and loop" is a unique mechanical fastener consisting of two tapes of material with many small plastic hooks and loops that stick together. Children's sneakers often use such fastening tape instead of laces.

Springs

A spring is an elastic mechanical device, normally a coil of wire, that returns to its original shape after being compressed or extended. There are many types of springs including the compression coil, spiral coil, flat spiral, extension coil, leaf spring, and torsional spring.

Springs are used for many applications such as car suspensions (compression coil and leaf springs), garage doors (extension coil and torsion springs), wind-up clocks (flat spiral and torsion springs), and some styles of retractable pens (compression coil).

In most questions on the ASVAB, you can assume that springs behave linearly. That is, if an extension spring stretches one inch under a pull of ten pounds, then it will stretch two inches under a pull of twenty pounds. In real life, if you pull too hard on a spring, it will not return to its original shape. This is called exceeding the spring's **elastic limit**.

If several springs are used for one application, they can be arranged in one of two ways: in series or in parallel. The easiest way to remember the difference is that if the springs are all hooked together, end to end, then you have a **series** of springs. The other option is for the springs not to be hooked together but to be lined up side by side, **parallel** to each other. If two springs are arranged in series, they will stretch much farther than the same two springs arranged in parallel under the same pulling force. This is because in series, the total pulling force passes through both springs. If the same springs are arranged in parallel, the pulling force is divided equally with half going through each spring.

Springs in Series:

Springs in Parallel:

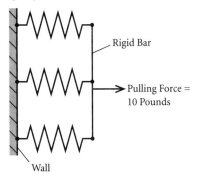

The key to solving spring problems is to draw a diagram of the arrangement, if one isn't already provided, and follow the pulling force through the system.

Valves

A valve is a mechanical device that controls the flow of liquids, gases, or loose material through piping systems. There are many types of valves including butterfly valves, gate valves, plug valves, ball valves, and check valves.

A valve is basically a gate that can be closed or opened in order to permit a fluid or gas to travel in a particular direction. Exam questions on valves typically require you to follow a piping flow diagram through several sets of valves. The best way to approach these problems is to methodically follow each branch of the piping system from start to finish.

Gauges and Pumps

Gauges and pumps may appear in the Mechanical Comprehension subtest. These devices are discussed in Chapter 10, "Auto and Shop Information."

Linkages

A linkage is a way of connecting objects in order to transfer energy. Belts and chains are commonly used in conjunction with gears and pulleys for this purpose. Chains are typically made of steel or some other metal, while belts are typically made of fiber-reinforced rubber. An example of the use of a belt is the fan belt on the engine of an automobile, which helps transfer the energy from the engine camshaft to the fan. A bicycle uses a chain to transfer the energy from the pedals to the wheel. Another mechanical linkage is the tie rod that connects the piston and crankshaft in an internal combustion engine.

Mechanical Motion

Motion simply means a change of position. The parameters that describe mechanical motion include velocity, direction, acceleration, and friction.

Velocity

Velocity means the rate at which an object is moving in such units as miles per hour or feet per minute. Exam questions on velocity might ask you to use velocity and time to determine the distance traveled. For instance, if a car travels at a constant velocity of 60 miles per hour for two hours, how far does it travel? The answer is velocity multiplied by time, or 60 mph times 2 hours for a total of 120 miles. You might also be asked about relative velocity in a question in which two objects travel at different speeds for different lengths of time.

Direction

If you want to travel quickly from Kansas City to Denver, your velocity is unimportant if you're not traveling in the right direction. When answering mechanical motion questions, always note the direction of travel of the object or objects, if this information is given. Again, drawing a sketch of the situation usually helps.

Acceleration

Acceleration is the rate of change of velocity or, in other words, how much faster you are going from one minute to the next. This is simpler than it sounds. If you are sitting in your car at a stop sign and then you press hard on the gas pedal, you get pushed back into the seat a bit. If you are traveling along the highway at a *constant* 50 mph, you don't have this feeling. However, if you hit the gas and accelerate to 65 mph, you are again pushed back into your seat. You have the same sensation when your airplane takes off on the runway. This sensation is the result of acceleration, an increase in how fast an object is traveling. The opposite of acceleration is **deceleration**, slowing down. Exam questions on acceleration may involve a little simple math.

Friction

Friction is the naturally occurring force that acts to hold back an object in motion. If you slide a block of wood across a floor, the friction between the floor and the block causes a drag on the movement of the block. There are two things you should remember if you encounter an exam question about friction:

- Friction always slows down movement.
- All movement experiences frictional force to some degree.

The drag force of friction varies depending on the materials involved. If you've ever tried to drag a piece of furniture from a room with a carpeted floor to another room with a wood floor, you found that the piece of furniture was much easier to drag on the wood floor than on the carpet. The carpet has a higher **coef-**ficient of friction than wood. Materials with a high coefficient of friction include such things as sandpaper and brick. Examples of materials with a low coefficient of friction include non-stick cooking surfaces and ice. The differing coefficients of fiction explain why it's more difficult to pull a wooden block across a rough surface such as sandpaper than across a slick surface such as ice.

Fluid Statics and Dynamics

The Mechanical Comprehension subtest includes questions on the behavior of fluids, including questions on pressure, density, and buoyancy.

Pressure

As a solid object is submerged below the surface of a fluid, the fluid exerts a **pressure** on it. Have you ever noticed that when diving in a swimming pool you feel more and more pressure on your ears as you go deeper? This is the effect of the pressure of the fluid, water in this case, on your body. The fluid has weight. As you go deeper, more of this weight presses on your body. All fluids behave this way. The deeper a solid object is submerged, the higher the pressure. This behavior of fluids affects the design of machines such as submarines.

The formula for pressure is: *pressure = density × depth.*

Density

Density is a proportion of weight to volume. If you are comparing two fluids, for example, a gallon of the one with the higher density weighs more than the same volume (a gallon) of another liquid. The density of a solid object or other fluid is usually compared to the density of water, 62.4 pounds per cubic foot. Density controls whether an a solid object or another fluid will sink or float in a given fluid. If a solid object sinks when placed in water, then its density is more than that of water. Conversely, if an object floats, then it is less dense than water. Some liquids, such as mercury, are more dense than water. If mercury and water are combined in a jar, the water will float on top of the mercury. Other fluids, such as gasoline or motor oil, are slightly less dense than water. That is why when an oil tanker has a spill, it leaves an oil slick—the oil is floating on the surface of the water.

Density influences the amount of pressure a fluid exerts on an object. The denser the fluid, the faster the pressure increases on an object as it is submerged. Exam questions on density may include simple mathematical calculations, such as computing pressure by multiplying density times depth. Or they may simply ask you to compare the effects of pressure at different depths and densities.

Buoyancy

Buoyancy is the force that acts to push an object submerged in a fluid to the surface. When you force a beach ball under water and then let it go, it springs to the surface. That's the effect of buoyancy.

Here's an example that shows how buoyancy works for an object that is denser than water. Let's say you have a glass that is completely full of water, and the water in the glass weighs one pound. Now put in a eight-pound steel ball, which occupies half of the volume of the glass. When the ball sinks, what happens? Half of the water in the glass, a half-pound worth, spills over the edge of the glass because the ball occupies half the volume of the glass. Now, here's a definition: the uplifting buoyant force acting on this ball is equal to the weight of the water displaced out of the glass by the ball. By definition, therefore, this ball weighs half a pound less when submerged in water than it does just sitting on the table.

The ball weighs less underwater, but it still sinks. Why? Because the ball weighs more than the water it displaces. How, then, is it possible to make a ship that floats in water out of steel, when steel is more dense than water? Simple. Take a thin sheet of steel and form it into a kind of bowl shape. As this thin shell is lowered into the water, it will displace enough water to make it float.

Properties of Materials

Mechanical components and systems can be fabricated using many different materials such as steel, wood, concrete, and plastic. All of these materials react differently to stress, temperature changes, and other external factors. You must understand the properties of materials—weight, strength, density, and thermal properties—in order to answer test questions about them.

Weight

The **weight** of an object is simply a measure of its heaviness.

Strength

The loads and stresses placed on a material must be less than the strength of the material in order to prevent failure. A material's strength can be measured in several ways. A concrete building foundation has lots of weight compressing on it and must have high **compressive** strength. A steel construction girder has a large pulling force acting on it and must therefore have a high **tensile** strength. The materials selected for a given project depend in part on the loads the structure will have to bear.

Density

Think of a one-gallon bottle full of feathers and another full of steel. Which bottle would be heavier? Both bottles have the same volume, but the one full of steel would obviously weigh more, because steel has a higher **density** (weight per unit volume) than feathers. Feathers have a low density; it would take a large volume—a big stack of them—to amount to any significant weight. On the other hand, a small volume of steel, which has a fairly high density, is reasonably heavy. Just remember that a material with a higher density will hurt more if you drop it on your toe!

In the English system of units, density is typically measured in pounds per cubic foot or pounds per cubic inch.

Thermal Properties

The **thermal properties** of materials—how they respond to changes in termperature—affect their suitability for various applications. Most materials expand slightly as the temperature increases and contract as the temperature decreases. This amount of expansion and contraction varies for each material but is typically very small; you could not see it with your eyes.

The effect of even this small amount of expansion or contraction can be significant on some mechanical systems. For instance, the internal combustion engine of a vehicle generates heat as it operates. All of the parts of the engine must be manufactured so that they fit together properly at both high and low temperatures. Likewise, an airplane experiences very low temperatures when flying at high altitudes, so that the metal of its body contracts a bit. The designers of the airplane must take this effect into account.

The strength of some materials is also affected by changes in temperature. Most materials get weaker as the temperature increases because the bonds between the individual molecules that make up the material get weaker as the molecules move more rapidly. This is why some building materials, such as steel, are coated with insulation during construction. If the building catches fire, the insulation will help maintain the strength of the steel girders.

Choosing Materials for a Given Application

In deciding what materials to use for a given application, weight, strength, density, and thermal properties must all be taken into consideration. For instance, if you wanted to build an airplane wing, you might consider using either steel or aluminum. Steel is stronger than aluminum. However, aluminum has a lower density; that is, an aluminum wing would be lighter than a steel wing of the same size. Therefore, you could use more aluminum to provide adequate strength and still have a lighter total weight.

Other factors, such as cost and how easy the materials are to work with, are also taken into account when selecting materials for a project.

Structural Support

Mechanical systems such as buildings and bridges require proper structural support in so they can hold up heavy loads. An object's center of gravity and its weight distribution affect the design of structural support.

Center of Gravity

The **center of gravity** of an object is the point at which all of the object's weight appears to act. For instance, you can balance a pencil on your finger by placing your finger under the pencil at the middle of its length. The center of gravity of that pencil is halfway along its length. Likewise, a round ball has its center of gravity at its center. Other objects that are not so symmetrical also have a center of gravity, which can be located through calculations.

Exam questions on center of gravity usually involve symmetrical objects so that the math does not become complicated. Take your time, draw a sketch of the object, and use common sense.

Weight Distribution

The **distribution of weight** on a structure such as on a bridge is also important to understand. If there are three trucks uniformly spaced across the length of a bridge that is supported only at its ends, then each support bears an equal amount of the load. However, if the trucks are all located close to one end of the bridge, then the support on that end will be holding up a higher load than the support on the opposite end.

Bridges and buildings have highly variable loads. The worst-case weight distribution must be accounted for—for instance, trucks standing nose to tail for the whole length of the bridge—even if that isn't very likely to happen

As with most Mechanical Comprehension questions, using the picture given, or drawing one if it's not provided, will help you see the location and distribution of the objects.

▶ Brushing Up on Related Topics

Some mechanical comprehension questions may require the use of math or science to determine the correct answer. This chapter cannot cover all the possible questions you might be asked on the ASVAB, but here are suggestions for ways to increase your knowledge of math and science and your general mechanical comprehension.

Math

The math you may need for Mechanical Comprehension questions are simple arithmetic (addition, subtraction, multiplication, and division) and geometry (angles and shapes). If you had trouble with arithmetic or geometry in your past schooling, you can brush up by reading the math chapter of this book. If you still want more help, pull out your old high school math book or check out a math book from the library.

Science

Science subjects such as physics, materials science, thermodynamics, and chemistry are confusing for some people, but they needn't be. Science is real, everyday life. You see science in action dozens of times every day. A car is stopped by brakes, which use friction—that's physics. A magnet adheres to the refrigerator door due to the properties of the magnet and carbon steel of which the door is made—that's materials science. A pot of water boils when you set it on the stove and turn on the burner—that's thermodynamics. A cake rises through the release of carbon dioxide from the baking powder or baking soda reacting with heat or an acid—that's chemistry. This chapter has reviewed many of the scientific concepts that are involved in mechanical devices. Again, as with math, you may have science books from previous schooling that you can use to help you solidify your scientific knowledge. If not, the library is full of scientific resources.

General Mechanical Comprehension

Mechanical devices are such an integral part of everyday life that there are many real-life sources you can investigate to gain more knowledge of their design and use. A construction site is a great place to visit for a day to learn more about hand tools, cranes, pumps, and other devices. Ask the construction supervisor if you can take a tour.

Another possibility would be to visit a local manufacturer in your town. Examples include a foundry, a sheet metal fabricator, an automotive manufacturer, or a pump manufacturer. Look in the yellow pages under "manufacturing" for possibilities.

▶ Practice Questions

Try the Mechanical Comprehension questions below. Answers and explanations are at the end of the chapter.

1. How can gears be used to change the speed of a machine?
   a. use more gears
   b. use two gears of the same size
   c. use two gears of different sizes
   d. use two large gears

2. Steve has a lever whose pivot point is 3 feet from the 50-pound box he wants to lift. Steve is standing at the other end of the lever, 6 feet from the pivot point. How much force must he apply to lift the box?

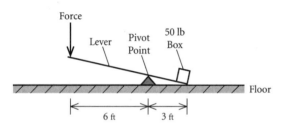

   a. 50 pounds
   b. 25 pounds
   c. 100 pounds
   d. 6 pounds

3. When three identical springs are arranged in series and a pulling force of 10 pounds is applied, the total stretch is 9 inches. If these same three springs are arranged in parallel and the same 10-pound force is applied to the new arrangement, what will be the total distance of stretch?

Springs in Series:

Springs in Parallel:

   a. 3 inches
   b. 4.5 inches
   c. 9 inches
   d. 18 inches

4. Jan and Shirley begin traveling from the same point. Jan travels east at 30 mph for half an hour and Shirley travels west at 40 mph for one hour. How far apart are they at the end of their travels?
   a. 25 miles
   b. 55 miles
   c. 70 miles
   d. 120 miles

5. If each of the following objects weighed the same, which would be easiest to drag?

 a. a wood object on a carpeted floor

 b. a wood object on a wood floor

 c. a glass object on a brick floor

 d. a glass object on a tiled floor

6. A ball is submerged beneath 6 feet of a fluid that has a density of 110 pounds per cubic foot. What pressure does the fluid exert on the ball?

 a. 6 pounds per square foot

 b. 18 pounds per square foot

 c. 110 pounds per square foot

 d. 660 pounds per square foot

7. Jar A contains a volume of 2 cubic feet of liquid and weighs 128 pounds. Jar B contains a volume of 3 cubic feet of liquid and weighs 216 pounds. Which liquid has a higher density?

 a. Jar A

 b. Jar B

 c. They have the same density.

 d. There is not enough information to answer the question.

8. Which of the following best explains why wood floats on water?

 a. Wood is less dense than water.

 b. Water is less dense than wood.

 c. Water exerts more pressure than wood.

 d. Water is more buoyant than wood.

9. Which of the following best describes the effect of heating a bar of steel?

 a. The bar will contract.

 b. The bar will expand.

 c. The bar will warp.

 d. The bar will remain unchanged.

10. A cube-shaped box, 12 inches on each side, is full of corn kernels. If you wanted to pick up this box with a single attachment point without having it tilt to one side, where would you attach the lifting device?

 a. in the center of the top of the box

 b. near one of the upper corners of the box

 c. near one of the lower corners of the box

 d. anywhere on the bottom of the box

How to Answer Mechanical Aptitude Questions

- Read each problem carefully. Questions may contain words such as *not, all,* or *mostly,* which can be tricky unless you pay attention.
- Read the entire question once or even a few times before trying to pick an answer. Decide exactly what the question is asking. Take notes and draw pictures on scratch paper. That way you won't waste time by going in the wrong direction.
- Use common sense. Some mechanical concepts can seem intimidating at first but are really a combination of a few more simple ideas. Try to break complicated questions down into smaller, manageable pieces.
- Answer the questions that are easiest for you first. You do not have to go in order from start to finish. Read each question and, if you are not sure what to do, move on to the next question. You can go back to harder questions if you have time at the end.
- Many mechanical concepts are commonly used in everyday life. You do not have to be a mechanic or an engineer to use these devices. If something seems unfamiliar, try to think of items around your house that might be similar.
- Don't be intimidated by unfamiliar terms. In most instances, there are clues in the question that will point you towards the correct answer, and some of the answers can be ruled out by common sense.

▶ Answers

1. **c.** Changing gears on a ten-speed bicycle is a good example of using different size gears to change speed.

2. **b.** Apply the distance formula, $w \times d_1 = f \times d_2$, to come up with the equation $50 \times 3 = f \times 6$. Solve for the unknown f by multiplying 3 times 50 to get 150 and then dividing by 6 to get 25 pounds.

3. **a.** The total pulling force will be divided equally, with each spring experiencing one-third of the total force. Since the force is divided by 3, the amount of movement will be divided by 3 also. The original configuration stretched 9 inches, so the new arrangement will stretch only 3 inches.

4. **b.** Jan has traveled 15 miles to the east of the starting point, and Shirley has traveled 40 miles west of their starting point. Since east and west are in opposite directions, this puts a distance of 55 miles between them. If both had been traveling in the same direction at the given velocity and time, the distance separating them would have been only 25 miles.

5. **d.** Glass and tile both have relatively low coefficients of friction.

6. **d.** Apply the formula for *pressure = density × depth*. 110 pounds per cubic foot times 6 feet equals 660 pounds per square foot.

7. **b.** Divide the weight of each jar by its volume. The liquid in Jar A has density of 64 pounds per cubic foot, and the liquid in Jar B has a density of 72 pounds per cubic foot.

8. **a.** Wood floats because it is less dense than the water it is floating on.

9. **b.** Most materials expand when heated.

10. **a.** If you lifted from the center of the box, you would be lifting upward through the center of gravity, and you could lift the box without tilting it to one side.

CHAPTER

12▶ Electronics Information Review

CHAPTER SUMMARY

We use electricity every day of our lives. Lightbulbs produce light from electricity. Many ovens use electricity to produce heat. Our televisions and computers use electricity. Our cars use electricity to ignite the fuel in the engine. Batteries produce electricity to power games and calculators. This chapter will add to your knowledge of electronics and review what you already know so that you can get a top score on the Electronics Information subtest of the ASVAB.

The electricity used in the United States is predominately produced from three resources: fossil fuels, such as oil, natural gas, and coal; nuclear materials, primarily uranium; and hydropower from water.

Almost 80 percent of the electrical power used in the United States is produced from the burning of fossil fuels. Fossil fuels are burned to produce heat. The heat is used to produce steam that turns a turbine. The turbine transforms rotational mechanical energy into electric energy which in turn is fed into a power grid.

Nuclear power plants produce about 7 percent of the electricity we consume. A nuclear power plant uses a nuclear reaction (fission) to produce heat that generates steam. The process described above is then used to convert steam into electricity.

About 15 percent of the electricity we use is from hydropower. The kinetic energy of falling water is used to turn turbines that produce the electrical power.

> **Kinetic Energy:** the energy produced by a body in motion.

▶ Basic Electrical Theory

Understanding electricity and electronics is not dependent on understanding the complex structure of the atom—understanding the basics is sufficient. All materials on Earth are made up of atoms. An atom is made up in part of electrons and protons. These two subatomic particles each have an electric charge, or electric polarity. The charge of an electron has a negative polarity while the charge of a proton has a positive polarity. Electricity is essentially the management of positive and negative electric charges.

Charge

Most everyone has experienced the buildup of electric charge when shuffling across a carpet. Your body develops a static charge. It is static because the charge is not moving. When you touch a light switch, the static charge moves, creating a current. You have produced and used electricity.

The symbol for electric charge is **q** or **Q**. Charge is measured in coulombs, **C**. A coulomb of electrons has a negative charge and a coulomb of protons has a positive charge. A coulomb is defined as 6.25×10^{18} electrons or protons:

the charge of 6.25×10^{18} electrons = Q = 1C

Example: What is the charge, in coulombs, of one electron?
You remember that

6.25×10^{18} electrons = 1 Coulomb

To get the charge of one electron, divide both sides by 6.25×10^{18}:

1 electron = 0.16×10^{-18} C

Voltage

An electric charge has the potential to do work by forcing another charge to move. Opposite charges attract each other and like charges repel each other, just like magnets. Thus, a positive and a negative charge would attract each other, while two negative charges would repel each other. The potential of an electric charge to do work is the **voltage** or the **potential difference**. A battery produces a voltage. This voltage can be thought of as the force that moves electrons from one terminal to the other. This force is called the electromotive force (emf). The accepted symbol for voltage is **V**. The schematic symbol for a DC voltage is:

$$+ \mathbin{\vert}$$
$$- \mathbin{\top}$$

> **Voltage:** the potential of an electric charge to do work.

Current

All batteries have two terminals, a positive and a negative one. On a flashlight battery, for example, one end (usually marked with a + sign) is the positive terminal, and the other end (usually marked with a − sign) is the negative terminal.

When a battery is connected to a load with wires, the potential difference, or voltage, between the two terminals (the two opposite charges) forces a third charge to move. The charge in motion is called an electric **current**. Current is produced when a potential difference moves an electric charge. Picture a battery connected with wires to a light bulb:

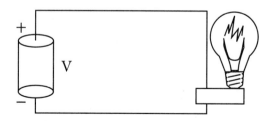

The battery produces a voltage, which forces the free electrons in the wire to move. The mobile free electrons moving in the wire are the current. The current is always a continuous flow of electrons, and at every point in the circuit, the current is the same.

Load: the resistance in an electric circuit.

Electric current is measured in amperes. An **ampere** is defined to be 6.25×10^{18} electrons moving past any given point in one second. This is the same as one coulomb of charge moving past any given point in one second. The symbol for current is **I** or *i*. Mathematically, current is expressed as:

$I = \frac{Q}{T}$ where I is current in amperes (A), Q is charge in coulombs (C), and T is time in seconds (s).

Example: What is the current if 10 coulombs of charge flow through a light bulb every 5 seconds?

$I = \frac{Q}{T}$
$I = \frac{10\,C}{5\,s}$
$I = 2\,A$

The charge, or number of electrons, can be determined using the equation above:

$I = \frac{Q}{T}$

multiply both sides of the equation by time

$I \times T = \frac{Q}{T} \times T$
$IT = Q \times 1$
$IT = Q$

Therefore, if we solve for charge, or Q, this same equation tells us that charge is equal to current multiplied by time. In other words, charge equals the amount of current during a given time period.

Example: How many electrons are flowing through the light bulb when the current is 2 amperes?

$Q = I \times T$
$Q = 2\,A \times 1\,s$
$Q = 2$ Coulombs
and
$2\,C = 2 \times 6.25 \times 10^{18}$
$2\,C = 12.5 \times 10^{18}$ electrons

Alternating Current (AC) and Direct Current (DC)

A battery is an example of a direct voltage source. The terminals of the battery always maintain the same polarity, so the current flow from one terminal to the other is always in the same direction. On the other hand, an alternating voltage source periodically reverses its polarity. The current resulting from an alternating voltage also periodically changes its direction of flow.

The electricity generated in a power plant is by nature an alternating voltage. The magnetic fields developed in a rotating turbine always produce an alternating voltage. The voltage we most often use in our homes is 110 volt 60 Hz. The 60 Hz, or Hertz, refers to the frequency that an alternating voltage changes polarity. In this case the polarity changes from positive to negative and back to positive 60 times a second.

One advantage of producing an alternating voltage is that it is more easily changed to a different value than a direct voltage can be changed. This is very important because power plants produce thousands of volts, while we can safely use just 110 or 220 volts in our homes. Most of our appliances then convert the 110 or 220 volts to even a smaller voltage. Simple transformers are used to step up or down alternating voltages. A direct voltage must first be converted to an alternating voltage before its value can be changed. This adds complexity and cost to using direct voltages.

Another benefit of using alternating voltages and currents is that they can be easily and inexpensively converted into direct voltage and current. A diode is a semiconductor device that allows current to flow in only one direction. When the direction of current flow changes, the diode acts like an insulator and stops the current. Two or four diodes can be used to transform alternating voltages and currents into direct voltages and currents. This process is referred to as **rectifying** an alternating voltage.

Basic electrical theory is most easily understood by studying direct voltages and currents. The study of alternating voltages and currents can become very complex. The rest of this chapter will discuss only direct voltages and currents.

Conductors, Insulators, and Semiconductors

A copper wire is an example of a conductor. A **conductor** is a material that has electrons that can easily move. Metals are very good conductors. Copper is used to make most of the wires we use because it has high conductance and is relatively inexpensive. Aluminum was used in the 1950s to make wires for our homes because it was less expensive than copper; however, it is not as good a conductor.

An **insulator** is a material whose electrons do not move freely. Glass, rubber, wood, and porcelain are all examples of insulators. Insulators are used to prevent the flow of current.

A **semiconductor** is a material that conducts less than a metal conductor but more than an insulator. Silicon is the most recognized semiconductor. Most transistors, diodes, and integrated circuits are produced from semiconductor materials such as silicon or germanium.

Resistance

Resistance is the opposition to current. A copper wire has very little resistance; therefore it is a good conductor. Insulators have a large resistance. The symbol for resistance is **R**. Resistance is measured in **ohms**. The symbol for ohms is the Greek letter omega, Ω. The schematic symbol for resistance is:

A good copper wire has a resistance of about one-hundredth of an ohm, or 0.01 Ω per foot. For comparison, the resistive heating element used in a medium-size hair dryer has a resistance of about 14 Ω.

Resistors are fabricated using many different materials. The most common types of resistors are wire-wound resistors, carbon-composition resistors, and film resistors. Wire-wound resistors are generally used in high-power applications. Carbon resistors are the most common. They are used in most electronic circuits due to their low cost. Carbon resistors can't typically be built with an exact resistance value. Film resistors are used when a more exact resistance is needed. Resistors are easily built with resistance values from 0.01 Ω to many millions of ohms.

Analog Electrical Circuits

All electrical circuits have the three following components:

1. A potential difference or voltage.
2. A closed path for current to flow from one side of the potential difference to the other.
3. Resistance, which is often referred to as a "load."

Ohm's law defines the relationships between voltage, current, and resistance in a simple electrical circuit.

The illustration below shows a flashlight, where the voltage source is a battery and the load is a lightbulb:

The current flows along the circuit path...

This is the battery; it provides the voltage

This is the lightbulb; it provides the resistance

Ohm's law states that:

potential difference (or voltage) = current × resistance

or

$$V = I \times R$$

This can be rewritten as:

$$\text{current} = \frac{\text{potential difference}}{\text{resistance}}$$

or

$$I = \frac{V}{R}$$

Example: The battery in the flashlight below supplies 4.5 volts and the light bulb has a resistance of 1.5 Ω. How much current flows in the circuit?

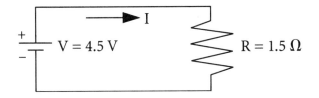

Ohm's law states that current (remember that current is measured in amperes) equals voltage over resistance:

$$I = \frac{V}{R}$$

$$I = \frac{4.5 \text{ V}}{1.5 \text{ }\Omega}$$

$$I = 3A$$

According to Ohm's law, 3 amperes of current flows through this circuit.

Series Resistance Circuits

Multiple resistance elements may be used in an electric circuit. An example of this type of circuit is the *series resistance circuit*, as represented schematically below:

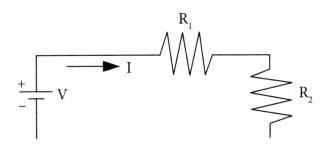

R_1 and R_2 are both in the same current path, providing more total resistance than a single resistance element. It is crucial to remember, however, that in a series resistance circuit, the current is the same everywhere in the circuit. In other words, the current flowing through R_1 is the same as the current through R_2. The total circuit resistance is the sum of the resistance of each individual resistance element.

Example: Christmas tree lights are a good example of a series resistance circuit. The following circuit represents four bulbs in a string connected to a 20-volt source; each bulb provides 5 ohms of resistance. What is the current flowing through the string of lights?

Again, Ohm's law states that the current equals the voltage over the resistance, and in this circuit the total resistance is equal to the sum of the resistance of each of the four bulbs.

$$I = \frac{V}{R_T}$$
$$I = \frac{V}{R_1 + R_2 + R_3 + R_4}$$
$$I = \frac{20\ V}{5\ \Omega + 5\ \Omega + 5\ \Omega + 5\ \Omega}$$
$$I = \frac{20\ V}{20\ \Omega}$$
$$I = 1A$$

The voltage across each of the light bulbs in the example above can also be easily calculated using Ohm's law:

$$V_1 = I \times R_1$$
$$V_1 = 1\ A \times 5\ \Omega$$
$$V_1 = 5\ V$$

Notice that the sum of the voltages across each bulb equals the total voltage. This can be stated:

$$V_T = V_1 + V_2 + V_3 + V_4$$
or
$$V_T = 5\ V + 5\ V + 5\ V + 5\ V$$
$$V_T = 20\ V$$

Parallel Resistance Circuits

A **parallel** resistance circuit has two or more loads connected across a single voltage source. An example of this is plugging your coffee pot and toaster into the same electric outlet. Consider the circuit below, where R_1 is the coffee pot and R_2 is the toaster.

The **voltage** across each resistor of a *parallel* resistance circuit is the same. On the other hand, the **current** through each resistor of a *series* resistance circuit is the same. The current through each resistor in a *parallel* circuit may be different, depending on the resistance of the loads. The total current of the circuit is the sum of the current through each resistor.

$$I_T = I_1 + I_2$$

Again, the voltage across both R_1 and R_2 is the same, it is V. The current through each resistor can still be calculated using Ohm's law.

$$I_1 = \frac{V}{R_1}$$
$$I_2 = \frac{V}{R_2}$$

Example: What is the total current, I_T, that a 120-volt source must supply if a coffee pot with a resistance of 30 ohms and a toaster with a resistance of 20 ohms are plugged into the same outlet?

The total current:
$$I_T = I_1 + I_2$$
$$I_T = \frac{V}{R_1} + \frac{V}{R_2}$$
$$I_T = \frac{120\ V}{30\ \Omega} + \frac{120\ V}{20\ \Omega}$$
$$I_T = 4\ A + 6\ A$$
$$I_T = 10\ A$$

The resultant total resistance of the toaster and coffee pot is the value a single resistor would have if the toaster and coffee pot were combined. Look at the previous example and determine the total resistance. The total resistance is equivalent to the total voltage divided by the total current; therefore, using the coffee pot and toaster:

$$R_T = \frac{V}{I_T}$$
$$R_T = \frac{120\ V}{10\ A}$$
$$R_T = 12\ \Omega$$

We can redraw our circuit now with a single load replacing the coffee pot and toaster. Notice that the equivalent resistance of 12 Ω is indeed less than the resistance of either the toaster or coffee pot.

Electrical circuits many times combine series and parallel resistance. Determining the total current depends on first solving for the total resistance. The parallel resistances must first be combined and then added to the series resistance to determine the total resistance.

Ohm's law in a parallel resistance circuit really means that the voltage is constant and the total current is the sum of the currents through each resistor. Ohm's law in a series resistance circuit implies that the current is constant and the total voltage is the sum of the voltages across each resistance.

Electrical Power

The measurement of **power** (**P**) should be familiar to everyone. Light bulbs are used according to their wattage. Electrical power is measured in **watts** (**W**). A watt is defined to be the work done in one second by one volt to move one coulomb of charge. It is written mathematically:

$$P = V \times \frac{Q}{T}$$

or

$$\text{Power} = \text{Voltage} \times \frac{\text{Change}}{\text{Time}}$$

Remember that current is:

$$I = \frac{Q}{T}$$

Substitute I for $\frac{Q}{T}$ into the equation above to give:

$$P = V \times I$$

This is called the power equation; power, or the number of watts, is equal to voltage multiplied by current.

> **Watt:** the work done in one second by one volt to move one coulomb of charge.

Example: Calculate how many watts a light bulb uses when it is connected to a 120-volt circuit with 0.5 A flowing.

$$P = V \times I$$
$$P = 120\ V \times 0.5\ A$$
$$P = 60\ \text{watts}$$

One of the most important circuit characteristics an electrical designer must consider is the power dissipated in a resistor when current flows through it. A resistor will heat up when current flows. The heat is equivalent to the power lost in the resistor. We can use the power equation (P = V × I) and Ohm's law (V = $\frac{I}{R}$) to determine the power dissipated in a resistor.

When we substitute Ohm's law into the power equation to calculate power in terms of current:

$$P = V \times I$$

Ohm's law is V = I × R. Substitute (I × R) for V in the power equation giving:

$$P = (I \times R) \times I$$
$$P = I^2 R$$

We can also use Ohm's law to solve the power equation in terms of voltage:

$$P = V \times I$$

Ohm's law is $I = \frac{V}{R}$. Substitute $\frac{V}{R}$ for I in the power equation giving

$$P = V \times \frac{V}{R}$$
$$P = \frac{V^2}{R}$$

The heat generated in a resistor is sometimes harmful and sometimes beneficial. When too much power is lost in a resistor, it can burn up and destroy an appliance. A toaster is an example of using the heat generated in a resistor for benefit. The heating element in a toaster is nothing more than a large resistor.

Example: How much power does the heating element of the toaster use in the following circuit?

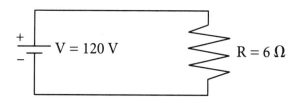

$$P = \frac{V^2}{R}$$
$$P = \frac{120^2\ V}{6W}$$
$$P = 2,400 \text{ watts}$$

▶ Miscellaneous Electrical Components

Capacitors
Most practical circuits contain devices other than voltage sources, resistors, and wires. Capacitors, for instance, are widely used. A **capacitor** is an electrical device that can store electrical charge. A capacitor's function is limited to AC circuits. A common application for capacitors is building filter circuits to protect appliances from voltage spikes. The symbol for a capacitor (C) is similar to a voltage source.

Fuses
Fuses are used to protect almost every electrical item we use. A **fuse** is typically a small piece of wire that will burn up and stop conducting electricity when too much current is forced to flow through it. Fuses are rated to blow at a given current, up to a maximum voltage. For example, a typical fuse in a television may be rated to blow, or open, at 3.0 amperes at any voltage up to 120 volts to protect the television from currents over 3 amperes and voltages over 120 V. An ideal fuse has zero resistance of its own and opens instantly when excess current flows. Some fuses are designed to allow a large current surge to safely flow for a small period of time. This is important because many appliances and motors have what is called an in-rush current surge. A **"slo-blo" fuse** will allow a large current to flow for a few seconds before opening.

Switches
Most circuits wouldn't be practical if we couldn't turn them on and off. **Switches** are used to break a circuit path to stop current flow to a load, such as a lightbulb. There are many types of switches, depending on the application. The most common switches are single-pole-single-throw and double-pole-double-throw switches. The dial used to turn the channel on older televisions is a called a rotary switch. A rotary switch opens and closes contacts when it is turned.

► Electronic Manufacturing and Testing

A common workshop will have most of the tools needed to work on electrical equipment. Pliers, screwdrivers, wire cutters, and wrenches are all needed. In addition, a few specialty tools are required. For instance, a wire stripper is a very useful tool. It is used to remove the insulation from a wire in preparation for joining the wire to a circuit element.

Solder

Solder and a soldering iron are used to physically connect most circuit components. **Solder** is a metal alloy usually containing almost equal amounts of tin and lead. Solder is usually specified to be either 40 percent tin and 60 percent lead, 50 percent each, or 60 percent tin and 40 percent lead. The latter mixture does the best soldering job because it melts the easiest, flows the best, and hardens the fastest. However, it is more expensive than the other mixtures. A soldering iron melts solder by heating it to 500 or 600 degrees Fahrenheit; the solder is fused to the metal leads of the electronic components and wires as it cools to permanently bond them together. A joint that has been properly soldered will appear shiny and smooth. A flux must also be used when soldering to remove oxidation from the components to be joined. The flux is typically contained in the solder. One must be careful to not use acid flux when joining electronic components because the acid will eventually corrode the solder joint. A rosin flux is preferred for electronic uses.

Wires and Printed Circuit Boards

Wires have historically been used to connect the components of a circuit. Today's modern technology has

Mastering Zeros

MASTERING ZEROS

The numbers used for circuit analysis are often either very large or very small. Writing out all the zeroes before or after the decimal point can be extremely tedious. Prefixes are used to simplify the writing out of all the zeros. For example a billion words can be written as any of the following:

>   1,000,000,000 words

or

>   1,000 million words

or

> 1×10^9 words

or better yet

>   1G words

The following table lists the prefixes that are typically used to simplify measurement terminology.

prefix	symbol	multiplier
giga	G	10^9
mega	M	10^6
kilo	k	10^3
milli	m	10^{-3}
micro	u	10^{-6}
nano	n	10^{-9}
pico	p	10^{-12}

replaced most wires with **printed circuit boards (PCBs)**. Printed circuit boards are thin, typically fiberglass boards with electronic components soldered to them and copper circuit paths, called traces, that replace discrete wires. Complex circuits can be built using multi-layer PCBs. The copper traces can be sandwiched and laminated between more boards. Typical multi-layer circuit boards may have three to seven layers of circuit paths. If you take the top off a computer or television you will see large and small PCBs and relatively few discrete wires. Wires are mostly used today to join PCBs to connectors.

Testing Instruments

The testing of electronic circuits requires a few specialized test instruments. Measuring basic DC circuit parameters can be accomplished with the following instruments:

- ammeter: measures currents
- ohmmeter: measures resistance
- voltmeter: measures voltage

Voltage is the easiest parameter to test. A voltmeter can easily be connected across the device being tested at any point in the current. An ammeter must be connected in series to give a true indication of the current in the circuit. An ohmmeter is typically used on an unpowered device to measure its resistance. Many times the device being measured must be completely removed from the circuit to get an accurate resistance measurement. Power in a circuit is typically calculated after measuring the voltage and current.

Testing AC circuits and digital circuits requires much more complex and expensive test equipment. An oscilloscope is used to display AC and complex voltage waveforms. It is an indispensable tool for analyzing most of the circuits found in today's electronic products. The test equipment needed to test tomorrow's circuits will become more and increasingly specialized with the continued rapid growth of technology.

▶ Radio

The radio was invented by Guglielmo Marconi in the late 1800s.

The theory behind radio is simple; however, the experience needed to fully understand radio may take years of study to develop. The simple drawing below shows how radio communication works.

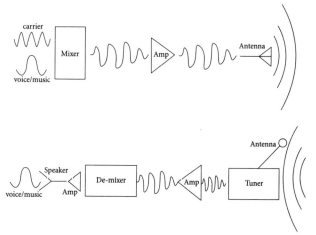

The voice or music signal is combined with a carrier wave and fed into an amplifier and then to an antenna. The antenna transmits the combined signal into the air. The receiving antenna catches the weak signal out of the air and sends it to an amplifier. The signal is amplified, and then the carrier wave is removed, leaving the original voice or music signal intact. The original signal can then be amplified again and listened to through a speaker.

Radio: communication between two or more points using electromagnetic waves as the transmission medium.

Radio communication was first used on ships to communicate at sea. The importance of radio was proven when assistance was requested by the Titanic when it was sinking. Radio communication is not limited to the AM and FM radios we listen to. Television and cellular phones are also examples of radio communication.

► Practice Questions

Now use what you've learned to answer the following electronics questions. Answers are at the end of the chapter.

1. What natural resource is used to generate the majority of the electricity used in the United states?
   a. water
   b. wind
   c. fossil fuels
   d. nuclear materials

2. How many electrons are there in four coulombs of charge?
   a. 13.1×10^{18}
   b. 6.25×10^{18}
   c. 6.25×10^{-18}
   d. 2.5×10^{19}

3. Which of the following values would provide the greatest resistance?
   a. $1 \, k\Omega$
   b. $1 \, m\Omega$
   c. $1 \, u\Omega$
   d. $1 \, M\Omega$

4. How much current will flow when an 8-ohm speaker is connected in series with a 24-volt potential source?
   a. 0.33 A
   b. 8 A
   c. 1.5 A
   d. 3 A

5. Which of the following is a statement of Ohm's law?
   a. $I = \frac{Q}{T}$
   b. $P = V \times I$
   c. $V = I \times R$
   d. $P = I^2 \times R$

6. Electricity is unique among energy sources. Which of the following is NOT a unique characteristic of electricity?
   a. It is instantly available.
   b. It is easily controlled.
   c. It is extremely limited in its use.
   d. It is easily transmitted.

7. Film resistors are typically used when
   a. a large resistance is required.
   b. a small resistance is required.
   c. an exact resistance is required.
   d. cost is the most important consideration.

8. A high tension power line has 100 amperes flowing through it. The resistance of the power line is $0.01 \, \Omega$/foot. How much power, in watts, is lost in one foot of wire?
   a. 1 watt
   b. 10 watts
   c. 100 watts
   d. 1,000 watts

9. When testing a DC circuit, which of the following parameters is the simplest to measure accurately?
   a. voltage
   b. current
   c. resistance
   d. power

10. Special "slo-blo" fuses are required when a circuit exhibits which characteristic?
a. a short circuit
b. in-rush current
c. voltage fluctuations
d. open circuits

11. Which of the following is NOT an example of radio communication?
a. AM radio
b. cellular phones
c. a tape recorder
d. television

12. Which electrical component allows current to flow in only one direction?
a. a capacitor
b. a resistor
c. a diode
d. a wire

▶ Answers

1. c. Fossil fuels are used to generate about 80 percent of the electricity we use. Water is used for 7 percent. Nuclear materials provide 7 percent. Wind is used for a very small percentage.

2. d. One coulomb is 6.25×10^{18} electrons. Four times $6.25 \times 10^{18} = 25 \times 10^{18} = 2.5 \times 10^{19}$.

3. d. The multipliers are: k $\times$ 1,000
m $\times$ .001
u $\times$ .000001
M $\times$ 1,000,000

4. d. $I = \frac{V}{R} = \frac{24\,V}{8\,\Omega} = 3\,A$.

5. c. Ohm's law is $V = I \times R$

6. c. Electricity is instantly available, easily controlled, and easily transmitted.

7. c. Resistors of all types can be made to have large or small resistances. Carbon resistors are used when cost is the most important consideration.

8. c. $P = I^2 \times R = (100\,A)^2 \times .01\,\Omega = 100$ watts.

9. a. Current must be measured by attaching an ammeter in *series*. A resistance to be measured must often be removed from the circuit. Power can be calculated from the current and the voltage.

10. b. Regular fuses are used to protect against short circuits and voltage fluctuations. Open circuits do not need to be protected by a fuse.

11. c. Tape recorders do not use electromagnetic waves as the transmission medium.

12. c. A diode allows current to flow in one direction only.

13 ▶ ASVAB Practice Test 2

CHAPTER SUMMARY

Here's another sample ASVAB for you to practice with. After working through the review material in the previous chapters, take this test to see how much your score has improved.

Like the practice test in Chapter 5, this practice ASVAB contains the eight subtests of the types you will find on the ASVAB, for a total of 200 questions. For this test, simulate the actual test-taking experience as closely as you can. Find a quiet place to work where you won't be disturbed. If you own this book, tear out the answer sheet on the following pages and find some number 2 pencils to fill in the circles with. Use a timer or stopwatch to time each section. The times are marked at the beginning of each section.

After you take the test, use the detailed answer explanations that follow to review any questions you missed.

▶ Part 1: General Science

1.	ⓐ	ⓑ	ⓒ	ⓓ	10.	ⓐ	ⓑ	ⓒ	ⓓ	19.	ⓐ	ⓑ	ⓒ	ⓓ
2.	ⓐ	ⓑ	ⓒ	ⓓ	11.	ⓐ	ⓑ	ⓒ	ⓓ	20.	ⓐ	ⓑ	ⓒ	ⓓ
3.	ⓐ	ⓑ	ⓒ	ⓓ	12.	ⓐ	ⓑ	ⓒ	ⓓ	21.	ⓐ	ⓑ	ⓒ	ⓓ
4.	ⓐ	ⓑ	ⓒ	ⓓ	13.	ⓐ	ⓑ	ⓒ	ⓓ	22.	ⓐ	ⓑ	ⓒ	ⓓ
5.	ⓐ	ⓑ	ⓒ	ⓓ	14.	ⓐ	ⓑ	ⓒ	ⓓ	23.	ⓐ	ⓑ	ⓒ	ⓓ
6.	ⓐ	ⓑ	ⓒ	ⓓ	15.	ⓐ	ⓑ	ⓒ	ⓓ	24.	ⓐ	ⓑ	ⓒ	ⓓ
7.	ⓐ	ⓑ	ⓒ	ⓓ	16.	ⓐ	ⓑ	ⓒ	ⓓ	25.	ⓐ	ⓑ	ⓒ	ⓓ
8.	ⓐ	ⓑ	ⓒ	ⓓ	17.	ⓐ	ⓑ	ⓒ	ⓓ					
9.	ⓐ	ⓑ	ⓒ	ⓓ	18.	ⓐ	ⓑ	ⓒ	ⓓ					

▶ Part 2: Arithmetic Reasoning

1.	ⓐ	ⓑ	ⓒ	ⓓ	11.	ⓐ	ⓑ	ⓒ	ⓓ	21.	ⓐ	ⓑ	ⓒ	ⓓ
2.	ⓐ	ⓑ	ⓒ	ⓓ	12.	ⓐ	ⓑ	ⓒ	ⓓ	22.	ⓐ	ⓑ	ⓒ	ⓓ
3.	ⓐ	ⓑ	ⓒ	ⓓ	13.	ⓐ	ⓑ	ⓒ	ⓓ	23.	ⓐ	ⓑ	ⓒ	ⓓ
4.	ⓐ	ⓑ	ⓒ	ⓓ	14.	ⓐ	ⓑ	ⓒ	ⓓ	24.	ⓐ	ⓑ	ⓒ	ⓓ
5.	ⓐ	ⓑ	ⓒ	ⓓ	15.	ⓐ	ⓑ	ⓒ	ⓓ	25.	ⓐ	ⓑ	ⓒ	ⓓ
6.	ⓐ	ⓑ	ⓒ	ⓓ	16.	ⓐ	ⓑ	ⓒ	ⓓ	26.	ⓐ	ⓑ	ⓒ	ⓓ
7.	ⓐ	ⓑ	ⓒ	ⓓ	17.	ⓐ	ⓑ	ⓒ	ⓓ	27.	ⓐ	ⓑ	ⓒ	ⓓ
8.	ⓐ	ⓑ	ⓒ	ⓓ	18.	ⓐ	ⓑ	ⓒ	ⓓ	28.	ⓐ	ⓑ	ⓒ	ⓓ
9.	ⓐ	ⓑ	ⓒ	ⓓ	19.	ⓐ	ⓑ	ⓒ	ⓓ	29.	ⓐ	ⓑ	ⓒ	ⓓ
10.	ⓐ	ⓑ	ⓒ	ⓓ	20.	ⓐ	ⓑ	ⓒ	ⓓ	30.	ⓐ	ⓑ	ⓒ	ⓓ

▶ Part 3: Word Knowledge

1.	ⓐ	ⓑ	ⓒ	ⓓ	10.	ⓐ	ⓑ	ⓒ	ⓓ	19.	ⓐ	ⓑ	ⓒ	ⓓ
2.	ⓐ	ⓑ	ⓒ	ⓓ	11.	ⓐ	ⓑ	ⓒ	ⓓ	20.	ⓐ	ⓑ	ⓒ	ⓓ
3.	ⓐ	ⓑ	ⓒ	ⓓ	12.	ⓐ	ⓑ	ⓒ	ⓓ	21.	ⓐ	ⓑ	ⓒ	ⓓ
4.	ⓐ	ⓑ	ⓒ	ⓓ	13.	ⓐ	ⓑ	ⓒ	ⓓ	22.	ⓐ	ⓑ	ⓒ	ⓓ
5.	ⓐ	ⓑ	ⓒ	ⓓ	14.	ⓐ	ⓑ	ⓒ	ⓓ	23.	ⓐ	ⓑ	ⓒ	ⓓ
6.	ⓐ	ⓑ	ⓒ	ⓓ	15.	ⓐ	ⓑ	ⓒ	ⓓ	24.	ⓐ	ⓑ	ⓒ	ⓓ
7.	ⓐ	ⓑ	ⓒ	ⓓ	16.	ⓐ	ⓑ	ⓒ	ⓓ	25.	ⓐ	ⓑ	ⓒ	ⓓ
8.	ⓐ	ⓑ	ⓒ	ⓓ	17.	ⓐ	ⓑ	ⓒ	ⓓ					
9.	ⓐ	ⓑ	ⓒ	ⓓ	18.	ⓐ	ⓑ	ⓒ	ⓓ					

▶ Part 4: Paragraph Comprehension

1.	ⓐ	ⓑ	ⓒ	ⓓ	6.	ⓐ	ⓑ	ⓒ	ⓓ	11.	ⓐ	ⓑ	ⓒ	ⓓ
2.	ⓐ	ⓑ	ⓒ	ⓓ	7.	ⓐ	ⓑ	ⓒ	ⓓ	12.	ⓐ	ⓑ	ⓒ	ⓓ
3.	ⓐ	ⓑ	ⓒ	ⓓ	8.	ⓐ	ⓑ	ⓒ	ⓓ	13.	ⓐ	ⓑ	ⓒ	ⓓ
4.	ⓐ	ⓑ	ⓒ	ⓓ	9.	ⓐ	ⓑ	ⓒ	ⓓ	14.	ⓐ	ⓑ	ⓒ	ⓓ
5.	ⓐ	ⓑ	ⓒ	ⓓ	10.	ⓐ	ⓑ	ⓒ	ⓓ	15.	ⓐ	ⓑ	ⓒ	ⓓ

▶ Part 5: Auto and Shop Information

1.	ⓐ	ⓑ	ⓒ	ⓓ	10.	ⓐ	ⓑ	ⓒ	ⓓ	19.	ⓐ	ⓑ	ⓒ	ⓓ
2.	ⓐ	ⓑ	ⓒ	ⓓ	11.	ⓐ	ⓑ	ⓒ	ⓓ	20.	ⓐ	ⓑ	ⓒ	ⓓ
3.	ⓐ	ⓑ	ⓒ	ⓓ	12.	ⓐ	ⓑ	ⓒ	ⓓ	21.	ⓐ	ⓑ	ⓒ	ⓓ
4.	ⓐ	ⓑ	ⓒ	ⓓ	13.	ⓐ	ⓑ	ⓒ	ⓓ	22.	ⓐ	ⓑ	ⓒ	ⓓ
5.	ⓐ	ⓑ	ⓒ	ⓓ	14.	ⓐ	ⓑ	ⓒ	ⓓ	23.	ⓐ	ⓑ	ⓒ	ⓓ
6.	ⓐ	ⓑ	ⓒ	ⓓ	15.	ⓐ	ⓑ	ⓒ	ⓓ	24.	ⓐ	ⓑ	ⓒ	ⓓ
7.	ⓐ	ⓑ	ⓒ	ⓓ	16.	ⓐ	ⓑ	ⓒ	ⓓ	25.	ⓐ	ⓑ	ⓒ	ⓓ
8.	ⓐ	ⓑ	ⓒ	ⓓ	17.	ⓐ	ⓑ	ⓒ	ⓓ					
9.	ⓐ	ⓑ	ⓒ	ⓓ	18.	ⓐ	ⓑ	ⓒ	ⓓ					

▶ Part 6: Mathematics Knowledge

1.	ⓐ	ⓑ	ⓒ	ⓓ	13.	ⓐ	ⓑ	ⓒ	ⓓ	25.	ⓐ	ⓑ	ⓒ	ⓓ
2.	ⓐ	ⓑ	ⓒ	ⓓ	14.	ⓐ	ⓑ	ⓒ	ⓓ	26.	ⓐ	ⓑ	ⓒ	ⓓ
3.	ⓐ	ⓑ	ⓒ	ⓓ	15.	ⓐ	ⓑ	ⓒ	ⓓ	27.	ⓐ	ⓑ	ⓒ	ⓓ
4.	ⓐ	ⓑ	ⓒ	ⓓ	16.	ⓐ	ⓑ	ⓒ	ⓓ	28.	ⓐ	ⓑ	ⓒ	ⓓ
5.	ⓐ	ⓑ	ⓒ	ⓓ	17.	ⓐ	ⓑ	ⓒ	ⓓ	29.	ⓐ	ⓑ	ⓒ	ⓓ
6.	ⓐ	ⓑ	ⓒ	ⓓ	18.	ⓐ	ⓑ	ⓒ	ⓓ	30.	ⓐ	ⓑ	ⓒ	ⓓ
7.	ⓐ	ⓑ	ⓒ	ⓓ	19.	ⓐ	ⓑ	ⓒ	ⓓ	31.	ⓐ	ⓑ	ⓒ	ⓓ
8.	ⓐ	ⓑ	ⓒ	ⓓ	20.	ⓐ	ⓑ	ⓒ	ⓓ	32.	ⓐ	ⓑ	ⓒ	ⓓ
9.	ⓐ	ⓑ	ⓒ	ⓓ	21.	ⓐ	ⓑ	ⓒ	ⓓ	33.	ⓐ	ⓑ	ⓒ	ⓓ
10.	ⓐ	ⓑ	ⓒ	ⓓ	22.	ⓐ	ⓑ	ⓒ	ⓓ	34.	ⓐ	ⓑ	ⓒ	ⓓ
11.	ⓐ	ⓑ	ⓒ	ⓓ	23.	ⓐ	ⓑ	ⓒ	ⓓ	35.	ⓐ	ⓑ	ⓒ	ⓓ
12.	ⓐ	ⓑ	ⓒ	ⓓ	24.	ⓐ	ⓑ	ⓒ	ⓓ					

▶ Part 7: Mechanical Comprehension

1.	ⓐ	ⓑ	ⓒ	ⓓ	10.	ⓐ	ⓑ	ⓒ	ⓓ	19.	ⓐ	ⓑ	ⓒ	ⓓ
2.	ⓐ	ⓑ	ⓒ	ⓓ	11.	ⓐ	ⓑ	ⓒ	ⓓ	20.	ⓐ	ⓑ	ⓒ	ⓓ
3.	ⓐ	ⓑ	ⓒ	ⓓ	12.	ⓐ	ⓑ	ⓒ	ⓓ	21.	ⓐ	ⓑ	ⓒ	ⓓ
4.	ⓐ	ⓑ	ⓒ	ⓓ	13.	ⓐ	ⓑ	ⓒ	ⓓ	22.	ⓐ	ⓑ	ⓒ	ⓓ
5.	ⓐ	ⓑ	ⓒ	ⓓ	14.	ⓐ	ⓑ	ⓒ	ⓓ	23.	ⓐ	ⓑ	ⓒ	ⓓ
6.	ⓐ	ⓑ	ⓒ	ⓓ	15.	ⓐ	ⓑ	ⓒ	ⓓ	24.	ⓐ	ⓑ	ⓒ	ⓓ
7.	ⓐ	ⓑ	ⓒ	ⓓ	16.	ⓐ	ⓑ	ⓒ	ⓓ	25.	ⓐ	ⓑ	ⓒ	ⓓ
8.	ⓐ	ⓑ	ⓒ	ⓓ	17.	ⓐ	ⓑ	ⓒ	ⓓ					
9.	ⓐ	ⓑ	ⓒ	ⓓ	18.	ⓐ	ⓑ	ⓒ	ⓓ					

▶ Part 8: Electronics Information

1.	ⓐ	ⓑ	ⓒ	ⓓ	8.	ⓐ	ⓑ	ⓒ	ⓓ	15.	ⓐ	ⓑ	ⓒ	ⓓ
2.	ⓐ	ⓑ	ⓒ	ⓓ	9.	ⓐ	ⓑ	ⓒ	ⓓ	16.	ⓐ	ⓑ	ⓒ	ⓓ
3.	ⓐ	ⓑ	ⓒ	ⓓ	10.	ⓐ	ⓑ	ⓒ	ⓓ	17.	ⓐ	ⓑ	ⓒ	ⓓ
4.	ⓐ	ⓑ	ⓒ	ⓓ	11.	ⓐ	ⓑ	ⓒ	ⓓ	18.	ⓐ	ⓑ	ⓒ	ⓓ
5.	ⓐ	ⓑ	ⓒ	ⓓ	12.	ⓐ	ⓑ	ⓒ	ⓓ	19.	ⓐ	ⓑ	ⓒ	ⓓ
6.	ⓐ	ⓑ	ⓒ	ⓓ	13.	ⓐ	ⓑ	ⓒ	ⓓ	20.	ⓐ	ⓑ	ⓒ	ⓓ
7.	ⓐ	ⓑ	ⓒ	ⓓ	14.	ⓐ	ⓑ	ⓒ	ⓓ					

▶ Part 1: General Science

Time: 11 minutes

1. In order to be considered organic, a compound must contain which element?
   a. carbon
   b. hydrogen
   c. sodium
   d. nitrogen

2. What is a solution called when it can dissolve no more solutes?
   a. unsaturated
   b. supersaturated
   c. saturated
   d. volatile

3. Which of the following is NOT true of the Sun?
   a. The Sun is almost 110 times the diameter of Earth.
   b. Most of the mass of our solar system can be attributed to the Sun.
   c. The Sun is a typical star that is predicted to shine for approximately nine billion years.
   d. The solid surface of the Sun has a temperature of approximately 15,000,000 K.

4. Which of the following symbols represents one of the elements present in NH_4Cl?
   a. C
   b. Cl
   c. NH
   d. NHCl

5. What is the total number of atoms present in the molecule CH_3NH_2?
   a. 4
   b. 5
   c. 6
   d. 7

6. Which of the following plants lacks a vascular system?
   a. moss
   b. fern
   c. fir tree
   d. peanut plant

7. On the Celsius temperature scale, at what temperatures does water freeze and boil?
   a. It freezes at −10 degrees and boils at 100 degrees.
   b. It freezes at 0 degrees and boils at 100 degrees.
   c. It freezes at 0 degrees and boils at 212 degrees.
   d. It freezes at 32 degrees and boils at 212 degrees.

8. It is harder to stop a car moving at 60 miles per hour than a car moving at 15 miles per hour because the car moving at 60 miles per hour has more
   a. momentum.
   b. deceleration.
   c. mass.
   d. velocity.

9. The force that opposes the motion of an object is called
   a. gravity.
   b. momentum.
   c. inertia.
   d. friction.

10. When a tapeworm lives in the intestines of a cow, this is an example of
   a. commensalism.
   b. mutualism.
   c. parasitism.
   d. succession.

11. In a food chain, which of the following are the Producers?
   a. green plants
   b. bits of dead organic matter
   c. plant-eating animals
   d. meat-eating animals

12. What is the primary purpose of anticoagulants?
   a. to cause amnesia
   b. to paralyze the muscles
   c. to prevent the blood from clotting
   d. to prevent the heart from stopping

13. Which of the following are the blood vessels that carry blood toward the heart?
   a. arteries
   b. veins
   c. capillaries
   d. arterioles

14. Which of the following is the junction between two adjacent nerve cells?
   a. a neurotransmitter
   b. a dendrite
   c. an axon
   d. a synapse

15. Which of the following is the lowest level of Earth's atmosphere?
   a. the stratosphere
   b. the troposphere
   c. the ionsphere
   d. the exosphere

16. What is the latitude of any point on Earth's equator?
   a. 0 degrees
   b. 90 degrees
   c. 180 degrees
   d. 360 degrees

17. The conversion of a vapor to a liquid is called
   a. melting.
   b. condensation.
   c. evaporation.
   d. freezing.

18. What does a barometer measure?
   a. humidity
   b. wind speed
   c. air pressure
   d. temperature

19. The movement of water from a region of high concentration to an area of lower concentration is called
   a. osmosis.
   b. photosynthesis.
   c. respiration.
   d. diffusion.

20. What substance forms the skeletal system of sharks and reduces friction in human joints?
   a. scales
   b. collagen
   c. bone marrow
   d. cartilage

21. Where are the majority of nutrients absorbed in the human digestive system?
   a. in the large intestine
   b. in the mouth
   c. in the small intestine
   d. in the stomach

22. An elevator uses which of the following simple machines?
   a. a pulley
   b. a lever
   c. a wheel and axle
   d. an inclined plane

23. The product of an object's mass and its speed is equal to its
  a. distance.
  b. work.
  c. momentum.
  d. power.

24. What is the process called when a light bulb heats up a lamp shade?
  a. insulation
  b. radiation
  c. convection
  d. conduction

25. Rickets in children, characterized by weak and deformed bones, may be attributed to a deficiency of which vitamin?
  a. A
  b. B
  c. C
  d. D

▶ Part 2: Arithmetic Reasoning

Time: 36 minutes

1. What is the estimated product when 157 and 817 are rounded to the nearest hundred and multiplied?
  a. 160,000
  b. 180,000
  c. 16,000
  d. 80,000

2. A large coffee pot holds 120 cups. It is about two-thirds full. About how many cups are in the pot?
  a. 40 cups
  b. 80 cups
  c. 60 cups
  d. 90 cups

3. Mr. Tupper is purchasing gifts for his family. He stops to consider what else he has to buy. A quick mental inventory of his shopping bag so far reveals the following:

- 1 cashmere sweater, valued at $260
- 3 diamond bracelets, each valued at $365
- 1 computer game, valued at $78
- 1 cameo brooch, valued at $130

Later, having coffee in the Food Court, he suddenly remembers that he has purchased only 2 diamond bracelets, not 3, and that the cashmere sweater was on sale for $245. What is the total value of the gifts Mr. Tupper has purchased so far?
  a. $833
  b. $1,183
  c. $1,198
  d. $1,563

This is a list of ingredients needed to make 16 brownies. Use this list to answer questions 4 and 5.

Deluxe Brownies
$\frac{2}{3}$ cup butter
5 squares (1 ounce each) unsweetened chocolate
$1\frac{1}{2}$ cups sugar
2 teaspoons vanilla
2 eggs
1 cup flour

4. How much sugar is needed to make 8 brownies?
  a. $\frac{3}{4}$ cup
  b. 3 cups
  c. $\frac{2}{3}$ cup
  d. $\frac{5}{8}$ cup

5. What is the greatest number of brownies that can be made if the baker has only 1 cup of butter?
  a. 12
  b. 16
  c. 24
  d. 32

6. One lap on an outdoor track measures a quarter of a mile around. To run a total of three and a half miles, how many laps must a person complete?
a. 7
b. 10
c. 13
d. 14

7. The state of Connecticut will pay two-fifths of the cost of a new school building. If the city of New Haven is building a school that will cost a total of $15,500,000, what will the state pay?
a. $3,100,000
b. $7,750,000
c. $6,200,000
d. $4,550,000

8. Body mass index (BMI) is equal to weight in kilograms/(height in meters)^2. A man who weighs 64.8 kilograms has a BMI of 20. How tall is he?
a. 1.8 meters
b. 0.9 meters
c. 2.16 meters
d. 3.24 meters

9. A floor plan is drawn to scale so that $\frac{1}{4}$-inch represents 2 feet. If a hall on the plan is 4 inches long, how long will the actual hall be when it is built?
a. 2 feet
b. 8 feet
c. 16 feet
d. 32 feet

10. Newly hired nurses have to buy duty shoes at the full price of $84.50, but nurses who have served at least a year get a 15 percent discount. Nurses who have served at least three years get an additional 10 percent off the discounted price. How much does a nurse who has served at least three years have to pay for shoes?
a. $63.78
b. $64.65
c. $71.83
d. $72.05

11. There are 176 men and 24 women serving in a particular battalion. What percentage of the battalion's force is women?
a. 12%
b. 14%
c. 16%
d. 24%

12. The basal metabolic rate (BMR) is the rate at which our body uses calories. The BMR for a man in his twenties is about 1,700 calories per day. If 204 of those calories should come from protein, about what percent of this man's diet should be protein?
a. 1.2%
b. 8.3%
c. 12%
d. 16%

13. The condition Down's syndrome occurs in about 1 in 1,500 children when the mothers are in their twenties. About what percent of all children born to mothers in their twenties are likely to have Down's syndrome?
a. 0.0067%
b. 0.67%
c. 6.7%
d. 0.067%

14. If a population of yeast cells grows from 10 to 320 in a period of 5 hours, what is the rate of growth?
   a. It doubles its numbers every hour.
   b. It triples its numbers every hour.
   c. It doubles its numbers every two hours.
   d. It triples its numbers every two hours.

15. How much water must be added to 1 liter of a 5 percent saline solution to get a 2 percent saline solution?
   a. 1 L
   b. 1.5 L
   c. 2 L
   d. 2.5 L

16. In the first week of his exercise program, John went on a 15-mile hike. The next week, he increased the length of his hike by 20%. How long was his hike in the second week?
   a. 17 miles
   b. 18 miles
   c. 30 miles
   d. 35 miles

17. All of the rooms in a building are rectangular, with 8-foot ceilings. One room is 9 feet wide by 11 feet long. What is the combined area of the four walls, including doors and windows?
   a. 99 square feet
   b. 160 square feet
   c. 320 square feet
   d. 72 square feet

18. What is the volume of a pyramid that has a rectangular base of 10 inches by 12 inches and a height of 10 inches? ($V = \frac{1}{3}lwh$)
   a. 40 cubic inches
   b. 320 cubic inches
   c. 400 cubic inches
   d. 1,200 cubic inches

19. A child has a temperature of 40 degrees C. What is the child's temperature in degrees Fahrenheit? ($F = \frac{9}{5}C + 32$)
   a. 101 degrees F
   b. 102 degrees F
   c. 103 degrees F
   d. 104 degrees F

20. If jogging for one mile uses 150 calories and brisk walking for one mile uses 100 calories, a jogger has to go how many times as far as a walker to use the same number of calories?
   a. $\frac{1}{2}$
   b. $\frac{2}{3}$
   c. $\frac{3}{2}$
   d. 2

21. A dosage of a certain medication is 12 cc per 100 pounds. What is the dosage for a patient who weighs 175 pounds?
   a. 15 cc
   b. 18 cc
   c. 21 cc
   d. 24 cc

22. A hiker walks 40 miles on the first day of a five-day trip. On each day after that, he can walk only half as far as he did the day before. On average, how far does he walk each day?
   a. 10 miles
   b. 15.5 miles
   c. 20 miles
   d. 24 miles

23. A woman drives west at 45 miles per hour. After half an hour, her husband starts to follow her. How fast must he drive to catch up to her three hours after he starts?
   a. 52.5 miles per hour
   b. 55 miles per hour
   c. 60 miles per hour
   d. 67.5 miles per hour

24. A family's gas and electricity bill averages $80 a month for seven months of the year and $20 a month the rest of the year. If the family's bills were averaged over the entire year, what would the monthly bill be?
a. $45
b. $50
c. $55
d. $60

25. Jason is six times as old as Kate. In two years, Jason will be twice as old as Kate is then. How old is Jason now?
a. 3 years old
b. 6 years old
c. 9 years old
d. 12 years old

26. During her first three months at college, a student's long distance phone bills are $103.30, $71.60, and $84.00. Her local phone bill is $18.00 each month. What is her average total monthly phone bill?
a. $86.30
b. $92.30
c. $98.30
d. $104.30

27. A car uses 16 gallons of gas to travel 448 miles. How many miles per gallon does the car get?
a. 22 miles per gallon
b. 24 miles per gallon
c. 26 miles per gallon
d. 28 miles per gallon

28. Land in development is selling for $60,000 per acre. If Jack purchases $1\frac{3}{4}$ acres, how much will he pay?
a. $45,000
b. $135,000
c. $105,000
d. $120,000

29. For every dollar Kyra saves, her employer contributes a dime to her savings, with a maximum employer contribution of $10 per month. If Kyra saves $60 in January, $130 in March, and $70 in April, how much will she have in savings at the end of that time?
a. $270
b. $283
c. $286
d. $290

30. Jackie is paid $822.40 twice a month. If she saves $150.00 per paycheck and pays $84.71 on her student loan each month, how much does she have left to spend each month?
a. $1,175.38
b. $1,260.09
c. $1,410.09
d. $1,560.09

▶ Part 3: Word Knowledge

Time: 11 minutes

1. According to the code of conduct, "Every officer will be <u>accountable</u> for his or her decisions."
a. applauded
b. compensated
c. responsible
d. approached

2. <u>Scrutinize</u> most nearly means
a. vanish.
b. examine.
c. neglect.
d. weak.

3. <u>Enumerate</u> most nearly means
a. pronounce.
b. count.
c. explain.
d. plead.

4. <u>Emulate</u> most nearly means
   a. imitate
   b. authorize
   c. fascinate
   d. punish

5. The residents of that area were considered to be <u>compliant</u> in regard to the seat belt law.
   a. skeptical
   b. obedient
   c. forgetful
   d. appreciative

6. Following the disturbance, town officials felt the need to <u>augment</u> the laws pertaining to mass demonstrations.
   a. repeal
   b. evaluate
   c. supplement
   d. criticize

7. <u>Aversion</u> most nearly means
   a. harmony
   b. greed
   c. weariness
   d. dislike

8. <u>Validate</u> most nearly means
   a. confirm.
   b. retrieve.
   c. communicate.
   d. appoint.

9. <u>Antagonist</u> most nearly means
   a. comrade.
   b. opponent.
   c. master.
   d. perfectionist.

10. <u>Perseverance</u> most nearly means
   a. unhappiness.
   b. fame.
   c. persistence.
   d. humility.

11. As soon as the details of the affair were released to the media, the newspaper was <u>inundated</u> with calls from a curious public.
   a. provided
   b. bothered
   c. rewarded
   d. flooded

12. <u>Homogeneous</u> most nearly means
   a. alike.
   b. plain.
   c. native.
   d. dissimilar.

13. <u>Ominous</u> most nearly means
   a. ordinary.
   b. gracious.
   c. quarrelsome.
   d. threatening.

14 When people heard that timid Bob had taken up sky-diving, they were <u>incredulous</u>.
   a. fearful
   b. outraged
   c. disbelieving
   d. inconsolable

15. <u>Recluse</u> most nearly means
   a. prophet.
   b. fool.
   c. intellectual.
   d. hermit.

16. The company recruited her because she was <u>proficient</u> in the use of computers.
a. experienced
b. unequaled
c. efficient
d. skilled

17. <u>Defray</u> most nearly means
a. pay.
b. defend.
c. cheat.
d. disobey.

18. <u>Placid</u> most nearly means
a. flabby.
b. peaceful.
c. wise.
d. obedient.

19. The City Council has given <u>tentative</u> approval to the idea of banning smoking from all public buildings.
a. provisional
b. ambiguous
c. wholehearted
d. unnecessary

20. <u>Vast</u> most nearly means
a. attentive.
b. immense.
c. steady.
d. slight.

21. <u>Contemptuous</u> most nearly means
a. respectful.
b. unique.
c. scornful.
d. insecure.

22. Regarding the need for more free coffee and doughnuts, the group's opinion was <u>unanimous</u>.
a. divided
b. uniform
c. adamant
d. clear-cut

23. <u>Distinct</u> most nearly means
a. satisfied.
b. frenzied.
c. recognizable.
d. uneasy.

24. Various methods to <u>alleviate</u> the situation were debated.
a. ease
b. tolerate
c. clarify
d. intensify

25. <u>Enlighten</u> most nearly means
a. relocate.
b. confuse.
c. comply.
d. teach.

▶ **Part 4: Paragraph Comprehension**

Time: 13 minutes

The supervisors have received numerous complaints over the last several weeks about buses on several routes running hot. Drivers are reminded that each route has several check points at which drivers should check the time. If the bus is ahead of schedule, drivers should delay at the check point until it is the proper time to leave.

1. In the passage, saying a bus is "running hot" means
   a. the engine is over-heating.
   b. the bus is running ahead of schedule.
   c. the air conditioning is not working.
   d. there is no more room for passengers.

2. According to the passage
   a. every bus stop is also a check point.
   b. it is important to keep customer complaints to a minimum.
   c. drivers tend to rush their routes so they can leave work early.
   d. each bus route has several points at which drivers should check the time.

Drivers are responsible for refueling their trucks at the end of each shift. All other routine maintenance is performed by maintenance department personnel, who are also responsible for maintaining service records. If a driver believes a truck is in need of mechanical repair, he or she should fill out the pink "Repair Requisition" form and turn it in to the shift supervisor.

3. If a truck is due to have the oil changed, it will be done by
   a. maintenance department personnel.
   b. truck drivers.
   c. shift supervisors.
   d. outside contractors.

4. The passage indicates that trucks
   a. are refueled when they have less than half a tank of gas.
   b. have the oil changed every 1,000 miles.
   c. are refueled at the end of every shift.
   d. are in frequent need of repair.

Hazardous waste is defined as any waste designated by the United States Environmental Protection Agency as hazardous. If a worker is unclear whether a particular item is hazardous, he or she should not handle the item but should instead notify the supervisor and ask for directions.

5. Hazardous waste is
   a. anything too dangerous for workers to handle.
   b. picked up by special trucks.
   c. defined by the United States Environmental Protection Agency.
   d. not allowed with regular residential garbage.

6. A sanitation worker comes upon a container of cleaning solvent along with the regular garbage in front of a residence. The container does not list the contents of the cleaner. He should
   a. assume the solvent is safe and deposit it in the sanitation truck.
   b. leave a note for the residents, asking them to list the contents.
   c. contact the supervisor for directions.
   d. leave the container on the curb.

Many people hesitate to adopt a retired racing greyhound because they worry that it will be nervous and will need a large space to run. This is a false impression. Greyhounds have naturally sweet, mild dispositions and are sprinters rather than distance runners; they are sufficiently exercised with a few laps around a fenced-in backyard every day. Greyhounds do not make good watchdogs, but they are very good with children, get along well with other dogs (and usually cats as well), and are very affectionate and loyal.

7. According to the passage, adopting a greyhound is a good idea for people who
 a. do not have children.
 b. live in apartments.
 c. do not usually like dogs.
 d. already have another dog or a cat.

8. One drawback of adopting a greyhound is that they
 a. are not good watch dogs.
 b. are very old when they retire from racing.
 c. are very competitive.
 d. need lots of room to run.

One easy way to plan healthy menus is to shop only in the outer aisles of the grocery store. In most supermarkets, fresh fruit and vegetables, dairy, fresh meat, and frozen foods are in the outer aisles. Grains, like pasta, rice, bread, and cereal, are located on the next aisles, the first inner rows. The inside aisles are where you'll find chips and snacks, cookies and pastries, soda pop and drink mixes—foods that nutritionists say one should eat rarely, if at all. A side benefit of shopping this way is that grocery shopping takes less time.

9. A good title for this article would be
 a. "Why You Should Shop in a Health Food Store"
 b. "How to Complete Your Grocery Shopping in Less Time"
 c. "How to Shop for Healthy Food"
 d. "How to Cook Healthy Food"

10. According to the passage, the best way to shop in the grocery store is to
 a. make a list and stick to it.
 b. stay in the outside aisles.
 c. look for the best prices.
 d. check the newspaper ads each week.

Law enforcement officers often do not like taking time from their regular duties to testify in court, but testimony is an important part of an officer's job. To be good witnesses, officers should keep complete notes detailing any potentially criminal incidents. When on the witness stand, officers may refer to these notes to refresh their memory about particular events. It is also very important for officers to listen carefully to the questions asked by the lawyers and to provide only the information requested.

11. According to the passage, an officer who is testifying in court
 a. will be questioned by the judge.
 b. may refer to his or her notes while on the witness stand.
 c. must do so without pay.
 d. appreciates taking a break from routine assignments.

12. This passage is probably taken from a(n)
 a. memo entitled "Proper Arrest Procedure."
 b. newspaper article.
 c. best-selling novel.
 d. officers' training manual.

13. According to the passage, testifying in court is
 a. an important part of a police officer's job.
 b. difficult, because lawyers try to trick witnesses.
 c. less stressful for police officers than for other witnesses.
 d. a waste of time, because judges usually let criminals off.

In the summer, the northern hemisphere is slanted toward the Sun, making the days longer and warmer than in winter. The first day of summer is called summer solstice and is also the longest day of the year. However, June 21 marks the beginning of winter in the southern hemisphere, when that hemisphere is tilted away from the Sun.

14. According to the passage, when it is summer in the northern hemisphere, in the southern hemisphere it is
a. spring.
b. summer.
c. autumn.
d. winter.

15. It can be inferred from the passage that, in the southern hemisphere, June 21 is the
a. autumnal equinox.
b. winter solstice.
c. vernal equinox.
d. summer solstice.

▶ Part 5: Auto and Shop Information

Time: 11 minutes

1. Engine overheating can be caused by which of the following?
a. a low fuel level
b. too much motor oil
c. a faulty transmission
d. a faulty thermostat

2. Which of the following automotive systems uses lubrication fluid?
a. the transmission system
b. the exhaust system
c. the suspension system
d. the electrical system

3. Which automotive system uses fuses and an alternator?
a. the steering system
b. the cooling system
c. the electrical system
d. the engine

4. What is the function of the spark plugs in the internal combustion engine in a car?
a. to transfer electricity to the alternator
b. to increase the cylinder size
c. to cool the engine
d. to ignite the fuel

5. Which fluid is contained in a car radiator?
a. transmission fluid
b. cooling fluid
c. brake fluid
d. steering fluid

6. What is the primary function of the water pump in a car?
a. to circulate coolant
b. to evacuate waste water
c. to remove exhaust
d. to filter water

7. Mortar is typically used in conjunction with which other building material?
a. brick construction
b. wood siding
c. steel beams
d. asphalt road basc

8. Concrete is typically used in conjunction with which of the following building materials in order to provide a stronger product?
a. bronze reinforcement
b. aluminum reinforcement
c. steel reinforcement
d. plastic reinforcement

9. Concrete is made up of which of the following components?
a. cement, water, and steel
b. gravel and sand
c. gravel, water, and glass
d. cement, sand, gravel, and water

10. Which material may be used as the outer material on a roof in order to keep out rain?
 a. tile
 b. wood
 c. asphalt
 d. all of the above

11. A come-along wrench is used to perform which of the following actions?
 a. pushing
 b. pulling
 c. sliding
 d. prying

12. How often should the oil in a car engine be changed?
 a. after every 300 miles of driving
 b. after every 3,000 miles of driving
 c. after every 30,000 miles of driving
 d. after every 300,000 miles of driving

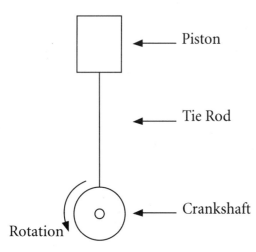

13. The figure above shows a piston that is connected to a crankshaft by a tie rod. The crankshaft has a radius of 1.0 inch. If the crankshaft rotates 180 degrees (one half of a revolution), how far downward will the piston be pulled?
 a. 0.5 inches
 b. 1.0 inch
 c. 1.33 inches
 d. 2.0 inches

14. Which system on an automobile uses shock absorbers?
 a. the suspension system
 b. the exhaust system
 c. the electrical system
 d. the braking system

15. Which automotive system uses universal joints, a drive shaft, and a clutch?
 a. the steering system
 b. the cooling system
 c. the transmission system
 d. the braking system

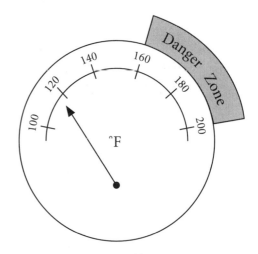

16. On the temperature gauge above, what is the maximum recommended operating temperature (degrees Fahrenheit) for this gauge in order to remain in a safe zone?
 a. 120
 b. 140
 c. 160
 d. 180

17. Of which automotive system does the driver have the most direct control while driving?
 a. the exhaust system
 b. the cooling system
 c. the suspension system
 d. the braking system

18. Which pair of systems listed below is directly connected to each other in an automobile?
    a. the steering and cooling systems
    b. the transmission and exhaust systems
    c. the exhaust and engine systems
    d. the brake and heating systems

19. Which of the following systems connects directly to the internal combustion engine in an automobile?
    a. the cooling system
    b. the suspension system
    c. the steering system
    d. the braking system

20. The gauge above is
    a. a pressure gauge.
    b. an altitude gauge.
    c. a temperature gauge.
    d. a flow meter gauge.

21. In the typical workshop, a plane is used for what purpose?
    a. welding metal
    b. curing concrete
    c. removing thin strips of wood
    d. loosening bolts

22. The turn signal on an automobile is connected to which of the following automotive systems?
    a. the braking system
    b. the transmission system
    c. the suspension system
    d. the electrical system

23. On which of the following types of material in a workshop would a shear, a brake, a form, and a punch be used?
    a. sheet metal
    b. wood
    c. plastic
    d. angle iron

24. A crimp, a bond, and a weld are all examples of
    a. cutting methods.
    b. fastening methods.
    c. grinding methods.
    d. drilling methods.

25. What are scales, calipers, micrometers, and dial indicators all used to measure?
    a. weight
    b. time
    c. length
    d. surface roughness

▶ Part 6: Mathematics Knowledge

Time: 24 minutes

1. Which pair of lines is parallel?

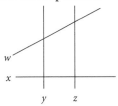

    a. w and x
    b. x and y
    c. x and z
    d. y and z

2. Choose the answer to the following problem:
$4\frac{1}{3} + 3\frac{3}{10} =$
a. $7\frac{2}{15}$
b. $7\frac{4}{13}$
c. $7\frac{2}{3}$
d. $7\frac{19}{30}$

3. $\frac{4}{5}$ is equal to
a. 0.80
b. 0.50
c. 0.90
d. 0.45

4. Choose the answer to the following problem:
$x(3x^2 + y) =$
a. $4x^2 + xy$
b. $4x^2 + x + y$
c. $3x^3 + 2xy$
d. $3x^3 + xy$

5. 35 percent of what number is equal to 14?
a. 4
b. 40
c. 49
d. 400

6. $\frac{1}{4}$ is equal to
a. 0.15
b. 0.25
c. 0.20
d. 0.75

7. If $8n + 25 = 65$, then n is
a. 5
b. 10
c. 40
d. 90

8. What is the reciprocal of $3\frac{7}{8}$?
a. $\frac{31}{8}$
b. $\frac{8}{31}$
c. $\frac{8}{21}$
d. $-\frac{31}{8}$

9. $3\frac{3}{10}$ is equal to
a. 3.10
b. 0.30
c. 2.30
d. 3.30

10. Which of these angle measures forms a right triangle?
a. 45 degrees, 50 degrees, 85 degrees
b. 40 degrees, 40 degrees, 100 degrees
c. 40 degrees, 50 degrees, 90 degrees
d. 20 degrees, 30 degrees, 130 degrees

11. What is another way to write $3\sqrt{12}$?
a. $12\sqrt{3}$
b. $6\sqrt{3}$
c. $2\sqrt{10}$
d. 18

12. Which is another was to write $\frac{4}{25}$?
a. 4%
b. 16%
c. 40%
d. 100%

13. What is another way to write 3^4?
a. 12
b. 24
c. 27
d. 81

14. What is the decimal form of $-1\frac{1}{3}$ rounded to the nearest hundredth?

    a. 1.33
    b. −1.33
    c. 3.67
    d. −3.67

15. $1\frac{3}{4} =$

    a. 1.75
    b. 0.75
    c. 1.34
    d. 1.25

16. Triangles *RST* and *MNO* are similar. What is the length of line segment *MO*?

    a. 10 cm
    b. 20 cm
    c. 32 cm
    d. 40 cm

17. Which number sentence is true?

    a. 4.3 < 0.43
    b. 0.43 < 0.043
    c. 0.043 > 0.0043
    d. 0.0043 > 0.43

18. 0.40 =

    a. $\frac{1}{4}$
    b. $\frac{1}{5}$
    c. $\frac{2}{5}$
    d. $\frac{3}{4}$

19. Which of these has a 9 in the thousandths place?

    a. 3.0095
    b. 3.0905
    c. 3.9005
    d. 3.0059

20. 0.75 =

    a. $\frac{1}{4}$
    b. $\frac{1}{5}$
    c. $\frac{2}{7}$
    d. $\frac{3}{4}$

21. Which of the following means $5n + 7 = 17$?

    a. 7 more than 5 times a number is 17
    b. 5 more than 7 times a number is 17
    c. 7 less than 5 times a number is 17
    d. 12 times a number is 17

22. Lines *a*, *b*, and *c* intersect at point *O*. Which of these are NOT adjacent angles?

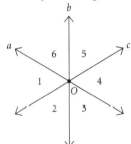

    a. ∠1 and ∠6
    b. ∠1 and ∠4
    c. ∠4 and ∠5
    d. ∠2 and ∠3

23. 2.25 =

    a. $2\frac{1}{4}$
    b. $2\frac{1}{5}$
    c. $\frac{2}{5}$
    d. $1\frac{3}{4}$

24. What is the value of y when $x = 3$ and $y = 5 + 4x$?
   a. 6
   b. 9
   c. 12
   d. 17

25. 6^3 is equal to
   a. 36
   b. 1,296
   c. 18
   d. 216

26. What percentage of 50 is 12?
   a. 4%
   b. 14%
   c. 24%
   d. 34%

27. Choose the answer to the following problem:
$(14 \times 7) + 12 =$
   a. 98
   b. 266
   c. 110
   d. 100

28. $0.125 =$
   a. $\frac{1}{25}$
   b. $\frac{1}{8}$
   c. $\frac{2}{5}$
   d. $\frac{1}{5}$

29. $3.3 =$
   a. $\frac{3}{33}$
   b. $1\frac{3}{10}$
   c. $3\frac{3}{10}$
   d. $\frac{3}{3}$

30. Which of the following is 14% of 232?
   a. 3.248
   b. 32.48
   c. 16.57
   d. 165.7

31. One side of a square bandage is 4 inches long. What is the perimeter of the bandage?
   a. 4 inches
   b. 8 inches
   c. 12 inches
   d. 16 inches

32. 33 is 12% of which of the following?
   a. 3,960
   b. 396
   c. 275
   d. 2,750

33. The radius of a circle is 13. What is the approximate area of the circle?
   a. 81.64
   b. 530.66
   c. 1,666.27
   d. 169

34. 17^2 is equal to
   a. 34
   b. 68
   c. 136
   d. 289

35. If the two triangles below are similar, with ∠A equal to ∠D, what is the perimeter of triangle *DEF*?

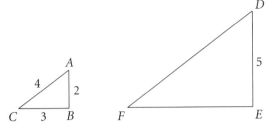

a. 12
b. 21
c. 22.5
d. 24.75

▶ Part 7: Mechanical Comprehension

Time: 19 minutes

1. A concrete beam has a maximum strength of 3,000 psi (pounds per square inch). In an experiment, a 500-pound weight is placed in the center of the beam, and the stress in the beam is measured to be 1,000 psi. If the stresses in the beam continue to increase at the same rate with added weight, how much additional weight can be added to the same location on the beam before the beam will break?
a. 500 pounds
b. 1,000 pounds
c. 1,500 pounds
d. 3,000 pounds

2. Two cars have the same weight and the same type of engine and travel at the same speed. One is a boxy minivan and the other a low, sleek sports car. Which factor below best explains why the sports car gets better gas mileage than the minivan?
a. friction
b. wind resistance
c. acceleration
d. all of the above

3. Which principle of mechanical motion is used in the design of a roller coaster?
a. momentum
b. friction
c. acceleration
d. all of the above

4. Two balls of the same density, one large and one small, are rolled towards each other at the same speed. When they collide, what will happen to the smaller ball?
a. It will be propelled backwards in the opposite direction.
b. It will continue forward in the same direction.
c. It will stop and stay at the point of impact.
d. It will jump over the heavier ball.

5. A seesaw works best when both people weigh the same. This demonstrates which principle of mechanical motion?
a. relative velocity
b. centrifugal force
c. acceleration
d. equilibrium

6. A grandfather clock typically has a long pendulum that swings back and forth to keep time. Which description below best describes the action of this pendulum?
a. periodic motion
b. relative velocity
c. free-falling body
d. all of the above

7. Which term below best describes the OPPOSITE of "an increase in speed"?
a. velocity
b. friction
c. deceleration
d. rotation

8. When a load is applied to a structural beam, which of the following does the beam experience?
a. deflection
b. stress
c. strain
d. all of the above

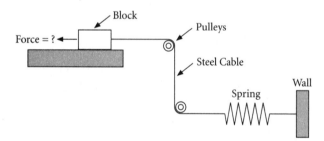

9. In the diagram above, the spring is very stiff and can be stretched 1 inch by a pulling force of 100 pounds. How much force must be applied to the block in order to move the box 3.5 inches to the left?
a. 100 pounds
b. 300 pounds
c. 350 pounds
d. 3.5 pounds

10. The simple mechanical device used to block the wheels of an airplane to keep it from rolling is best known as a
a. wedge.
b. piston.
c. gear.
d. pulley.

11. A pump is typically used to accomplish which of the following tasks?
a. to move liquids downhill
b. to separate liquids
c. to clarify liquids
d. to move liquids uphill

12. When a cannon ball is fired at an upward angle from the surface of the Earth, which of the following causes it to come back to the surface of the Earth?
a. friction
b. centrifugal force
c. gravity
d. momentum

13. A valve is used to perform which of the following functions?
a. increase the temperature of a liquid
b. control the flow of a liquid
c. decrease the density of a liquid
d. aid evaporation of a liquid

14. Which of the following best describes the location of the center of gravity of a steel bar that is four feet long and is the same diameter along its length?
a. two feet from the left end of the bar
b. three feet from the right end of the bar
c. on the right end of the bar
d. on the left end of the bar

15. Which of the following materials is the LEAST elastic?
  a. silly putty
  b. wax
  c. rubber
  d. paper

16. Block A is twice as big as Block B. Block B is made of a material that is three times as dense as the material in Block A. Which block is heavier?
  a. Block A
  b. Block B
  c. both blocks weigh the same amount
  d. not enough information

17. A block of steel has a density of 0.29 pounds per cubic inch. If the block has dimensions of 1 inch by 1 inch by 2 inches, what is its weight?
  a. 0.29 pounds
  b. 0.58 pounds
  c. 2.0 pounds
  d. 4.0 pounds

18. What is the structural principle behind the use of snowshoes?
  a. to spread the load out on the snow
  b. to increase the weight on the snow
  c. to slow down the person using them
  d. to prevent slippage in the snow

19. There are three beams that are each 10 feet long and all of the same size. One is made of wood, another of steel, and the third of concrete. If identical loads are applied to these three beams, which of the following will occur?
  a. The concrete beam will deflect more than the other two.
  b. The wood beam will deflect less than the steel beam.
  c. The steel beam will deflect less than the wood beam.
  d. The wood beam will deflect less than the concrete beam.

20. In the diagram above, Joe must lift a 100-pound box using a lever. How many pounds of force must Joe apply to the left side of the lever to lift the box? ($w \times d_1 = f \times d_2$)
  a. 100 pounds
  b. 200 pounds
  c. 50 pounds
  d. 33 pounds

21. Two springs are arranged in series as shown above. Spring #1 is very stiff and will become 1 inch longer when a tension force of 10 pounds is applied to it. Spring #2 is very soft and will become 2 inches longer when a tension force of 5 pounds is applied to it. What will be the change in length of the two springs (that is, how far will point A move to the right) when a force of 20 pounds is applied?
  a. 10 inches
  b. 6 inches
  c. 8 inches
  d. 3 inches

22. Which mechanical device listed below is used to control the flow of liquids and gases in a piping system?
  a. a gear
  b. a valve
  c. a piston
  d. a spring

23. A solar panel, a wind mill, an atomic reactor, a dam on a river, and a steam turbine are all examples of methods that could be used to create which of the following?
a. ice
b. electricity
c. steel
d. rain

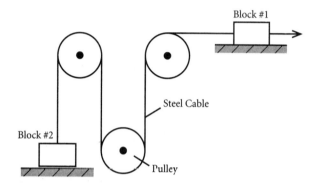

Block #1

Steel Cable

Block #2

Pulley

24. In the diagram above, if block #1 is moved 10 feet to the right, how far upward is block #2 lifted?
a. 3 feet
b. 5 feet
c. 10 feet
d. 20 feet

25. Which of the following groups of items listed below consists entirely of fasteners—that is, of devices that are used to connect two items together?
a. chairs, tables, and windows
b. string, scissors, and glue
c. rivets, levers, and bolts
d. snaps, buckles, and buttons

▶ Part 8: Electronics Information

Time: 9 minutes

1. The heating element in one toaster is 5 Ω. The heating element in a second toaster is 10 Ω. Which of the following statements is true when the same voltage is applied to both toasters?
a. The first toaster uses twice as much power as the second toaster.
b. The first toaster uses one-half as much power as the second toaster.
c. The first toaster uses the same power as the second toaster.
d. The first toaster uses four times as much power as the second toaster.

2. An ammeter reads 287 microamps. Which of the following is equivalent to the meter reading?
a. 0.00287 A
b. 0.287 A
c. 0.0287 A
d. 0.000287 A

3. A wire stripper is used to
a. cut a wire.
b. remove the insulation from a wire.
c. join two wires together.
d. add insulation to a wire so that it won't short out.

4. The two most commonly used metals in solder are
a. gold and lead.
b. tin and nickel.
c. gold and silver.
d. tin and lead.

5. Why shouldn't acid flux be used when soldering electronic components?
   a. It will make the solder joint brittle.
   b. It will corrode the solder joint.
   c. It will soften the solder joint.
   d. It does not flow well.

6. Printed circuit boards are typically made out of
   a. fiberglass.
   b. laminated paper.
   c. glass.
   d. copper.

7. An ideal fuse has what resistance when it is operating normally?
   a. zero Ω
   b. 0.01 Ω
   c. 0.1 Ω
   d. 1.0 Ω

8. A properly soldered connection will appear
   a. dull.
   b. shiny.
   c. oily.
   d. black.

9. Two different wattage light bulbs are connected in series to a voltage source. The first bulb is a 60-watt bulb. The second bulb is a 40-watt bulb. What is the total power the voltage source must supply?
   a. 40 watts
   b. 60 watts
   c. 100 watts
   d. 120 watts

10. An oscilloscope is typically used to analyze
   a. simple circuits.
   b. resistance.
   c. power in a circuit.
   d. complex waveforms.

11. In series circuit A a 10 Ω load dissipates 1 watt. In series circuit B a 10 Ω load dissipates 2 watts. What can be said about the current through the load in circuit A if the voltages in both circuits are equal?
   a. the current through load A is equal to the current through load B
   b. the current through load A is twice the current through load B
   c. the current through load A is half the current through load B
   d. the current through load A is zero

12. Which electronic component can store charge?
   a. a resistor
   b. a capacitor
   c. a transistor
   d. a transformer

13. Which of the following resistors would allow the most current to flow if connected in series with a 1.5 V battery?
   a. 1 Ω
   b. 2 Ω
   c. 5 Ω
   d. 10 Ω

14. A current meter is connected to a circuit as shown. What does the current meter read?

   a. 3.0 amperes
   b. 4.5 amperes
   c. 13.5 amperes
   d. 15 amperes

15. The letters AC stand for
  a. ampere coil.
  b. ampere charge.
  c. alternating current.
  d. alternating charge.

16. Two 8-ohm speakers are connected in parallel to an amplifier with a 24-volt output. What is the voltage across each speaker?
  a. 3 volts
  b. 6 volts
  c. 12 volts
  d. 24 volts

17. Which of the following is NOT a type of switch?
  a. single pole-single throw
  b. rotary
  c. double pole-double throw
  d. linear

18. Electrons have a _____ charge while protons have a _____ charge.
  a. neutral, positive
  b. negative, neutral
  c. positive, negative
  d. negative, positive

19. The force between an electron and a proton in close proximity will cause them to
  a. move apart.
  b. come together.
  c. stay static.
  d. split.

20. What is the frequency of the alternating voltage and current typically used in the United States?
  a. 20 Hz
  b. 40 Hz
  c. 60 Hz
  d. 110 Hz

► Answers

Part 1: General Science

1. a. Organic chemistry is the study of carbon compounds.

2. c. The dissolved is in equilibrium with the undissolved in saturated solutions.

3. d. The Sun has no solid surface, as it is composed entirely of gas. The core temperature of the Sun is 15,000,000 K, compared to its outer atmosphere temperature of 1,000,000 K.

4. b. The elements that make up NH_4Cl are nitrogen (N), hydrogen (H), and chlorine (Cl). Choice **a** is the symbol for carbon, which is not present at all. Choice **c** is the symbol for two of the elements present, not one. Choice **d** is the symbol for all three elements in NH_4Cl.

5. d. The molecule CH_3NH_2 contains 1 atom of carbon, 1 atom of nitrogen, and 5 atoms of hydrogen, for a total of 7 atoms.

6. a. Mosses are bryophytes, which are characterized by their lack of a vascular system.

7. b. The Celsius scale is part of the metric system. On the Celsius scale, the freezing point of water is 0°; the boiling point is 100°.

8. a. Momentum equals mass (amount of matter in an object) times velocity (speed in a given direction).

9. d. Friction is the force that opposes the motion of an object.

10. c. A tapeworm is a parasite. It causes harm to its host. Commensalism is a relationship in which one organism benefits from a host; mutualism is an interaction in which two organisms depend on each other.

11. a. A Producer is a living thing that can make its own food.

12. c. Anticoagulants are defined as any substance that stops the blood from forming clots.

13. b. Veins carry blood in the direction of the heart.

14. d. The synapse is the area between the axon on one nerve cell sending a signal and the beginning dendrite of the next nerve cell that is receiving the signal.

15. b. The troposphere is the lowest level of the atmosphere in which most of the weather occurs. The stratosphere is directly above it.

16. a. All points on the equator have a latitude of 0 degrees. The North Pole has a latitude of 90 degrees north. The South Pole has a latitude of 90 degrees south.

17. b. Condensation is the change of vapor or gas into a liquid. Evaporation is the process by which water changes to a vapor or gas.

18. c. A barometer is a device for measuring atmospheric or air pressure. Humidity is measured by a hygrometer. Wind speed is measured by an anemometer.

19. a. Osmosis is the net movement of water molecules traveling from an area of high concentration to an area of low concentration. Diffusion is the process of any particles moving from higher to lower concentration until uniform concentration is reached.

20. d. Cartilage, a firm, flexible connective tissue, cushions joints and forms the skeleton of cartilaginous fish such as sharks. Bone marrow is a soft tissue in the central internal cavity of a bone.

21. c. The small intestine is the primary site of nutrient absorption in the human digestive system. Saliva breaks down food particles in the mouth, and enzymes and other chemicals break down food in the stomach. The large intestine reabsorbs water and forms the feces.

22. a. An elevator uses a pulley, consisting of a wheel with a flat, crowned, or grooved rim with a belt, rope, or chain that lifts a load. A seesaw or crowbar is an example of a lever.

23. c. Mass × speed = momentum. Force × distance = work.

24. b. Radiation is heat carried by electromagnetic waves from a hot source, such as a light bulb, into surrounding material, such as a lampshade. Conduction is when a hot and cold object come into contact and become an equal temperature.

25. d. Vitamin D aids in the uptake of calcium from the digestive system. Insufficient amounts of vitamin D is characterized by brittle or deformed bones.

Part 2: Arithmetic Reasoning

1. a. Here, 157 is rounded to 200; 817 is rounded to 800. $(200)(800) = 160,000$.

2. b. Multiply 120 by $\frac{2}{3}$. Thus, $\frac{120}{1} \times \frac{2}{3} = \frac{240}{3} = 80$; 120 is written as a fraction with a denominator of 1. The fraction $\frac{240}{3}$ is simplified by dividing 240 by 3 to get 80 cups.

3. b. Add the corrected value of the sweater ($245) to the value of the two, not three, bracelets ($730), plus the other two items ($78 and $130).

4. a. The recipe is for 16 brownies. Half of that, 8, would reduce the ingredients by half. Half of $1\frac{1}{2}$ cups of sugar is $\frac{3}{4}$ cup.

5. c. The recipe for 16 brownies calls for $\frac{2}{3}$ cup butter. An additional $\frac{1}{3}$ cup would make 8 more brownies, for a total of 24 brownies.

6. d. To solve this problem, you must convert $3\frac{1}{2}$ to $\frac{7}{2}$ and then divide $\frac{7}{2}$ by $\frac{1}{4}$. The answer, $\frac{28}{2}$, is then reduced to the number 14.

7. c. Multiply $15,500,000 by $\frac{2}{5}$; $\frac{15,500,000}{1} \times \frac{2}{5} =$ $6,200,000

8. a. Substituting known quantities into the formula yields $20 = \frac{64.8}{x^2}$. Next, you must multiply through by x^2 to get $20x^2 = 64.8$. Now divide through by 20 to get $x^2 = \frac{64.8}{20} = 3.24$. Now take the square root of both sides to get x equals 1.8.

9. d. Four inches is equal to 16 quarter inches. Each quarter inch is 2 feet, so 16 quarter inches is 32 feet.

10. b. You can't just take 25% off the original price, because the 10% discount after three years of service is taken off the price that has already been reduced by 15%. Figure the problem in two steps: after the 15% discount the price is $71.83; 90% of that—subtracting 10%—is $64.65.

11. a. Add the number of men and women to get the total number: 200. The number of women, 24, is 12 percent of 200.

12. c. The problem is solved by dividing 204 by 1,700. The answer, 0.12, is then converted to a percentage.

13. d. The simplest way to solve this problem is to divide 1 by 1,500, which is 0.0006667, and then count off two decimal places to arrive at the percentage, which is 0.06667 percent. Since the question asks *about what percentage*, the nearest value is 0.067 percent.

14. a. You can use trial and error to arrive at a solution to this problem. After the first hour, the number would be 20, after the second hour 40, after the third hour 80, after the fourth hour 160, and after the fifth hour 320. The other answer choices do not have the same outcome.

15. b. Use the equation $.05(1) = .02(x)$, where x is the total amount of water in the resulting 2% solution. Solving for x, you get 2.5. Subtracting the 1 liter of water already present in the 5% solution, you will find that 1.5 liters need to be added.

16. b. Twenty percent of 15 miles is 3 miles; adding 3 to 15 gives 18 miles.

17. c. Each 9-foot wall has an area of 9(8) or 72 square feet. There are two such walls, so those two walls combined have an area of 144 square feet. Each 11-foot wall has an area of 11(8) or 88 square feet, and again there are two such walls: 88 (2) = 176. Finally, add 144 and 176 to get 320 square feet.

18. c. Using the formula, $V = \frac{1}{3}(10)(12)(10) = 400$.

19. d. Substituting 40 for C in the equation yields $F = (\frac{9}{5})(40) + 32 = 72 + 32 = 104$.

20. b. Here, $150x = (100)(1)$, where x is the part of a mile a jogger has to go to burn the calories a walker burns in 1 mile. If you divide both sides of this equation by 150, you get $x = \frac{100}{150}$. Cancel 50 from both the numerator and denominator to get $\frac{2}{3}$. This means that a jogger has to jog only $\frac{2}{3}$ of a mile to burn the same number of calories a walker burns in a mile of brisk walking.

21. c. The ratio is $\frac{12\,cc}{100\,pounds} = \frac{x}{175\,pounds}$, where x is the number of cc's per 175 pounds. Multiply both sides by 175 to get $(175)(\frac{12}{100})$ equals x, so x equals 21.

22. b. On the first day, the hiker walks 40 miles. On the second day, he walks 20 miles. On the third day, he walks 10 miles. On the fourth day, he walks 5 miles. On the fifth day, he walks 2.5 miles. The sum of the miles walked, then, is 77.5 miles. The average over 5 days is 77.5 divided by 5, or 15.5 miles per day.

23. a. The woman will have traveled 3.5 hours at 45 miles per hour for a distance of 157.5 miles. To reach her in 3 hours, her husband must travel at 157.5 miles per 3 hours, or 52.5 mph.

24. c. Eighty dollars per month times 7 months is $560. Twenty dollars per month times the remaining 5 months is $100. Add $560 and $100, which equals $660 for the entire year, so $660 divided by 12 months is $55.

25. a. $J = 6K$. $J + 2 = 2(K + 2)$, so $6K + 2 = 2K + 4$, which means K equals $\frac{1}{2}$. J equals $6K$, or 3.

26. d. Add each monthly bill plus $54 for total local service to get $312.90 for three months. Dividing by 3 gives an average of $104.30.

27. d. Here, 448 miles divided by 16 gallons is 28 miles per gallon.

28. c. Multiply the cost per acre by the number of acres; $60,000 \times 1\frac{3}{4}$.

29. b. Kyra saves $60 + $130 + $70 = $260. In January, her employer contributes $6 and in April, $7. In March, her employer contributes only $10, the maximum amount. The total in savings is $260 + $6 + $7 + $10 = $283.

30. b. Jackie is paid and saves twice a month, while she pays her student loan only once a month. Her monthly salary is $1,644.80. Subtract $300 in savings and $84.71 for the student loan to get $1,260.09.

Part 3: Word Knowledge

1. c. To be held *accountable* is to be held *responsible*.

2. b. To *scrutinize* is to inspect or *examine* in detail.

3. b. To *enumerate* is to ascertain the number of or *count*.

4. a. To *emulate* a person is to strive to equal that person or to *imitate* that person.

5. b. When one is *compliant*, one is acquiescent or *obedient*.

6. c. To *augment* something is to add to or *supplement* it.

7. d. To have an *aversion* to something is to have a feeling of repugnance for it or to *dislike* it.

8. a. To *validate* something is to *confirm* the authenticity of it.

9. b. To have an *antagonist* is to have an *opponent*, or one who opposes you.

10. c. To have *perseverance* is to be steadfast in your course or to have *persistence*.

11. d. To be *inundated* is to be overwhelmed or *flooded*.

12. a. *Homogeneous* means of the same or a similar kind, *alike*.

13. d. *Ominous* means foreshadowing evil, *threatening*.

14. c. When one is *incredulous*, one is skeptical or *disbelieving*.

15. d. A *recluse* is a person who lives withdrawn or shut up from the world, a *hermit*.

16. d. When one is *proficient* at something, one is expert or *skilled* at it.

17. a. To *defray* is to provide for the payment of something, to *pay*.

18. b. *Placid* means serenely free of disturbance; calm, *peaceful*.

19. a. When something is *tentative* it is of an experimental or *provisional* nature.

20. b. Something that is *vast* is huge or *immense*.

21. c. When one is *contemptuous*, one is disdainful or *scornful*.

22. b. When a group's opinion is *unanimous*, it is in accord or *uniform*.

23. c. When something is *distinct*, it is explicit or *recognizable*.

24. a. To *alleviate* something is to make it more bearable or *ease* it.

25. d. To *enlighten* someone is to impart wisdom to that person or to *teach*.

Part 4: Paragraph Comprehension

1. b. The passage explains the procedure for bus drivers to follow when their bus gets ahead of schedule. Therefore, "running hot" means running ahead of schedule.

2. d. The passage indicates that each route contains several check points at which drivers should check the time to see if they are running on schedule.

3. a. The second sentence states that routine maintenance is performed by the maintenance department.

4. c. The first sentence states that drivers are responsible for refueling at the end of each shift; this implies trucks are refueled at the end of every shift.

5. c. According to the passage, hazardous waste is defined by the United States Environmental Protection Agency.

6. c. According to the passage, he should call his supervisor for directions because he is unclear whether the solvent is unsafe.

7. d. See the last sentence. The passage does not mention choice **b** or choice **c**. Choice **a** is clearly wrong; the passage states the opposite.

8. a. See the last sentence. Choices **b** and **c** are not mentioned, and choice **d** is directly contradicted in the third sentence of the passage.

9. c. This title most nearly captures the main idea of the passage. The other choices either are not mentioned or are secondary ideas in the passage.

10. b. This is the point of the first sentence of the passage.

11. b. The third sentence of the passage states that officers may refer to their notes.

12. d. The passage provides information for law enforcement officers; therefore it is probably not from either a newspaper article or a novel. Choice **a** refers to a memo directed to police officers, but the subject matter is incorrect.

13. a. The first sentence states the importance of officer testimony.

14. d. The first day of summer in the north is the first day of winter in the south.

15. b. The first day of summer is summer solstice; therefore, the first day of winter is winter solstice.

Part 5: Auto and Shop Information

1. d. A faulty thermostat can cause engine overheating. If the thermostat is stuck in the closed position, the coolant cannot circulate and cool the engine.

2. a. The transmission has many moving parts (gears and shafts), which must be lubricated by transmission fluid in order to prevent excessive wear and allow the parts to move smoothly.

3. c. The fuses are used as links in the electrical system to prevent damage to other key components. The alternator is used to recharge the battery when the car is running.

4. d. The spark plug sends a spark into the cylinder, igniting the fuel.

5. b. The radiator is part of the cooling system. The cooling fluid is stored in the radiator and is then pumped through the cooling system by the water pump. As air passes over the radiator, the fluid is cooled, which prevents engine overheating.

6. a. The water pump pumps the engine coolant (a combination of water and antifreeze) out of the radiator and around the engine block in order to cool the engine.

7. a. Mortar is composed of cement, sand, and water and is used to hold together brick walls or floors.

8. c. Steel is most often used to provide additional strength in concrete slabs and walls due to its high strength and relatively low cost.

9. d. Cement, sand, gravel, and water are the four primary ingredients in concrete.

10. d. Tile shingles are expensive but have a long life. Wooden "shake shingles" are also used as roofing material. The most common outer roofing material is asphalt shingles since they are low in cost and provide good protection.

11. b. A come-along wrench is used to exert a pulling force on heavy objects of not more than five tons.

12. b. Oil's lubricating properties break down over time, and the oil must therefore be replaced. The recommended interval is normally about 3,000 miles.

13. d. The crankshaft has a radius of 1.0 inch, which means that the diameter is 2.0 inches. If the crankshaft rotates one-half revolution (180 degrees) from its starting point, the attachment of the tie rod to the crankshaft will move from the top of the crankshaft down to the bottom. This is equivalent to the diameter of the crankshaft, which is 2.0 inches.

14. a. The shock absorbers are the components in the suspension that dampen the vibrations in the system.

15. c. The clutch is used to engage and disengage the transmission. The drive shaft is used to transfer power from the engine to the wheels. Universal joints are special linkages in the transmission system.

16. c. The indicated danger zone on the gauge is from 160 degrees to 200 degrees Fahrenheit. Thus, it is acceptable to operate up to 160 degrees for this gauge.

17. d. The braking system can be controlled by the driver by pressing the brake pedal. The other systems listed cannot typically be directly controlled while operating the automobile.

18. c. The exhaust and engine systems are directly connected. The four cycles of an internal combustion engine produce exhaust when the fuel burns. The exhaust exits the engine through the manifold and then continues through the exhaust system, which is comprised of the tail pipe and muffler.

19. a. The cooling system circulates water around the engine to prevent it from overheating. None of the other systems is connected directly to the engine.

20. c. That this gauge measures temperature can be determined by the units of degrees Fahrenheit and degrees Celsius shown on the gauge.

21. c. A plane is a hand tool that has a sharp blade extending slightly below the bottom surface of the tool. The plane is pushed across the surface of a piece of wood and the blade removes a thin layer of wood from the surface.

22. d. The power from the battery of the electrical system is what makes the turn signal indicator blink.

23. a. The tools listed are all used to form, cut, and punch thin sheets of metal.

24. b. These are all ways to fasten things together (such as wood, plastic, metal, and so forth).

25. c. These are common shop tools that are used to measure the length of various items.

Part 6: Mathematics Knowledge

1. d. The only parallel lines are y and z.

2. d. You must convert both fractions to thirtieths before adding.

3. a. Divide 4 by 5 in order to convert the fraction into a decimal. $4 \div 5 = 0.80$.

4. d. x times x^2 is x^3; x times y is xy.

5. b. Divide 14 by 35 and then multiply the answer by 100 to find the percent.

6. b. Divide 1 by 4 in order to convert the fraction into a decimal; $1 \div 4 = 0.25$.

7. a. The problem is solved by first determining that $8n$ equals 40 and then dividing 40 by 8.

8. b. Convert the mixed number $3\frac{7}{8}$ to the improper fraction $\frac{31}{8}$ and then invert.

9. d. This is a mixed number so it can be broken down into the whole number plus the fraction; $3\frac{3}{10} = 3.0 + \frac{3}{10}$; divide 3 by 10 in order to convert the fraction into a decimal; $3.00 \div 10 = 0.30$. Therefore, $3.0 + 0.30 = 3.30$.

10. c. This is the only choice that includes a 90-degree angle.

11. b. The square root of 12 is the same as the square root of 4 times 3, which is the same as the square root of 4 times the square root of 3. The square root of 4 is 2. So 3 times the square root of 12 is the same as 3 times 2 times the square root of 3.

12. b. Four divided by 25 equals 0.16 or 16%.

13. d. $(3)(3)(3)(3) = 81$.

14. b. $-1\frac{1}{3}$ is a mixed fraction and is equal to the whole number plus the fraction; $-1\frac{1}{3} = -(1 + \frac{1}{3})$. Convert $\frac{1}{3}$ into a decimal by dividing 1 by 3; $1 \div 3 = 0.333$; round this portion of the answer to the nearest hundredth, (two decimal places), to get 0.33; $-(1 + 0.33) = -1.33$.

15. a. The mixed number is equal to the whole number plus the fraction; $1\frac{3}{4} = 1.0 + \frac{3}{4}$. Convert the fraction to a decimal by dividing 3 by 4; $3 \div 4 = 0.75$; $1.0 + 0.75 = 1.75$.

16. a. The dimensions of triangle *MNO* are double those of triangle *RST*. Line segment *RT* is 5 cm; therefore line segment *MO* is 10 cm.

17. c. The farther to the right the digits go, the smaller the number.

18. c. To convert a decimal into a fraction, first note the number of place positions to the right of the decimal point. In 0.4, the 4 is in the tenths place, which is one place to the right of the decimal point. Therefore, the fraction would be $\frac{4}{10}$. Now, the fraction needs to be reduced to its lowest terms. The number 2 is the greatest common factor of 4 and 10, so divide the numerator and denominator by 2. The final fraction is $\frac{2}{5}$.

19. a. In choice **b**, the 9 is in the hundredths place. In choice **c**, it is in the tenths place. In choice **d**, it is in the ten-thousandths place.

20. d. In the decimal 0.75, the 75 is two places to the right of the decimal point. Therefore, the fraction would be $\frac{75}{100}$, which can then be reduced by dividing the top and bottom by 25, the greatest common factor of 75 and 100. $\frac{75 \div 25}{100 \div 25} = \frac{3}{4}$.

21. a. The expression $5n$ means 5 times *n*. The addition sign before the 7 indicates the phrase *more than*.

22. b. Angles 1 and 4 are the only ones NOT adjacent to each other.

23. a. The number 2.25 involves a whole number, which is the 2 to the left of the decimal. This means that the answer will be a mixed number—a whole number plus a fraction. Convert the 0.25 into a fraction; $\frac{25 \div 25}{100 \div 25} = \frac{1}{4}$; adding the whole number, 2, to this fraction gives the answer $2\frac{1}{4}$.

24. d. Substitute 3 for *x* in the expression $5 + 4x$ to determine that *y* equals 17.

25. d. 6^3 is equal to $(6)(6)(6) = 216$.

26. c. Divide 12 by 0.5 (50%) to get 24%.

27. c. Perform the operation in parentheses first: $(14)(7) = 98$, and then add 12 to get 110.

28. b. In the decimal, 0.125, the 125 is in the thousandths place, since it is three places to the right of the decimal point; 125 is the greatest common factor of 125 and 1,000. The fraction is $\frac{125 \div 125}{1,000 \div 125} = \frac{1}{8}$.

29. c. Since there is a number, 3, to the left of the decimal point, this is the whole number; 0.3 is to the right of the decimal point, so this part is the fraction. The 3 is in the tenths place, so the fraction is $\frac{3}{10}$. The final mixed number answer is the whole number (3) plus the fraction ($\frac{3}{10}$); $3 + \frac{3}{10} = 3\frac{3}{10}$.

30. b. Convert the percentage to a decimal: (232)(0.14) = 32.48.

31. d. The perimeter is the total length of all sides. In a square, all four sides are of equal length, so the perimeter is (4)(4) = 16.

32. c. Divide 33 by 0.12 (12%) to get 275.

33. b. The formula for finding the area of a circle is A = πr^2. First, square the radius: (13)(13) = 169. Then multiply by the approximate value of π, 3.14, to get 530.66.

34. d. 17^2 is equivalent to 17 times 17, which is 289.

35. c. *DE* is 2.5 times greater than *AB*; therefore, *EF* is 7.5 and *DF* is 10. Add the three sides together to arrive at the perimeter.

Part 7: Mechanical Comprehension

1. b. The first 500 pounds generated 1,000 psi of stress in the beam; therefore, 500 more pounds will increase the total stress to 2,000 psi. Another 500 pounds will increase the stress to 3,000 psi, which we are told is the maximum strength of the beam. Therefore, the maximum additional load that can be applied to this beam before it breaks is 1,000 pounds.

2. b. The cars both weigh the same, so friction and acceleration would be identical for both. The difference is that a sports car has a low, sleek shape compared to a minivan and therefore has less drag from the wind.

3. d. Acceleration must be considered in designing the maximum rise of the first hill. Momentum must be considered to ensure the train gets back to the starting point, since it has no motor. Friction must be considered in the design of the braking system.

4. a. This is a demonstration of momentum. Momentum is defined as mass (weight) multiplied by velocity. Since both balls have the same speed (velocity), the heavier ball (the larger one in this case, since both balls have the same density) will have more momentum. Therefore, upon impact, the heavier ball will be slowed but continue in the same direction and knock the smaller, lighter ball backwards.

5. d. When an object is at equilibrium, it has equal forces acting on it. When both people on a seesaw weigh the same, the seesaw is in equilibrium, and it is easier for each person to push off the ground.

6. a. In the equilibrium position, the pendulum hangs straight down. When displaced from this position, the pendulum does not simply return to the equilibrium position, but swings back and forth in a regular, repetitive manner. This is the definition of periodic motion.

7. c. By definition, deceleration means slowing down.

8. d. The beam will move, or deflect, under the load. The beam will also undergo internal stresses and strains caused by the load.

9. c. Multiply 3.5 inches by 100 pounds per inch, which equals 350 pounds.

10. a. A wedge is a triangular-shaped object that has many mechanical functions.

11. d. Pumps are not used to move liquids downhill since they will flow downhill by gravity. Also, pumps do not separate or clarify liquids, since they agitate and mix liquids.

12. c. On Earth, the force of gravity pulls objects toward its surface. The force of a cannon is not enough to allow the cannon ball to escape this pull.

13. b. Valves are placed in piping systems and can be opened or closed in order to control the flow of liquids or gasses.

14. a. The center of gravity of an object is loosely defined as "the middle of its weight" or "the point at which you could balance it on your finger"; in this case, that would be two feet from the left end (or two feet from the right end).

15. d. Elasticity is defined as "stretchiness." It is a measure of how easy it is to deform a material. Paper is the stiffest or least elastic of the material listed.

16. b. Block B is smaller, but we are told it is made of a material that is three times more dense (density is weight per unit volume) than Block A. Therefore, since Block A is only twice as big as Block B, it is actually 50 percent lighter.

17. b. The volume of the block can be calculated by multiplying its length by its width by its height, or 1 times 1 times 2, which equals 2 cubic inches. The weight is the density multiplied by its volume, which is 2 cubic inches multiplied by 0.29 pounds per cubic inch, which equals 0.58 pounds.

18. a. Snowshoes distribute the weight of the person over a larger area than boots alone and reduce the pressure on the snow. This keeps the person from sinking so far into the snow.

19. c. The steel beam will deflect less than the wood beam. Choice **a** is not correct since the concrete beam will deflect less that the wood beam—concrete is stiffer than wood.

20. c. The distance from the pivot point to the point of application of the force (20 feet) is twice the distance from the pivot point to the box (10 feet). Therefore, in order to lift the box, the required force will be one half of the weight of the box, or 50 pounds.

21. a. Because the springs are in series, their amount of stretch is additive. Spring #1 will stretch 1 inch under 10 pounds. So its total stretch under 20 pounds will be 2 inches. Spring #2 is being subjected to a load of 20 pounds, which is four times the load that will stretch it 2 inches. Therefore, its total stretch will be 8 inches. Adding the amount of stretch for the two springs together gives you 10 inches.

22. b. A valve is used to control the flow of liquids and gases in a piping system. An example is the faucet on a sink.

23. b. The systems listed produce electric power.

24. c. The two blocks are directly connected by a fixed length of steel cable. Therefore, regardless of the number of pulleys between the two blocks, the distance moved by one block will be the same as the other block.

25. d. The items listed that are *not* fasteners are chairs, tables, windows, scissors, and levers.

Part 8: Electronics Information

1. a. $P = \frac{V^2}{R}$. V^2 divided by 5 W will be twice as big as V^2 divided by 10 W.

2. d. The prefix "micro" means multiply by 10^{-6}, so 287 microamps equals 0.000287 A.

3. b. Wire cutters are used to cut wire. A soldering iron and solder are used to join wires. Heat shrink insulation can be added to wires.

4. d. Typical solders are almost equal parts tin and lead.

5. b. An acid flux will corrode the solder joint.

6. a. Fiberglass is used to make most printed circuit boards.

7. a. Ideally, a fuse should have zero resistance when it is operating normally.

8. b. Shiny joints indicate a properly soldered connection.

9. c. The total power in a series circuit is the sum of the power used by the two light bulbs.

10. d. An oscilloscope is used primarily to look at complex waveforms.

11. c. The power in circuit A is one half the power in B, so the current through A must be one half the current through B. If either circuit had no current flowing, there would be zero power dissipated.

12. b. A capacitor has the ability to store charge.

13. a. Resistance is the opposition to current, so the smallest resistance will allow the most current to flow.

14. b. The current through the meter is equal to the current through R_1. The current through R_1 is $\frac{45\text{ V}}{10\,\Omega} = 4.5$ A.

15. c. AC stands for alternating current.

16. d. Resistances in parallel have the same voltage across them.

17. d. Linear switches do not exist.

18. d. The charge polarity of electrons is negative; the charge polarity of protons is positive.

19. b. Electrons and protons have opposite charges and attract each other.

20. c. Electricity produced in the United States has a frequency of 60 Hz. Some foreign countries produce electricity at 50 Hz.

Scoring

Write your raw score (the number you got right) for each test in the blanks below. Then turn to Chapter 3 to find out how to convert these raw scores into the scores the armed services use.

1. General Science: _____ right out of 25
2. Arithmetic Reasoning: _____ right out of 30
3. Word Knowledge: _____ right out of 25
4. Paragraph Comprehension: _____ right out of 15
5. Auto and Shop Information: _____ right out of 25
6. Mathematics Knowledge: _____ right out of 35
7. Mechanical Comprehension: _____ right out of 25
8. Electronics Information: _____ right out of 20

14 ▶ ASVAB Practice Test 3

CHAPTER SUMMARY

This is the third of three practice test batteries based on the ASVAB. Take this test for more practice and additional improvement over your scores on the first two tests.

Like the previous practice ASVAB batteries, this one contains the eight subtests of the type you will find on the ASVAB, for a total of 200 items. For this exam, again simulate the actual test-taking experience as closely as you can. Work in a quiet place where you won't be interrupted. If you own this book, tear out the answer sheet and use your number 2 pencils to fill in the circles. As you did for the practice exam in Chapter 13, set a timer or stopwatch, and give yourself the appropriate amount of time marked at the beginning of each subtest.

After you take the test, use the detailed answer explanations that follow to review any questions you missed.

▶ Part 1: General Science

1.	ⓐ	ⓑ	ⓒ	ⓓ
2.	ⓐ	ⓑ	ⓒ	ⓓ
3.	ⓐ	ⓑ	ⓒ	ⓓ
4.	ⓐ	ⓑ	ⓒ	ⓓ
5.	ⓐ	ⓑ	ⓒ	ⓓ
6.	ⓐ	ⓑ	ⓒ	ⓓ
7.	ⓐ	ⓑ	ⓒ	ⓓ
8.	ⓐ	ⓑ	ⓒ	ⓓ
9.	ⓐ	ⓑ	ⓒ	ⓓ

10.	ⓐ	ⓑ	ⓒ	ⓓ
11.	ⓐ	ⓑ	ⓒ	ⓓ
12.	ⓐ	ⓑ	ⓒ	ⓓ
13.	ⓐ	ⓑ	ⓒ	ⓓ
14.	ⓐ	ⓑ	ⓒ	ⓓ
15.	ⓐ	ⓑ	ⓒ	ⓓ
16.	ⓐ	ⓑ	ⓒ	ⓓ
17.	ⓐ	ⓑ	ⓒ	ⓓ
18.	ⓐ	ⓑ	ⓒ	ⓓ

19.	ⓐ	ⓑ	ⓒ	ⓓ
20.	ⓐ	ⓑ	ⓒ	ⓓ
21.	ⓐ	ⓑ	ⓒ	ⓓ
22.	ⓐ	ⓑ	ⓒ	ⓓ
23.	ⓐ	ⓑ	ⓒ	ⓓ
24.	ⓐ	ⓑ	ⓒ	ⓓ
25.	ⓐ	ⓑ	ⓒ	ⓓ

▶ Part 2: Arithmetic Reasoning

1.	ⓐ	ⓑ	ⓒ	ⓓ
2.	ⓐ	ⓑ	ⓒ	ⓓ
3.	ⓐ	ⓑ	ⓒ	ⓓ
4.	ⓐ	ⓑ	ⓒ	ⓓ
5.	ⓐ	ⓑ	ⓒ	ⓓ
6.	ⓐ	ⓑ	ⓒ	ⓓ
7.	ⓐ	ⓑ	ⓒ	ⓓ
8.	ⓐ	ⓑ	ⓒ	ⓓ
9.	ⓐ	ⓑ	ⓒ	ⓓ
10.	ⓐ	ⓑ	ⓒ	ⓓ

11.	ⓐ	ⓑ	ⓒ	ⓓ
12.	ⓐ	ⓑ	ⓒ	ⓓ
13.	ⓐ	ⓑ	ⓒ	ⓓ
14.	ⓐ	ⓑ	ⓒ	ⓓ
15.	ⓐ	ⓑ	ⓒ	ⓓ
16.	ⓐ	ⓑ	ⓒ	ⓓ
17.	ⓐ	ⓑ	ⓒ	ⓓ
18.	ⓐ	ⓑ	ⓒ	ⓓ
19.	ⓐ	ⓑ	ⓒ	ⓓ
20.	ⓐ	ⓑ	ⓒ	ⓓ

21.	ⓐ	ⓑ	ⓒ	ⓓ
22.	ⓐ	ⓑ	ⓒ	ⓓ
23.	ⓐ	ⓑ	ⓒ	ⓓ
24.	ⓐ	ⓑ	ⓒ	ⓓ
25.	ⓐ	ⓑ	ⓒ	ⓓ
26.	ⓐ	ⓑ	ⓒ	ⓓ
27.	ⓐ	ⓑ	ⓒ	ⓓ
28.	ⓐ	ⓑ	ⓒ	ⓓ
29.	ⓐ	ⓑ	ⓒ	ⓓ
30.	ⓐ	ⓑ	ⓒ	ⓓ

▶ Part 3: Word Knowledge

1.	ⓐ	ⓑ	ⓒ	ⓓ
2.	ⓐ	ⓑ	ⓒ	ⓓ
3.	ⓐ	ⓑ	ⓒ	ⓓ
4.	ⓐ	ⓑ	ⓒ	ⓓ
5.	ⓐ	ⓑ	ⓒ	ⓓ
6.	ⓐ	ⓑ	ⓒ	ⓓ
7.	ⓐ	ⓑ	ⓒ	ⓓ
8.	ⓐ	ⓑ	ⓒ	ⓓ
9.	ⓐ	ⓑ	ⓒ	ⓓ

10.	ⓐ	ⓑ	ⓒ	ⓓ
11.	ⓐ	ⓑ	ⓒ	ⓓ
12.	ⓐ	ⓑ	ⓒ	ⓓ
13.	ⓐ	ⓑ	ⓒ	ⓓ
14.	ⓐ	ⓑ	ⓒ	ⓓ
15.	ⓐ	ⓑ	ⓒ	ⓓ
16.	ⓐ	ⓑ	ⓒ	ⓓ
17.	ⓐ	ⓑ	ⓒ	ⓓ
18.	ⓐ	ⓑ	ⓒ	ⓓ

19.	ⓐ	ⓑ	ⓒ	ⓓ
20.	ⓐ	ⓑ	ⓒ	ⓓ
21.	ⓐ	ⓑ	ⓒ	ⓓ
22.	ⓐ	ⓑ	ⓒ	ⓓ
23.	ⓐ	ⓑ	ⓒ	ⓓ
24.	ⓐ	ⓑ	ⓒ	ⓓ
25.	ⓐ	ⓑ	ⓒ	ⓓ

▶ Part 4: Paragraph Comprehension

1.	ⓐ	ⓑ	ⓒ	ⓓ
2.	ⓐ	ⓑ	ⓒ	ⓓ
3.	ⓐ	ⓑ	ⓒ	ⓓ
4.	ⓐ	ⓑ	ⓒ	ⓓ
5.	ⓐ	ⓑ	ⓒ	ⓓ

6.	ⓐ	ⓑ	ⓒ	ⓓ
7.	ⓐ	ⓑ	ⓒ	ⓓ
8.	ⓐ	ⓑ	ⓒ	ⓓ
9.	ⓐ	ⓑ	ⓒ	ⓓ
10.	ⓐ	ⓑ	ⓒ	ⓓ

11.	ⓐ	ⓑ	ⓒ	ⓓ
12.	ⓐ	ⓑ	ⓒ	ⓓ
13.	ⓐ	ⓑ	ⓒ	ⓓ
14.	ⓐ	ⓑ	ⓒ	ⓓ
15.	ⓐ	ⓑ	ⓒ	ⓓ

▶ Part 5: Auto and Shop Information

1.	ⓐ ⓑ ⓒ ⓓ	10.	ⓐ ⓑ ⓒ ⓓ	19.	ⓐ ⓑ ⓒ ⓓ
2.	ⓐ ⓑ ⓒ ⓓ	11.	ⓐ ⓑ ⓒ ⓓ	20.	ⓐ ⓑ ⓒ ⓓ
3.	ⓐ ⓑ ⓒ ⓓ	12.	ⓐ ⓑ ⓒ ⓓ	21.	ⓐ ⓑ ⓒ ⓓ
4.	ⓐ ⓑ ⓒ ⓓ	13.	ⓐ ⓑ ⓒ ⓓ	22.	ⓐ ⓑ ⓒ ⓓ
5.	ⓐ ⓑ ⓒ ⓓ	14.	ⓐ ⓑ ⓒ ⓓ	23.	ⓐ ⓑ ⓒ ⓓ
6.	ⓐ ⓑ ⓒ ⓓ	15.	ⓐ ⓑ ⓒ ⓓ	24.	ⓐ ⓑ ⓒ ⓓ
7.	ⓐ ⓑ ⓒ ⓓ	16.	ⓐ ⓑ ⓒ ⓓ	25.	ⓐ ⓑ ⓒ ⓓ
8.	ⓐ ⓑ ⓒ ⓓ	17.	ⓐ ⓑ ⓒ ⓓ		
9.	ⓐ ⓑ ⓒ ⓓ	18.	ⓐ ⓑ ⓒ ⓓ		

▶ Part 6: Mathematics Knowledge

1.	ⓐ ⓑ ⓒ ⓓ	13.	ⓐ ⓑ ⓒ ⓓ	25.	ⓐ ⓑ ⓒ ⓓ
2.	ⓐ ⓑ ⓒ ⓓ	14.	ⓐ ⓑ ⓒ ⓓ	26.	ⓐ ⓑ ⓒ ⓓ
3.	ⓐ ⓑ ⓒ ⓓ	15.	ⓐ ⓑ ⓒ ⓓ	27.	ⓐ ⓑ ⓒ ⓓ
4.	ⓐ ⓑ ⓒ ⓓ	16.	ⓐ ⓑ ⓒ ⓓ	28.	ⓐ ⓑ ⓒ ⓓ
5.	ⓐ ⓑ ⓒ ⓓ	17.	ⓐ ⓑ ⓒ ⓓ	29.	ⓐ ⓑ ⓒ ⓓ
6.	ⓐ ⓑ ⓒ ⓓ	18.	ⓐ ⓑ ⓒ ⓓ	30.	ⓐ ⓑ ⓒ ⓓ
7.	ⓐ ⓑ ⓒ ⓓ	19.	ⓐ ⓑ ⓒ ⓓ	31.	ⓐ ⓑ ⓒ ⓓ
8.	ⓐ ⓑ ⓒ ⓓ	20.	ⓐ ⓑ ⓒ ⓓ	32.	ⓐ ⓑ ⓒ ⓓ
9.	ⓐ ⓑ ⓒ ⓓ	21.	ⓐ ⓑ ⓒ ⓓ	33.	ⓐ ⓑ ⓒ ⓓ
10.	ⓐ ⓑ ⓒ ⓓ	22.	ⓐ ⓑ ⓒ ⓓ	34.	ⓐ ⓑ ⓒ ⓓ
11.	ⓐ ⓑ ⓒ ⓓ	23.	ⓐ ⓑ ⓒ ⓓ	35.	ⓐ ⓑ ⓒ ⓓ
12.	ⓐ ⓑ ⓒ ⓓ	24.	ⓐ ⓑ ⓒ ⓓ		

▶ Part 7: Mechanical Comprehension

1.	ⓐ ⓑ ⓒ ⓓ	10.	ⓐ ⓑ ⓒ ⓓ	19.	ⓐ ⓑ ⓒ ⓓ
2.	ⓐ ⓑ ⓒ ⓓ	11.	ⓐ ⓑ ⓒ ⓓ	20.	ⓐ ⓑ ⓒ ⓓ
3.	ⓐ ⓑ ⓒ ⓓ	12.	ⓐ ⓑ ⓒ ⓓ	21.	ⓐ ⓑ ⓒ ⓓ
4.	ⓐ ⓑ ⓒ ⓓ	13.	ⓐ ⓑ ⓒ ⓓ	22.	ⓐ ⓑ ⓒ ⓓ
5.	ⓐ ⓑ ⓒ ⓓ	14.	ⓐ ⓑ ⓒ ⓓ	23.	ⓐ ⓑ ⓒ ⓓ
6.	ⓐ ⓑ ⓒ ⓓ	15.	ⓐ ⓑ ⓒ ⓓ	24.	ⓐ ⓑ ⓒ ⓓ
7.	ⓐ ⓑ ⓒ ⓓ	16.	ⓐ ⓑ ⓒ ⓓ	25.	ⓐ ⓑ ⓒ ⓓ
8.	ⓐ ⓑ ⓒ ⓓ	17.	ⓐ ⓑ ⓒ ⓓ		
9.	ⓐ ⓑ ⓒ ⓓ	18.	ⓐ ⓑ ⓒ ⓓ		

▶ Part 8: Electronics Information

1.	ⓐ ⓑ ⓒ ⓓ	8.	ⓐ ⓑ ⓒ ⓓ	15.	ⓐ ⓑ ⓒ ⓓ
2.	ⓐ ⓑ ⓒ ⓓ	9.	ⓐ ⓑ ⓒ ⓓ	16.	ⓐ ⓑ ⓒ ⓓ
3.	ⓐ ⓑ ⓒ ⓓ	10.	ⓐ ⓑ ⓒ ⓓ	17.	ⓐ ⓑ ⓒ ⓓ
4.	ⓐ ⓑ ⓒ ⓓ	11.	ⓐ ⓑ ⓒ ⓓ	18.	ⓐ ⓑ ⓒ ⓓ
5.	ⓐ ⓑ ⓒ ⓓ	12.	ⓐ ⓑ ⓒ ⓓ	19.	ⓐ ⓑ ⓒ ⓓ
6.	ⓐ ⓑ ⓒ ⓓ	13.	ⓐ ⓑ ⓒ ⓓ	20.	ⓐ ⓑ ⓒ ⓓ
7.	ⓐ ⓑ ⓒ ⓓ	14.	ⓐ ⓑ ⓒ ⓓ		

▶ Part 1: General Science

Time: 11 minutes

1. On the pH scale, any substance above what number is considered alkaline?
   a. 5
   b. 7
   c. 15
   d. 0

2. What is the simplest aromatic compound (C_6H_6)?
   a. benzoic acid
   b. toulene
   c. phenol
   d. benzene

3. How many different elements are present in glucose, $C_6H_{12}O_6$?
   a. 3
   b. 6
   c. 12
   d. 24

4. 1 micrometer equals 1/1000 of a
   a. kilometer.
   b. meter.
   c. centimeter.
   d. millimeter.

5. What is the scientific notation for 617,000?
   a. 6.17×10^{-5}
   b. 0.617×10^2
   c. 0.617×10^3
   d. 6.17×10^5

6. If you throw a baseball forward, it will accelerate downward due to
   a. orbital motion.
   b. terminal velocity.
   c. gravity.
   d. Newton's third law of motion.

7. Which of these simple machines is NOT a lever?
   a. an ax blade
   b. a shovel
   c. a wheelbarrow
   d. a pair of pliers

8. The dense center of the Earth is called the
   a. mantle.
   b. core.
   c. crust.
   d. axis.

9. An instrument used to measure the speed of the wind is called
   a. a hydrometer.
   b. a barometer.
   c. a seismograph.
   d. an anemometer.

10. To which class do tigers belong?
    a. Carnivora
    b. Mammalia
    c. *tigris*
    d. Chordata

11. In vertebrates, which substance gives red blood cells their color?
    a. hemoglobin
    b. melanin
    c. carotene
    d. dopamine

12. What type of rock is formed by the cooling of lava? (An example is granite.)
   a. metamorphic
   b. sedimentary
   c. igneous
   d. salt

13. Which of the following is an organic compound?
   a. calcium (Ca)
   b. water (H_2O)
   c. salt (NaCl)
   d. glucose ($C_6H_{12}O_6$)

14. Which of the following animals are most closely related to crabs?
   a. beetles
   b. salmon
   c. frogs
   d. robins

15. What causes the human diseases polio and measles?
   a. bacterium
   b. virus
   c. fungus
   d. protozoan

16. What is the hormone that regulates the amount of sugar in the blood?
   a. estrogen
   b. adrenaline
   c. insulin
   d. androgen

17. Unoxygenated blood travels to the heart via which of the following?
   a. arteries
   b. veins
   c. capillaries
   d. aorta

18. What are animals called that feed ONLY on plant matter?
   a. carnivores
   b. omnivores
   c. decomposers
   d. herbivores

19. One hundred centimeters equals how many kilometers?
   a. 0.001
   b. 0.01
   c. 0.1
   d. 1.0

20. Yawning equalizes the air pressure in what structure?
   a. nasal cavity
   b. Eustachian tube
   c. windpipe
   d. cochlea

21. James Watson and Francis Crick discovered that DNA has which of the following structures?
   a. a helix
   b. a parabola
   c. a double helix
   d. a hexagon

22. Which of the following contains fiber?
   a. chicken breast
   b. raspberries
   c. steak
   d. butter

23. Which of the following ecosystems could be described as having a temperate climate and many leaf-shedding trees?
   a. a deciduous forest
   b. a tropical rain forest
   c. a tundra
   d. a taiga

24. Which of the following represents a chemical change?
- **a.** burning a piece of toast
- **b.** dissolving salt in water
- **c.** cutting an aspirin in half
- **d.** freezing water to make ice cubes

25. A human embryo will be female if the
- **a.** mother's egg contributes an X chromosome.
- **b.** mother's egg contributes a Y chromosome.
- **c.** father's sperm contributes an X chromosome.
- **d.** father's sperm contributes a Y chromosome.

▶ Part 2: Arithmetic Reasoning

Time: 36 minutes

1. Mr. Anthony Blake has inherited some musical instruments from his father. They are:

- ■ 1 violin valued at $3,500
- ■ 2 violin bows, each valued at $850
- ■ 2 music stands, each valued at $85
- ■ 1 cello valued at $2,300

In addition, Mr. Blake's father has left him a watch, valued at $250, and some old sheet music valued at $85 total. What is the value of Mr. Blake's inheritance?
- **a.** $6,735
- **b.** $7,070
- **c.** $7,670
- **d.** $8,005

2. On the cardiac ward, there are 7 nursing assistants. NA Basil has 8 patients; NA Hobbes has 5 patients; NA McGuire has 9 patients; NA Hicks has 10 patients; NA Garcia has 10 patients; NA James has 14 patients, and NA Davis has 7 patients. What is the average number of patients per nursing assistant?
- **a.** 7
- **b.** 8
- **c.** 9
- **d.** 10

3. If a particular woman's resting heartbeat is 72 beats per minute and she is at rest for $6\frac{1}{2}$ hours, about how many times will her heart beat during that period of time?
- **a.** 4,320
- **b.** 28,080
- **c.** 4,680
- **d.** 43,200

4. A patient's hospice stay cost $\frac{1}{4}$ as much as his visit to the emergency room. His home nursing cost twice as much as his hospice stay. If his total health care bill was $140,000, how much did his home nursing cost?
- **a.** 10,000
- **b.** 20,000
- **c.** 40,000
- **d.** 80,000

5. Chuck is making a patio using $1\frac{1}{2}$ foot cement squares. The patio will be 10 cement squares by 10 cement squares. If the cement squares are placed right next to each other without any space in between, what will the dimensions of the patio be?
- **a.** 10 ft by 10 ft
- **b.** 20 ft by 20 ft
- **c.** $12\frac{1}{2}$ ft by $12\frac{1}{2}$ ft
- **d.** 15 ft by 15 ft

6. At a certain school, half the students are female and one-twelfth of the students are from outside the state. What proportion of the students would you expect to be females from outside the state?

a. $\frac{1}{12}$

b. $\frac{1}{24}$

c. $\frac{1}{6}$

d. $\frac{1}{3}$

7. Which of the following has a 9 in the thousandths place?

a. 3.0095

b. 3.0905

c. 3.9005

d. 3.0059

8. Based on the information below, estimate the weight of a person who is 5'5" tall.

HEIGHT	WEIGHT
5'	110 pounds
6'	170 pounds

a. 125

b. 130

c. 135

d. 140

9. During exercise, a person's heart rate should be between sixty and ninety percent of the difference between 220 and the person's age. According to this guideline, what should a 30-year-old person's maximum heart rate be during exercise?

a. 114

b. 132

c. 171

d. 198

10. The local firefighters are doing a "fill the boot" fundraiser. Their goal is to raise $3,500. After three hours, they have raised $2,275. Which statement below is accurate?

a. They have raised 35% of their goal.

b. They have $\frac{7}{20}$ of their goal left to raise.

c. They have raised less than $\frac{1}{2}$ of their goal.

d. They have raised more than $\frac{3}{4}$ of their goal.

11. A certain water pollutant is unsafe at a level of 20 ppm (parts per million). A city's water supply now contains 50 ppm of this pollutant. What percentage improvement will make the water safe?

a. 30%

b. 40%

c. 50%

d. 60%

12. In half of migraine sufferers, a certain drug reduces the number of migraines by 50%. What percentage of all migraines can be eliminated by this drug?

a. 25%

b. 50%

c. 75%

d. 100%

13. Joey, Aaron, Barbara, and Stu have been collecting pennies and putting them in identical containers. Joey's container is $\frac{3}{4}$ full, Aaron's is $\frac{3}{5}$ full, Barbara's is $\frac{2}{3}$ full, and Stu's is $\frac{2}{5}$ full. Whose container has the most pennies?

a. Joey

b. Aaron

c. Barbara

d. Stu

14. Rosa kept track of how many hours she spent reading during the month of August. The first week she read for $4\frac{1}{2}$ hours, the second week for $3\frac{3}{4}$ hours, the third week for $8\frac{1}{2}$ hours, and the fourth week for $1\frac{1}{3}$ hours. How many hours altogether did she spend reading in the month of August?

a. $17\frac{47}{60}$

b. 16

c. $16\frac{1}{8}$

d. $18\frac{2}{15}$

15. A study shows that 600,000 women die each year in pregnancy and childbirth, one-fifth more than scientists previously estimated. How many such deaths did the scientists previously estimate?

a. 120,000

b. 300,000

c. 480,000

d. 500,000

16. A gram of fat contains 9 calories. An 1,800-calorie diet allows no more than 20% calories from fat. How many grams of fat are allowed in that diet?

a. 40 g

b. 90 g

c. 200 g

d. 360 g

17. What is 250 mg in terms of grams?

a. 0.0250 g

b. 0.250 g

c. 2.50 g

d. 250,000 g

18. After three days, a group of hikers discovers that they have used $\frac{2}{5}$ of their supplies. At this rate, how many more days can they go forward before they have to turn around?

a. 0.75 days

b. 3.75 days

c. 4.5 days

d. 7.5 days

19. A supply truck can carry 3 tons. A breakfast ration weighs 12 ounces, and the other two daily meals weigh 18 ounces each. On a ten-day trip, how many troops can be supplied by one truck?

a. 100

b. 150

c. 200

d. 320

20. A clerk can process 26 forms per hour. If 5,600 forms must be processed in an 8-hour day, how many clerks must you hire for that day?

a. 24 clerks

b. 25 clerks

c. 26 clerks

d. 27 clerks

21. On the same latitude, Company E travels east at 35 miles per hour and Company F travels west at 15 miles per hour. If the two companies start out 2,100 miles apart, how long will it take them to meet?

a. 42 hours

b. 60 hours

c. 105 hours

d. 140 hours

22. During the last week of training on an obstacle course, a recruit achieves the following times in seconds: 66, 57, 54, 54, 64, 59, and 59. The recruit's three best times this week are averaged for his final score on the course. What is his final score?
   a. 57 seconds
   b. 55 seconds
   c. 59 seconds
   d. 61 seconds

23. Mike types three times as fast as Nick. Together they type 24 pages per hour. If Nick learns to type as fast as Mike, how much will they be able to type per hour?
   a. 30 pages
   b. 36 pages
   c. 40 pages
   d. 48 pages

24. If you take recyclables to whichever recycler will pay the most, what is the greatest amount of money you could get for 2,200 pounds of aluminum, 1,400 pounds of cardboard, 3,100 pounds of glass, and 900 pounds of plastic?

	ALUM-INUM	CARD-BOARD	GLASS	PLASTIC
Recycler X	6 cents/pound	3 cents/pound	8 cents/pound	2 cents/pound
Recycler Y	7 cents/pound	4 cents/pound	7 cents/pound	3 cents/pound

   a. $440
   b. $447
   c. $454
   d. $485

25. Water is coming into a tank three times as fast as it is going out. After one hour, the tank contains 11,400 gallons of water. How fast is the water coming in?
   a. 3,800 gallons/hour
   b. 5,700 gallons/hour
   c. 11,400 gallons/hour
   d. 17,100 gallons/hour

26. A train must travel 3,450 miles in six days. How many miles must it travel each day?
   a. 525
   b. 550
   c. 600
   d. 575

27. A uniform requires 4 square yards of cloth. To produce uniforms for 84,720 troops, how much cloth is required?
   a. 330,880 square yards
   b. 336,880 square yards
   c. 338,880 square yards
   d. 340,880 square yards

28. A dormitory now houses 30 men and allows 42 square feet of space per man. If five more men are put into this dormitory, how much less space will each man have?
   a. 5 square feet
   b. 6 square feet
   c. 7 square feet
   d. 8 square feet

29. Ron is half as old as Sam, who is three times as old as Ted. The sum of their ages is 55. How old is Ron?
   a. 5
   b. 10
   c. 15
   d. 30

30. To lower a fever of 105 degrees, ice packs are applied for 1 minute and then removed for 5 minutes before being applied again. Each application lowers the fever by half a degree. How long will it take to lower the fever to 99 degrees?
a. 1 hour
b. 1 hour and 12 minutes
c. 1 hour and 15 minutes
d. 1 hour and 30 minutes

▶ Part 3: Word Knowledge

Time: 11 minutes

1. Erroneous most nearly means
a. digressive.
b. confused.
c. impenetrable.
d. faulty.

2. Grotesque most nearly means
a. extreme.
b. frenzied.
c. bizarre.
d. typical.

3. The Adamsville Kennel Club's computer system was outmoded.
a. worthless
b. unusable
c. obsolete
d. unnecessary

4. Garbled most nearly means
a. lucid.
b. unintelligible.
c. devoured.
d. outrageous.

5. Rigorous most nearly means
a. demanding.
b. tolerable.
c. lenient.
d. disorderly.

6. Flagrant most nearly means
a. secret.
b. worthless.
c. noble.
d. glaring.

7. Oration most nearly means
a. nuisance.
b. independence.
c. address.
d. length.

8. Although the police might be able to help Mr. Chen recover his stolen property, he obstinately refuses to file a complaint.
a. repeatedly
b. reluctantly
c. foolishly
d. stubbornly

9. The student's glib remarks irritated the teacher.
a. angry
b. superficial
c. insulting
d. dishonest

10. Composure most nearly means
a. agitation.
b. poise.
c. liveliness.
d. stimulation.

11. Eccentric most nearly means
a. normal.
b. frugal.
c. peculiar.
d. selective.

12. Commendable most nearly means
a. admirable.
b. accountable.
c. irresponsible.
d. noticeable.

13. Oblivious most nearly means
a. visible.
b. sinister.
c. aware.
d. ignorant.

14. Philanthropy most nearly means
a. selfishness.
b. fascination.
c. disrespect.
d. generosity.

15. Most members of the community thought the Neighborhood Guards' red hats were ostentatious.
a. hilarious
b. pretentious
c. outrageous
d. obnoxious

16. Passive most nearly means
a. resigned.
b. emotional.
c. lively.
d. woeful.

17. Proximity most nearly means
a. distance.
b. agreement.
c. nearness.
d. intelligence.

18. Negligible most nearly means
a. insignificant.
b. delicate.
c. meaningful.
d. illegible.

19. Rational most nearly means
a. deliberate.
b. invalid.
c. prompt.
d. sound.

20. Vigilant most nearly means
a. nonchalant.
b. alert.
c. righteous.
d. strenuous.

21. Astute most nearly means
a. perceptive.
b. inattentive.
c. stubborn.
d. elegant.

22. The prerequisite training to belong to this team is a three-hour course in volleyball.
a. required
b. optional
c. preferred
d. advisable

23. Coerce most nearly means
a. permit.
b. waste.
c. compel.
d. deny.

24. Collaborate most nearly means
a. cooperate.
b. coordinate.
c. entice.
d. elaborate.

25. Abrupt most nearly means
a. interrupt.
b. brusque.
c. extended.
d. corrupt.

▶ Part 4: Paragraph Comprehension

Time: 13 minutes

Police officers must read suspects their Miranda rights upon taking them into custody. When a suspect who is merely being questioned incriminates himself, he might later seek to have the case dismissed on the grounds of not having been apprised of his Miranda rights when arrested. Therefore, officers must take care not to give suspects grounds for later claiming they believed themselves to be in custody.

1. What is the main idea of the passage?
   a. Officers must remember to read suspects their Miranda rights.
   b. Suspects sometimes mistakenly believe they are in custody when in fact they are only being questioned.
   c. Officers who are merely questioning a suspect must not give the suspect the impression that he or she is in custody.
   d. Miranda rights needn't be read to all suspects before questioning.

2. When must police officers read Miranda rights to a suspect?
   a. while questioning the suspect
   b. while placing the suspect under arrest
   c. before taking the suspect to the police station
   d. before releasing the suspect

Dilly's Deli provides a dining experience like no other! Recently relocated to the old market area, Dilly's is especially popular for lunch. At the counter, you can place your order for one of Dilly's three daily lunch specials or one of several sandwiches, all at reasonable prices. Once you get your food, choose a seat at one of the four charming communal tables. By the time you are ready to carry your paper plate to the trash bin, you have experienced some of the best food and most charming company our city has to offer.

3. According to the passage, if you eat lunch at Dilly's Deli, you should expect to
   a. be surrounded by antiques.
   b. place your order with the waiter who comes to your table.
   c. carry your own food to your table.
   d. be asked out on a date by someone charming.

4. The main purpose of the passage is to
   a. profile the owner of Dilly's Deli.
   b. describe the kind of food served at Dilly's Deli.
   c. encourage people to eat at Dilly's Deli.
   d. explain the historical significance of the Dilly's Deli Building.

There are two types of diabetes, insulin-dependent and non-insulin-dependent. Between 90 and 95 percent of the estimated 13 to 14 million people in the United States with diabetes have non-insulin-dependent, or Type II, diabetes. Its symptoms often develop gradually and are hard to identify at first; therefore, nearly half of all people with diabetes do not know they have it. This can be particularly dangerous because untreated diabetes can cause damage to the heart, blood vessels, eyes, kidneys, and nerves. While the causes, short-term effects, and treatments of Type I and Type II diabetes differ, both types can cause the same long-term health problems.

5. According to the passage, which of the following may be the most dangerous aspect of Type II diabetes?
   a. Insulin shots are needed daily for treatment of Type II diabetes.
   b. In Type II diabetes the pancreas does not produce insulin.
   c. Type II diabetes interferes with digestion.
   d. Persons with Type II diabetes may not know they have it and will therefore not seek treatment.

6. Which of the following are the same for Type I and Type II diabetes?
  a. treatments
  b. long-term health risks
  c. short-term effects
  d. causes

Because crimes against adolescents are likely to be committed by offenders of the same age (as well as same sex and race), preventing violence among and aginst adolescents is a two-fold challenge. New violence-prevention programs in urban middle schools help reduce the crime rate by teaching both victims and perpetrators the skills of conflict resolution and how to apply reason to disputes, as well as by changing attitudes towards achieving respect through violence and towards the need to retaliate.

7. What is the main idea of the passage?
  a. Middle school violence-prevention programs are designed to help to lower the rate of crimes against adolescents.
  b. Adolescents are more likely to commit crimes than older people and must therefore be taught nonviolence in order to protect society.
  c. Middle school students appreciate the conflict resolution skills they acquire in violence-prevention programs.
  d. Violence against adolescents is increasing.

8. According to the passage, why is preventing violence against adolescents a *two-fold challenge*?
  a. because adolescents are as likely to be victims of violent crime as members of other age groups
  b. because adolescents must be prevented from both perpetrating and being victimized by violent crime
  c. because adolescents must change both their violent behavior and their attitudes towards violence
  d. because adolescents are vulnerable yet reluctant to listen to adult advice

Beginning next month, the department will institute a program intended to remove the graffiti from trucks. Any truck that finishes its assigned route before the end of the workers' shift will return to the lot where supervisors will provide materials for workers to use in cleaning the trucks. Because the length of time it takes to complete different routes varies, trucks will no longer be assigned to a specific route but will be rotated among the routes. Therefore, workers should no longer leave personal items in the trucks, as they will not necessarily be driving the same truck each day as in the past.

9. According to the passage, the removal of graffiti from trucks will be done by
  a. supervisors.
  b. workers.
  c. janitorial staff.
  d. prisoners doing community service.

10. According to the passage, routes
  a. vary in the amount of time they take to complete.
  b. all take seven hours to complete.
  c. are all of equal length.
  d. take longer to complete at certain times of the year.

11. According to the passage, prior to the graffiti clean-up program, workers
  a. were not responsible for cleaning the trucks.
  b. had to re-paint the trucks every month.
  c. usually drove the same truck each workday.
  d. were not allowed to leave personal belongings in the trucks.

Some people argue that retribution is the purpose of punishment of a person convicted of a crime, and that therefore the punishment must in some direct way fit the crime. Another view, the deterrence theory, promotes punishment in order to discourage commission of future crimes. In this view, punishment need not relate directly to the crime committed. However, punishment must necessarily be uniform and consistently applied, in order for the members of the public to understand how they would be punished if they committed a crime.

12. The passage suggests that a person who believes that the death penalty results in fewer murders most likely also believes in
   a. the deterrence theory.
   b. the retribution theory.
   c. giving judges considerable discretion in imposing sentences.
   d. the integrity of the criminal justice system.

13. A person who believes in the deterrence theory would probably also support
   a. non-unanimous jury verdicts.
   b. early release of prisoners because of prison overcrowding.
   c. a broad definition of the insanity defense.
   d. allowing television broadcasts of court proceedings.

The city ordinance reads, "Sanitation workers will not collect garbage in containers weighing more than 50 pounds." Workers are expected to use their best judgment in determining when a container weighs more than 50 pounds. If a container is too heavy, workers should attach one of the pre-printed warning messages (which are carried in all trucks) to the container, informing the household that the container weighs more than 50 pounds and cannot be collected.

14. According to the passage, in order to determine if a container is too heavy, sanitation workers should
   a. carry a scale in their truck to weigh containers.
   b. practice lifting 50 pounds at home to know what it feels like.
   c. assume any container he or she can lift weighs less than 50 pounds.
   d. use her or his best guess whether a container weighs more than 50 pounds.

15. According to the passage, if a sanitation worker believes that a container weighs more than 50 pounds, he or she should
   a. attach a pre-printed warning to the container and leave it where it is.
   b. write a note to the household, informing them of the weight limit.
   c. collect it anyway as the household probably did not know about the weight limit.
   d. notify a special collections truck to pick up the item.

▶ Part 5: Auto and Shop Information

Time: 11 minutes

1. The hand tool shown above is a
   a. crescent wrench.
   b. hammer.
   c. screwdriver.
   d. pair of pliers.

2. Which of the following building materials provides the best thermal insulation?
   a. brick
   b. steel
   c. concrete
   d. foam

3. In an internal combustion automobile engine, the engine displacement is actually the volume of which of the following components?
   a. the cylinders
   b. the exhaust manifold
   c. the radiator
   d. the oil reservoir

4. A tachometer is a gauge, sometimes found on an automobile, that measures
   a. engine temperature.
   b. road velocity.
   c. engine speed.
   d. oil pressure.

5. Which group of items listed below is essential for proper operation of an automobile's internal combustion engine?
   a. fuel, spark, and oxygen
   b. cooling, shocks, and transmission
   c. heat, fire, and spark
   d. fuel, distributor cap, and muffler

6. Which of the following items is part of the braking system is an automobile?
   a. calipers
   b. drums
   c. master cylinder
   d. all of the above

7. A fire engine has become stuck in a ditch. Which of the following tools would most likely be used to help extract the fire engine from the ditch?
   a. a clamp
   b. an electric winch
   c. a cam
   d. all of the above

8. The purpose of a spark plug in an internal combustion engine is to provide
   a. lubrication of the engine.
   b. rotation of the piston.
   c. cooling of the manifold.
   d. ignition of the fuel.

9. A carpenter's square is primarily used to
   a. insure that a cut is straight.
   b. measure the length of a stud.
   c. saw a board to the correct length.
   d. check that a building is level.

10. Which of the following items is used to measure angles?
   a. a lever
   b. a tachometer
   c. a gear
   d. a protractor

11. Which of the following is NOT a type of wrench?
   a. crescent
   b. box end
   c. channel lock
   d. ratchet

12. A turbocharger is a type of
   a. heavy equipment.
   b. air pump.
   c. switch.
   d. electric motor.

13. Which of the following is an electrical, as opposed to a mechanical, device?
   a. a wrench
   b. a clamp
   c. a hydraulic jack
   d. a battery

14. The purpose of a radiator on a car is to
   a. cool the engine.
   b. adjust the tire pressure.
   c. increase the engine horsepower.
   d. reduce engine noise.

15. The C-clamp shown above would most likely be used to
   a. temporarily hold two boards together.
   b. hold up a car in order to repair a flat tire.
   c. secure a heavy load as it is being transported.
   d. make a straight cut on a board.

16. Which mechanical device is NOT typically found on an automobile?
   a. a valve
   b. a pump
   c. a drill
   d. a fan

17. A hinge is most likely to be used on which of the following?
   a. a hand rail
   b. a cabinet door
   c. an electric clock
   d. a ceiling fan

18. Which of the following best describes the purpose of welding?
   a. cleaning
   b. lifting
   c. joining
   d. moving

19. Which hand tool listed below is used to tighten a nut and bolt?
   a. a crescent wrench
   b. a reamer
   c. calipers
   d. pipe clamps

20. One main purpose of a brace is to
   a. transport water on a construction project.
   b. aid in reading a directional compass.
   c. manually drill holes in wood.
   d. lift heavy loads in a warehouse.

21. A crane is primarily used to perform which of the following functions?
   a. pushing
   b. drilling
   c. welding
   d. lifting

22. Which of the following woodworking objects would most likely be created with a lathe?
   a. a door
   b. a table leg
   c. a building block
   d. a sign

Figure #1 **Figure #2**

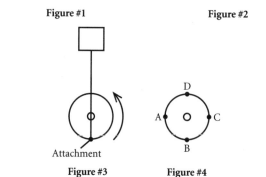

Attachment

Figure #3 **Figure #4**

23. On the gauge above, what is the maximum recommended operating pressure in psi, pounds per square inch, for this gauge to remain in a safe zone?

　a. 10 psi

　b. 20 psi

　c. 25 psi

　d. 30 psi

24. The function of a catalytic converter is primarily to

　a. change pollutants into substances that are less harmful.

　b. force air into the engine for better acceleration.

　c. improve the starting power of the automobile.

　d. control the amount of gasoline that flows into the engine.

25. Figure #1 above shows the initial position of a piston that is connected to a crankshaft by a connecting rod. Figure #2 shows the relative positions after the crankshaft is rotated 90 degrees (one quarter of a revolution) in the direction shown. Figure #3 shows the relative positions after another 90 degrees of rotation. In Figure #4, what will be the position of the connecting rod attachment to the crankshaft after yet another 90 degree rotation?

　a. position A

　b. position B

　c. position C

　d. position D

▶ Part 6: Mathematics Knowledge

Time: 24 minutes

1. Choose the answer to the following problem:
$$-\frac{5}{3} - \frac{1}{3} =$$
a. $\frac{4}{3}$
b. $-\frac{4}{3}$
c. 2
d. -2

2. The area of a region is measured in
a. units.
b. square units.
c. cubic units.
d. quadrants.

3. When calculating the area of a figure, you are finding
a. the distance around the object.
b. the length of a side.
c. the amount of space that the object covers.
d. the number of sides it has.

4. Choose the answer to the following problem:
$(25 + 17)(64 - 49) =$
a. 57
b. 630
c. 570
d. 63

5. Choose the answer to the following problem:
$12(84 - 5) - (3 \times 54) =$
a. 54,000
b. 841
c. 796
d. 786

6. Which of the following numbers is the smallest?
a. $\frac{6}{10}$
b. $\frac{8}{15}$
c. $\frac{33}{60}$
d. $\frac{11}{20}$

7. Which of the following is the equivalent of $\frac{13}{25}$?
a. 0.38
b. 0.4
c. 0.48
d. 0.52

8. What is another way to write 0.32×10^3?
a. 3.2
b. 32
c. 320
d. 3,200

9. How does the area of a rectangle change if both the base and the height of the original rectangle are tripled?
a. The area is tripled.
b. The area is six times larger.
c. The area is nine times larger.
d. The area remains the same.

10. When measuring the area of a football field, you would most likely use
a. square inches.
b. square millimeters.
c. square miles.
d. square yards.

11. On the number line below, point L is to be located halfway between points M and N. What number will correspond to point L?

a. $-\frac{1}{4}$

b. $-\frac{1}{2}$

c. $-1\frac{1}{4}$

d. 0

12. Which of the following statements is true?

a. Parallel lines intersect at right angles.

b. Parallel lines never intersect.

c. Perpendicular lines never intersect.

d. Intersecting lines have two points in common.

13. What is another way to write 2.75×100^2?

a. 275

b. 2,750

c. 27,500

d. 270,000

14. $(a^2b)^2(2ab)^3$ is equivalent to which of the following?

a. $2a^3b^5$

b. $5ab$

c. $6a^7b$

d. $8a^7b$

15. What is the next number in the series below?

　　3　16　6　12　12　8　_____

a. 4

b. 15

c. 20

d. 24

16. Which number sentence is true?

a. $4.3 < 0.43$

b. $0.43 < 0.043$

c. $0.043 > 0.0043$

d. $0.0043 > 0.043$

17. If $x = 6$, $y = -2$, and $z = 3$, what is the value of the following expression?

$$\frac{xz - xy}{z^2}$$

a. $-\frac{2}{3}$

b. $\frac{2}{3}$

c. $3\frac{1}{3}$

d. 5

18. What is the area of a triangle with a height of 10 inches and a base of 2 inches?

a. 10 square inches

b. 12 square inches

c. 20 square inches

d. 22 square inches

19. What is 0.716 rounded to the nearest tenth?

a. 0.7

b. 0.8

c. 0.72

d. 1.0

20. If $\frac{x}{2} + \frac{x}{6} = 4$, what is x?

a. $\frac{1}{24}$

b. $\frac{1}{6}$

c. 3

d. 6

21. Choose the answer to the following problem:
$10^5 \div 10^2 =$

a. 10

b. 10^3

c. 10^7

d. 10^{10}

22. If a population of cells grows from 10 to 320 in a period of five hours, what is the rate of growth?

a. It doubles its numbers every half hour.

b. It doubles its numbers every hour.

c. It triples its numbers every hour.

d. It doubles its numbers every two hours.

23. Choose the answer to the following problem:

$3.16 \div 0.079 =$

a. 0.025
b. 2.5
c. 4.0
d. 40

24. Choose the answer to the following problem:

$2\frac{5}{8} \div \frac{1}{3} =$

a. $7\frac{7}{8}$
b. $8\frac{1}{3}$
c. $5\frac{11}{24}$
d. $\frac{7}{8}$

25. $\frac{11}{5}$ is equal to

a. 2.25
b. 1.5
c. 1.15
d. 2.20

26. What is the area of the figure below?

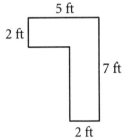

a. 19 square feet
b. 20 square feet
c. 24 square feet
d. 38 square feet

27. What is $7\frac{1}{5}\%$ of 465, rounded to the nearest tenth?

a. 32.5
b. 33
c. 33.5
d. 34

28. What kind of polygon is the figure below?

a. heptagon
b. octagon
c. hexagon
d. pentagon

29. Which of the following is equivalent to $2y^2$?

a. $2(y + y)$
b. $2y(y)$
c. $y^2 + 2$
d. $y + y + y + y$

30. For which of the following values of x is this number sentence true: $25 - x < 10$?

a. 16
b. 15
c. 14
d. 13

31. How much water must be added to 1 liter of a 5% saline solution to get a 2% saline solution?

a. 1 L
b. 2 L
c. 1.5 L
d. 2.5 L

32. What is the decimal form of $\frac{5}{6}$? (Round two decimal places.)

a. 0.65
b. 0.88
c. 0.83
d. 0.13

33. A 15 cc dosage must be increased by 20%. What is the new dosage?

a. 17 cc
b. 18 cc
c. 30 cc
d. 35 cc

34. What is the volume of liquid that is remaining in this cylinder?

10 cm

8 cm

    a. 64π cm^3

    b. 80π cm^3

    c. 96π cm^3

    d. 160π cm^3

35. $-0.05 =$

    a. $\frac{1}{20}$

    b. $-\frac{1}{20}$

    c. $\frac{1}{2}$

    d. $-\frac{1}{2}$

▶ Part 7: Mechanical Comprehension

Time: 19 minutes

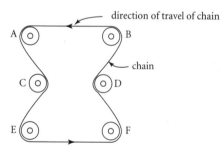

direction of travel of chain

chain

1. In the diagram above, which gears are turning clockwise?

    a. A, C, and E

    b. B, D, and F

    c. C and D

    d. E and F

2. What is the most accurate statement regarding the relationship between weight and density?

    a. Weight equals density divided by volume.

    b. A bathroom scale cannot measure density.

    c. Density can be measured in pounds.

    d. All of the above

3. Expansion is to contraction as

    a. pressure is to density.

    b. acceleration is to deceleration.

    c. weight is to center of gravity.

    d. direction is to velocity.

4. The center of gravity of a baseball bat would be best described as

    a. near the grip.

    b. near the fat end.

    c. near the skinny end.

    d. at the top.

5. Which is heavier, five pounds of feathers or five pounds of lead?

    a. the feathers

    b. the lead

    c. They weigh the same.

    d. It is not possible to compare the two.

6. Which material is best suited for use as a boat anchor?

    a. metal

    b. foam

    c. wood

    d. glass

7. A submarine would be most likely to use which of the following to aid in decreasing its submergence while under water?

    a. lead

    b. air

    c. steel

    d. none of the above

8. What would happen to a balloon full of air if you moved it from above a water surface to ten feet below the water surface?
   a. The balloon would explode.
   b. The volume of the balloon would stay the same.
   c. The volume of the balloon would increase.
   d. The volume of the balloon would decrease.

9. Which of the following groups of items could be used to form a common mechanical linkage?
   a. a crankshaft, a connecting rod, and a piston
   b. a chair, a desk, and a lamp
   c. a wheel, a screw, and a lever
   d. a window, a door, and a table

10. The sprocket on a bicycle is most similar to which of the simple mechanical devices listed below?
   a. a spring
   b. a lever
   c. a gear
   d. all of the above

11. The wheel of a bicycle rotates around which of the following mechanical components?
   a. a pulley
   b. an axle
   c. a cam
   d. a lever

12. Which mechanical components are typically used between a wheel and an axle to reduce friction?
   a. hinges
   b. levers
   c. springs
   d. bearings

13. Chains and belts are used in mechanical systems to do which of the following tasks?
   a. transfer energy
   b. transfer motion
   c. link gears and pulleys
   d. all of the above

14. What mechanical motion principle do the brakes in a car or on a bicycle use?
   a. friction
   b. centrifugal force
   c. acceleration
   d. momentum

15. Which of the following are types of springs?
   a. compression and leaf
   b. centrifugal and bilateral
   c. stem and root
   d. all of the above

16. In the diagram above, all valves are initially closed. Gravity will cause the water to drain down into the barrels when the valves are opened. Which barrels will be filled if valves A, B, E, F, and G are opened and valves C and D are left closed?
   a. barrels #1 and #2
   b. barrels #3 and #4
   c. barrels #1, #2, #3, and #4
   d. barrels #1, #2, and #3

17. A block of ice is slid across several different surfaces. Which type of surface will provide the least friction?
a. steel
b. concrete
c. wood
d. ice

18. A hoist is typically used for which of the operations shown below?
a. reducing wind resistance
b. cutting metal objects
c. lifting heavy objects
d. heating water

19. Which of the following are examples of plastic deformation?
a. a car crash
b. squeezing a ball of silly putty
c. crushing a soft drink can
d. all of the above

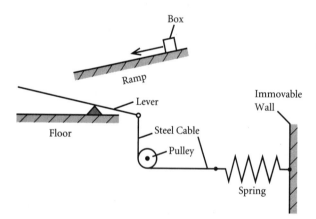

20. In the diagram above, if the box slides down the ramp and drops onto the left side of the lever, what will happen to the spring?
a. It will touch the box.
b. It will remain as it is.
c. It will be compressed, or shortened.
d. It will be stretched, or lengthened.

21. A total of seven columns will be used to support a new bridge. How much of the total bridge weight will each column support?
a. one-half
b. one-fifth
c. one-seventh
d. not enough information

22. Velocity, direction, and acceleration are all topics that fall into which of the following categories?
a. mechanical motion
b. rotary motion
c. torque
d. angular momentum

23. Which of the following mechanical devices is used to open a common soft drink can?
a. a winch
b. a lever
c. a wrench
d. a piston

24. An elevator is most similar to which of the following mechanical devices?
a. a lever
b. a hydraulic jack
c. a crane
d. a spring

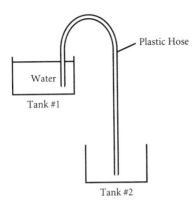

Tank #1

Plastic Hose

Water

Tank #2

25. What mechanical device could be used to transfer water from tank #1 to tank #2?

a. a pulley

b. a siphon

c. a lever

d. a spring

▶ Part 8: Electronics Information

Time: 9 minutes

1. What should the temperature of a typical soldering iron be when joining two wires together?

a. 150–200 degrees F

b. 300–400 degrees F

c. 500–600 degrees F

d. 900–1,000 degrees F

2. A digital multimeter combines an ammeter, an ohmmeter, and a voltmeter into one device. Which parameter CANNOT be directly measured by a multimeter?

a. voltage

b. current

c. capacitance

d. resistance

3. What is the voltage across the load R and the current through R when the switch is open in the following circuit?

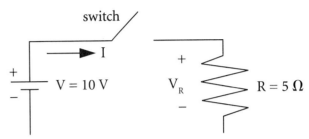

a. The current is 0 A; the voltage is 10 V.

b. The current is 2 A; the voltage is 10 V.

c. The current is 2 A; the voltage is 2 V.

d. The current is 0 A; the voltage is 0 V.

4. Which of the following is NOT a series resistance circuit?

a.

b.

c.

d.

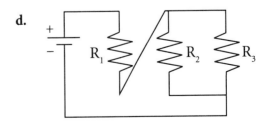

5. A 120 V light bulb is rated for 60 watts. What is the light bulb's rated current?
  a. 0.5 A
  b. 1 A
  c. 2 A
  d. 4 A

6. A toaster has two amperes flowing through it. If the current is doubled and the voltage source does not change, what happens to the power dissipated by the toaster?
  a. It does not change.
  b. It is doubled.
  c. It is reduced by a factor of 2.
  d. It is increased by a factor of 4.

7. What is the voltmeter reading in the following circuit?

  a. 1 V
  b. 2 V
  c. 6 V
  d. 12 V

8. Which of the following fossil fuels is NOT heavily used to produce electrical power?
  a. oil
  b. propane
  c. natural gas
  d. coal

9. Which of the following is NOT needed to produce electrical power from fossil fuels?
  a. a dam
  b. a turbine
  c. steam
  d. heat

10. What is the total current for a parallel resistance circuit with three parallel paths that each have four amperes flowing through them?
  a. 2 A
  b. 12 A
  c. 4 A
  d. 8 A

11. Most wires today are manufactured from
  a. gold
  b. copper
  c. aluminum
  d. silver

12. An AC voltmeter is connected across an outlet in your home. Which voltage will it read?
  a. 30 V
  b. 60 V
  c. 110 V
  d. 550 V

13. An AA battery produces a potential difference of 1.5 V. Four AA batteries are placed in series to power a portable FM radio. What is the total voltage of the radio?
  a. 0.75 V
  b. 1.5 V
  c. 3.0 V
  d. 6.0 V

14. A switch is used to turn on and off the light bulb in the following circuit. When the switch is open, _____ current flows, and when the switch is closed, _____ current flows.

- **a.** 0 A . . . 0.5 A
- **b.** 0.5 A . . . 2 A
- **c.** 0 A . . . 2 A
- **d.** 0.5 A . . . 0 A

15. A typical 12 V car battery is made up of eight individual cells, or batteries, connected in series. What is the voltage of each cell in a car battery?
- **a.** 1.5 V
- **b.** 12 V
- **c** 8 V
- **d.** 3 V

16. Lightning is a result of the power dissipated when an electrical circuit is established between a charged cloud and the ground. The air provides the circuit path. What is the resistance of the air if 0.1 amperes flow between a cloud and the earth with a potential difference of 100,000 volts?
- **a.** 10 K Ω
- **b.** 100 K Ω
- **c.** 0.1 M Ω
- **d.** 1 M Ω

17. Which of the following is the symbol for a resistor?

a.

b.

c.

d.

18. A large speaker at a concert is rated for a maximum of 1,000 watts. What is the maximum voltage that can be applied to the speaker if 10 amperes of current flow through it?
- **a.** 10 V
- **b.** 100 V
- **c.** 1,000 V
- **d.** 10,000 V

19. Which function does the receiving antenna provide in radio communication?
- **a.** It broadcasts the signal over the air.
- **b.** It mixes the signal and the carrier wave.
- **c.** It catches the signal out of the air.
- **d.** It separates the carrier wave from the signal.

20. Which of the following terms is the same as a potential difference?
- **a.** a conductor
- **b.** a voltage
- **c.** a resistance
- **d.** a capacitor

▶ Answers

Part 1: General Science

1. b. The pH scale ranges from 0 to 14, with 0 being acidic and 14 being alkaline (or basic). A pH of 7 is considered neutral. Anything above 7, then, is alkaline.

2. d. Benzene consists of a ring of six carbon atoms. This ring is the basis of all aromatic compounds.

3. a. $C_6H_{12}O_6$ contains 3 elements: carbon, hydrogen, and oxygen.

4. d. A micrometer is one-millionth of a meter; it is therefore one-thousandth of a millimeter, because a millimeter is one-thousandth of a meter.

5. d. To express a number in scientific notation, you move the decimal as many places as necessary until there is only one digit to the left of the decimal. For 617,000, you move the decimal to the left by 5 decimal places. The fact that you had to move it to the left means that the 10 should be raised to a positive power, so the result is 6.17×10^5.

6. c. Gravity pulls the ball downward as it moves forward.

7. a. An ax blade is an example of a wedge. A lever is usually a rigid bar used to exert pressure or sustain weight at one point by the application of force at a second point and a turning point at a third.

8. b. The core is the center; the crust is the outer layer; the mantle is the middle layer.

9. d. An anemometer measures wind. The other choices are instruments of measure, but they do not measure wind.

10. b. Tigers are in the phylum Chordata, class Mammalia, order Carnivora. Genus and species names are always underlined or in italics, as in the species name *tigris*.

11. a. Hemoglobin, used by all vertebrates and some invertebrates to transport oxygen and carbon dioxide in the body, gives red blood cells their color.

12. c. Igneous rocks make up a group of rocks formed from the crystallization of magma (lava). Sedimentary rock is formed by silt or rock fragments.

13. d. All organic compounds contain carbon (C). Calcium (Ca) is only a single element, and it does not contain carbon.

14. a. Beetles and crabs are both in the arthropod phylum. Arthropods are invertebrates characterized by having a hard exoskeleton (outer skeleton), at least six jointed legs, and a segmented body. Salmon, frogs, and robins are all in the chordate phylum; all chordates have a nerve cord (a spine) at some point in their development.

15. b. Viruses, microscopic organisms with no true cell structure, cause polio and measles. A fungus is a multi-cellular organism.

16. c. Insulin promotes the uptake of glucose (a sugar) in the body. Estrogen and androgen control the development of sex characteristics in women and men respectively.

17. b. Veins carry blood devoid of oxygen to the right atrium of the heart. Arteries, capillaries, and the aorta carry oxygenated blood from the heart to blood cells throughout the body.

18. d. Herbivores are animals that subsist on plant matter. Omnivores eat a variety of foodstuff, and carnivores eat other animals.

19. a. One hundred centimeters equals one meter, and 1,000 meters equals one kilometer.

20. b. The Eustachian tube connects the middle ear and throat. The cochlea is a fluid-filled structure in the inner ear.

21. c. The Watson-Crick model of DNA is a double-stranded twisted ladder, or double helix.

22. b. Fiber is found only in plants. Raw vegetables, fruit with seeds, whole cereals, and bread are other possible sources of fiber.

23. a. Deciduous forests are characterized by having mild temperatures and many trees that shed leaves periodically. Taigas are characterized by evergreen trees and long, harsh winters.

24. a. Burning a piece of toast changes the composition of the substance, so it is a chemical change. Choices **b**, **c**, and **d** are physical changes.

25. c. A human embryo's sex is always determined by the sperm. The egg always contributes an X chromosome, while the sperm contributes either an X (for a female) or a Y (for a male).

Part 2: Arithmetic Reasoning

1. d. Don't forget that there are two bows and two music stands, and remember to add the value of the watch and the sheet music.

2. c. First, add the number of patients to find the total: 63. Then divide the number of patients by the number of nursing assistants: 63 divided by 7 is 9.

3. b. This is a two-step multiplication problem. To find out how many heartbeats there would be in one hour, you must multiply 72 by 60 (minutes) and then multiply this result, 4,320, by 6.5 hours.

4. c. Let E = emergency room cost; H = hospice cost, which is $(\frac{1}{4})$E; N = home nursing cost, which is 2H, or $2(\frac{1}{4})$E. The total bill is E + H + N, which is E + $(\frac{1}{4})$E + $(\frac{2}{4})$E, = 140,000. Add the left side of the equation to get $\frac{7}{4}$E = 140,000. To solve for E, multiply both sides of the equation by $(\frac{4}{7})$. E = 140,000$(\frac{4}{7})$, or 80,000. H = $(\frac{1}{4})$E, or 20,000, and N = 2H, or 40,000.

5. d. Multiply $1\frac{1}{2}$ by 10. Change $1\frac{1}{2}$ to an improper fraction $(\frac{3}{2})$ and make 10 into a fraction by placing it over 1 $(\frac{10}{1})$; $\frac{3}{2} \times \frac{10}{1} = \frac{30}{2} = 15$ feet. Each side is 15 feet long, so the dimensions are 15 ft by 15 ft.

6. b. If half the students are female, then you would expect half of the out-of-state students to be female. One half of $\frac{1}{12}$ is $\frac{1}{24}$.

7. a. In choice **b**, the 9 is in the hundredths place; in choice **c**, it is in the tenths place; and in choice **d**, it is in the ten thousandths place.

8. c. A foot in height makes a difference of 60 pounds, or 5 pounds per inch of height over 5′.

A person who is 5′5″ is (5)(5 pounds), or 25 pounds, heavier than the person who is 5′, so add 25 pounds to 110 pounds to get 135 pounds.

9. c. The difference between 220 and this person's age is 190. The maximum heart rate is 90% of this: (0.9)(190) = 171.

10. a. The part of their goal that they have raised is $2,275 and the whole goal is $3,500. The fraction for this is $\frac{2,275}{3,500}$. The numerator and denominator can both be divided by 175 to get a simplified fraction of $\frac{13}{20}$. They have completed $\frac{13}{20}$ of their goal, which means that they have $\frac{7}{20}$ left to go $(\frac{20}{20} - \frac{13}{20} = \frac{7}{20})$.

11. d. Thirty ppm of the pollutant would have to be removed to bring the 50 ppm down to 20 ppm. Thirty ppm represents 60% of 50 ppm.

12. a. The drug is 50% effective for 50% of migraine sufferers, so it eliminates (0.50)(0.50), or 0.25 of all migraines.

13. a. Compare $\frac{3}{4}$, $\frac{3}{5}$, $\frac{2}{3}$, $\frac{2}{5}$ by finding a common denominator. The common denominator for 3, 4, and 5 is 60. Multiply the numerator and denominator of a fraction by the same number so that the denominator becomes 60. The fractions then become $\frac{45}{60}$, $\frac{36}{60}$, $\frac{40}{60}$, and $\frac{24}{60}$. The fraction with the largest numerator is the largest fraction; $\frac{45}{60}$ is the largest fraction. It is equivalent to Joey's fraction of $\frac{3}{4}$.

14. a. Add the number of hours together using a common denominator of $60; 4\frac{30}{60} + 3\frac{45}{60} + 8\frac{12}{60}$ = $1\frac{20}{60}$ = $16\frac{107}{60}$, which is simplified to $17\frac{47}{60}$ hours.

15. d. Let E = the estimate. *One-fifth more than the estimate* means $\frac{6}{5}$ or 120% of E, so 600,000 = (1.20)(E). Dividing both sides by 1.2 leaves E = 500,000.

16. a. 20% of 1,800, or (0.2)(1,800) = 360 calories are allowed from fat. Since there are 9 calories in each gram of fat, divide 360 by 9 to find that 40 grams of fat are allowed.

17. b. Here, 250 milligrams is $\frac{250}{1000}$ gram, or 0.250 g.

18. a. First find out how long the entire hike can be, based on the rate at which the hikers are using their supplies. If 1 = all supplies and x = entire hike, then $\frac{\frac{2}{5}}{3} = \frac{1}{x}$. Cross-multiply to get $\frac{2x}{5} = 3$, so that $x = \frac{(3)(5)}{2}$, or $7\frac{1}{2}$ days for the length of the entire hike. This means that the hikers could go forward for 3.75 days altogether before they would have to turn around. They have already hiked for 3 days, which leaves 0.75 for the amount of time they can now go forward before having to turn around.

19. c. Three tons is 6,000 pounds; 6,000 pounds multiplied by 16 ounces per pound is 96,000 ounces. The total weight of each daily ration is 48 ounces; 96,000 divided by 48 is 2,000 troops supplied; 2,000 divided by 10 days is 200 troops supplied.

20. d. Twenty-six forms multiplied by 8 hours is 208 forms per day per clerk; 5,600 divided by 208 is approximately 26.9, which means you have to hire 27 clerks for the day.

21. a. The companies' combined rate of travel is 50 miles per hour; 2,100 miles divided by 50 miles per hour is 42 hours.

22. b. The recruit's three best times are 54, 54, and 57. To find the average, add the 3 numbers and divide the sum by 3.

23. b. M = 3N; 3N + N = 24, so that N = 6. Since M = 3N, M = 18. If Nick catches up to Mike's typing speed, then both M and N will equal 18, and then the combined rate will be 36 pages per hour.

24. d. 2,200(0.07) = $154; $154 + 1400(0.04) = $210; $210 + 3100(0.08) = $458; $458 + $900(0.03) = $485.

25. d. 3W = water coming in; W = water going out; 3W − W = 11,400, which implies that W is 5,700 and 3W is 17,100.

26. d. Here, 3,450 miles divided by 6 days is 575 miles.

27. c. 84,720 troops multiplied by 4 square yards of cloth is 338,880 square yards of cloth required.

28. b. Thirty men multiplied by 42 square feet of space is 1,260 square feet of space; 1,260 square feet divided by 35 men is 36 square feet, so each man will have 6 less square feet of space.

29. c. Let T = Ted's age; S = Sam's age = 3T; R = Ron's age $= \frac{S}{2}$, or $\frac{3T}{2}$. The sum of the ages is 55, which means $T + 3T + \frac{3T}{2} = 55$. Find the common denominator (2) to add the left side of the equation. T = 10. If Ted is 10, then Sam is 30, and Ron is $\frac{3T}{2}$, which is 15 years old.

30. b. The difference between 105 and 99 is 6 degrees. The temperature is lowered by half a degree every six minutes, or 1 degree every 12 minutes; 6 degrees multiplied by 12 minutes per degree is 72 minutes, or 1 hour and 12 minutes.

Part 3: Word Knowledge

1. d. Something that is *erroneous* is wrong or *faulty*.

2. c. Something that is *grotesque* is distorted, misshapen, or *hideous*.

3. c. To be *outmoded* is to be out-of-date or *obsolete*.

4. b. A statement that is *garbled* is scrambled and confusing, or *unintelligible*.

5. a. Something that is *rigorous* is strict or *demanding*.

6. d. A thing that is *flagrant* is conspicuous or *glaring*.

7. c. An *oration* is a formal speech or an *address*.

8. d. When something is done *obstinately*, it is done in a refractory manner or *stubbornly*.

9. b. A *glib* remark is a quick and insincere, or *superficial*, one.

10. b. When someone has *composure*, that person has self-possession or *poise*.

11. c. To be *eccentric* is to be unconventional or *peculiar*.

12. a. If something is *commendable* it is praiseworthy or *admirable*.

13. d. To be *oblivious* of something is to be unaware or *ignorant* of it.

14. d. An act of *philanthropy* is an act of charity or *generosity*.

15. b. To be *ostentatious* is to be showy or *pretentious*.

16. a. To be *passive* is to be compliant or *resigned*.

17. c. When something is in *proximity* to something else, it is close or in *nearness* to it.

18. a. To be *negligible* is to be unimportant or *insignificant*.

19. d. A *rational* judgment is a logical or *sound* one.

20. b. To be *vigilant* is to be watchful or *alert*.

21. a. To be *astute* is to be keen-minded or *perceptive*.

22. a. A *prerequisite* is something that is necessary or *required*.

23. c. To *coerce* someone to do something is to force, pressure, or *compel* that person to do it.

24. a. To *collaborate* on a project is to work together or *cooperate* on it.

25. b. To be *abrupt* is to be curt or *brusque*.

Part 4: Paragraph Comprehension

1. a. While choices **b** and **c** are true, they are not the main idea. Choice **d** is contradicted in the last sentence.

2. b. See the first sentence of the passage.

3. c. This is the only one of the choices that is stated in the passage (in the third and fourth sentences). Choices **a** and **d** are not stated in the passage. Choice **b** is contradicted by the passage.

4. c. The whole tone of the passage is complimentary to Dilly's. Choices **a** and **d** are not mentioned in the passage. Although choice **b** is mentioned, it is not the main point.

5. d. The passage mentions that the symptoms of Type II diabetes may occur gradually and thus be attributed to other causes. Left untreated, diabetes can cause damage to several major organs in the body.

6. b. According to the passage, only the long-term health problems are the same for these two different disorders.

7. a. None of the other choices is mentioned in the passage.

8. b. This idea is explicitly stated in the first sentence.

9. b. See the second sentence of the passage.

10. a. See the third sentence of the passage.

11. c. The last sentence of the passage implies that, in the past, drivers usually drove the same truck each day.

12. a. This can be deduced from the second sentence of the passage.

13. d. The last sentence notes that the deterrence theory has the effect of teaching not only criminals but also the public.

14. d. Although the other options are not precluded by the passage, the passage only requires workers to make an educated guess as to the weight of the container.

15. a. See the third sentence of the passage.

Part 5: Auto and Shop Information

1. b. A hammer is used for driving nails and other general carpentry functions.

2. d. Of all the materials listed, foam has the most internal dead air space, which prevents heat from escaping. The other materials are fairly solid, and heat travels through them quickly.

3. a. The cylinder is the cavity in which the piston moves up and down. An engine with more cylinders (eight versus six or four) or bigger cylinders will have a bigger displacement and will generate more power.

4. c. This gauge measures engine speed in revolutions per minute (RPM).

5. a. The fuel is ignited by the spark from the spark plug. Oxygen is needed for the fuel to burn. The burning of the fuel pushes the piston up and down in the engine's cylinders, and that energy is transferred to the wheels by way of the transmission.

6. d. When the brake pedal is pressed, it operates the master cylinder, which forces the brake fluid through the lines out to each wheel. The pressure in the brake lines causes the calipers to move and press the brake shoes against the brake drum. This causes the automobile to slow down.

7. b. The other devices would not be useful in this situation.

8. d. The spark plug produces a spark inside the cylinder of the engine and causes the fuel to burn.

9. a. A carpenter's square is typically an L-shaped piece of metal which is used to draw a straight line on a board on which a cut is to be made.

10. d. A protractor is typically a half-circle made of metal or plastic that has tick marks around the edge spaced at one-degree intervals.

11. c. Channel lock is a type of pliers.

12. b. A turbocharger is a kind of air pump that increases combustion by forcing more air into the engine.

13. d. The other items listed are common mechanical devices.

14. a. The radiator contains fluid (water and anti-freeze) that is circulated around the engine block by the water pump. The fluid becomes hot as it passes around the engine and is then cooled as air passes through the radiator.

15. a. The C-clamp would be placed around the two boards and tightened by turning the screw with the handle.

16. c. A drill is a carpenter's hand tool. The other items are common parts of a car.

17. b. The function of a hinge is to connect two items together and to allow rotation of one of the items relative to the other.

18. c. Welding is the process of connecting two pieces of material such as metal or plastic.

19. a. A reamer is used to shape or enlarge holes; calipers are used to measure internal and external dimensions. Pipe clamps are used to clamp boards or framing together so they can be bonded by glue.

20. c. A brace can also be used to provide additional torque when driving screws.

21. d. A crane is used to raise and lower large items that are typically too heavy or awkward to lift by hand.

22. b. A lathe is a tool which is typically used to carve long, slender pieces of wood. The wood is attached to the lathe and an electric motor spins the piece of wood. A cutting blade is then used to remove parts of the wood, giving a decorative shape. A lathe would not be useful in making the other objects listed.

23. b. The gauge indicates that any pressure greater than 20 psi is in the danger zone.

24. a. The catalytic converter converts pollutants into less harmful substances.

25. c. Figure #3 shows the attachment of the connecting rod to the crankshaft at the bottom of the crankshaft. Another 90-degree counter-clockwise rotation would place the attachment point on the right side of the crankshaft at position C.

Part 6: Mathematics Knowledge

1. d. Subtract to get $-\frac{6}{3}$, which reduces to -2.

2. b. When calculating area, you are finding the number of square units that cover the region.

3. c. The area of a figure is the amount of space the object covers, in square units.

4. b. Perform the operations within the parentheses first, which gives you $(42)(15) = 630$.

5. d. Perform the operations in the parentheses first: $(12)(79) - 162 = 786$.

6. b. Fractions must be converted to the lowest common denominator, which allows you to compare the amounts: $\frac{36}{60}$, $\frac{32}{60}$, $\frac{33}{60}$, and $\frac{33}{60}$.

7. d. The fraction $\frac{13}{25}$ is equal to $\frac{52}{100}$.

8. c. $(0.32)(10^3) = 0.32 \times (10 \times 10 \times 10)$

9. c. Since both dimensions are tripled, there are two additional factors of 3. Therefore, the new area is $3 \times 3 = 9$ times as large as the original.

10. d. A football field would most likely be measured in square yards. Square inches and square millimeters are too small, and square miles are too large.

11. a. The halfway point on the number line is between 0 and $-\frac{1}{2}$, which is $-\frac{1}{4}$.

12. b. Corresponding points on parallel lines are always the same distance apart, so the lines can never intersect.

13. c. $100^2 = (100)(100)$, or 10,000; $(10,000)(2.75) =$ 27,500.

14. d. Multiply the powers of each set of parentheses to get $a^4b^2(8a^3b^{12})$. When multiplying the outside of the parentheses by the inside, add the exponents.

15. d. This series actually has two alternating sets of numbers. The first number is doubled, giving the third number. The second number has 4 subtracted from it, giving the fourth number. Therefore, the blank space will be 12 doubled, or 24.

16. c. The farther to the right the digits go, the smaller the number.

17. c. Beginning with the operations in the brackets, $[6(3)] - [6(-2)]$ divided by 9 becomes $18 - (-12)$ divided by 9; 30 divided by $9 = \frac{10}{3}$, which is $3\frac{1}{3}$.

18. a. The formula for the area of a triangle is $A = \frac{1}{2}bh$; $\frac{1}{2}(10)(2) = 10$.

19. a. Choice **c** is rounded to the thousandths place. Choice **d** is rounded to the nearest whole number. Choice **b** is rounded up rather than down.

20. d. To add the left side of the equation, find the common denominator, so that $\frac{3x}{6} + \frac{x}{6} = 4$; $\frac{4x}{6} = 4$; and $4x = 24$.

21. b. In a division problem like this, leave the whole number the same and subtract the exponents.

22. b. You can use trial and error to arrive at a solution to this problem. After the first hour, the number would be 20, after the second hour 40, after the third hour 80, after the fourth hour 160, and after the fifth hour 320. The other answer choices do not have the same outcome.

23. d. Create a division problem without decimals by moving the decimal point three places to the right: 3,160 divided by 79 is 40.

24. a. Convert the mixed number to a fraction: $\frac{21}{8}$ divided by $\frac{1}{3}$ is $(\frac{21}{8})(\frac{3}{1}) = \frac{63}{8}$, or $7\frac{7}{8}$.

25. d. Here, $\frac{11}{5}$ is an improper fraction. One way of solving this problem is to convert the improper fraction into a mixed number which can then be converted into a decimal. A quicker way is to divide the numerator by the denominator, paying close attention to the decimal point; $11 \div 5 = 2.20$.

26. b. Find the area of two rectangles and then add the results. Use an imaginary line to block off the first rectangle at the top of the figure. This rectangle measures (5 feet)(2 feet) = 10 square feet. The second rectangle is also (5 feet)(2 feet). Add the two together for a total of 20 square feet.

27. c. First, change the percent to a decimal: $(.072)(465) = 33.48$, which rounded to the nearest tenth is 33.5.

28. a. A heptagon has seven sides.

29. b. The expression y^2 means y times y.

30. a. $25 - 16 = 9$, which is the only choice that leaves you with a number less than 10.

31. c. Use the equation $(0.05)(1) = (0.02)x$: the left side represents 5% of 1 liter; the right side represents 2% of some amount of water. From the equation, $x = 2.5$. Subtracting the 1 liter of water already present in the 5% solution, you will find that 1.5 liters need to be added.

32. c. Divide 5 by 6 to convert the fraction into a decimal; $5 \div 6 = 0.833\overline{3}$. Round two decimal places to get 0.83.

33. b. Twenty percent of 15 cc is $(0.20)(15) = 3$. $15 + 3 = 18$ cc.

34. c. The volume of a cylinder equals πr^2h, where r is the radius of the cylinder and h is the height. The radius is half the diameter, so the radius of this cylinder is 4 cm. The height of the volume is $10 - 4 = 6$ (the height of the whole cylinder minus the height of space in which the liquid has been poured out). So the volume is $\pi(4)^2(6)$, or $\pi(16)(6) = 96\pi$ cm^3.

35. b. First convert -0.05 into a fraction; $\frac{5 \div 5}{100 \div 5} = \frac{1}{20}$. Then, do not forget to add the negative sign to get $-\frac{1}{20}$.

Part 7: Mechanical Comprehension

1. c. The other gears are turning counter-clockwise. It helps to follow the direction of the chain, which is connected to all of the gears.

2. b. Choice **a** is not correct, as weight is equal to density multiplied by volume. Choice **c** is not correct, as density is measured in weight (pounds) per unit volume.

3. b. Expansion and contraction are opposites, as are acceleration and deceleration. The other choices are not opposites.

4. b. The center of gravity is the place on an object where there is equal weight on either side.

5. c. Weight is measured in pounds, and the question states that both the feathers and the lead weigh five pounds.

6. a. Foam and wood float and would therefore make poor boat anchors. Glass is not strong enough to be used as a boat anchor.

7. b. Steel and lead are heavier than water and would therefore not aid in moving upward through the water. Air, which is lighter than water, can be injected into the ballast tanks, which will cause the submarine to rise.

8. d. The volume of the balloon would decrease. The pressure of the water would press inward on the balloon and cause it to shrink in volume.

9. a. The crankshaft, connecting rod, and piston are components of an internal combustion engine. They form a linkage because the piston pushes down on the connecting rod, which the causes the crankshaft to rotate.

10. c. A bicycle sprocket is the classic example of a gear, which is defined as a toothed wheel or cylinder that meshes with a chain or with another toothed element to transfer energy or motion.

11. b. An axle is typically a metal rod located at the center of a wheel around which the wheel rotates. The ends of the axle are then attached to the vehicle.

12. d. A set of bearings is typically a set of small metal balls packed in a groove and lubricated with grease or oil. The wheel rubs against one side of each ball, and the axle rubs against the other side. The net effect is that the wheel rolls much more easily.

13. d. All of the choices are correct.

14. a. When the brakes are applied, the brake pads rub on the wheel and the frictional force of this rubbing slows down the vehicle.

15. a. A compression spring is the type used on a ballpoint pen or on a pogo stick. A leaf spring is typically used on the rear suspension of pickup trucks.

16. a. Since valve D is closed, water will not flow to barrels #3 and #4. Water will flow through valve B but be stopped at valve C. Water will flow through valve A into barrels #1 and #2.

17. d. A low coefficient of friction between two surfaces means that the drag force between the two surfaces is low. A block of ice sliding over an ice surface will slide farther than a block of ice sliding across wood, concrete, or steel.

18. c. A hoist is usually a steel frame with a steel cable running over a pulley with a lifting hook on the end of the cable. The hook is placed around the heavy object to be lifted, and either a hand crank or an electric motor is used to reel in the cable, thus lifting the object.

19. d. Plastic deformation occurs when a material is deformed, or bent, beyond the point of springing back to its original shape. All of the answers listed give examples in which materials are plastically deformed.

20. d. The box will force the left side of the lever down and the right side of the lever up, which will pull the cable up. The cable will pass across the pulley and apply a pulling force on the spring, which will stretch the spring.

21. d. If we were told that the columns were uniformly spaced along the length of the bridge, then each column would support one-seventh of the total weight. Since this is not specified, there is not enough information to answer the question.

22. a. Velocity, direction, and acceleration are the terms used to describe mechanical motion such as vehicular travel, motion of a clock pendulum, or projectile motion of a bullet.

23. b. The little tab you use to pry open the can is a lever. You lift on one end of the lever, which rotates around a pivot point and forces the other end of the lever downward, so that the can pops open.

24. c. An elevator is simply a crane that raises and lowers people.

25. b. To use a siphon, you would first submerge the entire length of hose in tank #1 in order to completely fill it with water. You would then place one end of the hose in tank #1 and the other end in tank #2, as shown in the diagram. Since the end of the hose in tank #2 is lower than the end in tank #1, the extra weight of the water in the right side of the hose will cause the water to flow into tank #2.

Part 8: Electronics Information

1. c. The solder should be melted with a soldering iron heated to 500–600 degrees F.

2. c. An ammeter measures current. An ohmmeter measures resistance, and a voltmeter measures voltage.

3. d. When the switch is open, no current flows. The voltage V_R is I times R, which equals $0(5\,\Omega) = 0$.

4. d. R_2 and R_3 are in parallel; therefore, the circuit is a series parallel resistance circuit.

5. a. P = VI. Therefore, $I = \frac{P}{V} = \frac{60\text{ watts}}{120\text{ V}}$, or 0.5 A.

6. d. $P = I^2R$. The original current was 2 A, so power P = 4R. When the current is doubled to 4 A, the power P = 16R. The power is increased by a factor of four.

7. c. The voltage drop across the 6 Ω resistor is V = IR, which equals 1 A times 6 Ω, which equals 6 V. The total voltage in a series resistance circuit is equal to the sum of the voltages around the circuit. The voltage across the voltmeter is therefore 12 V – 6 V, which equals 6 V.

8. b. Coal, natural gas, and oil are the primary fossil fuels used to produce electrical power.

9. a. Dams are used to produce power from water.

10. b. The total current is equal to the sum of the currents through each resistance. Therefore, 4 A + 4 A + 4 A = 12 A.

11. b. Most wires are made of copper because it has high conductivity and is relatively inexpensive.

12. c. The voltages most commonly used in the home are 110 V and 220 V.

13. d. Voltages in series are added to determine the total voltage. 1.5 V + 1.5 V + 1.5 V + 1.5 V = 6.0 V.

14. a. When the switch is open, no current can flow because there is not a closed path. When the switch opens, $I = \frac{V}{R}$, which is $\frac{10\text{ V}}{20\text{ W}}$, which is 0.5 A.

15. a. Voltages in series are added to determine the total voltage, so divide 12 volts by 8 cells to get 1.5 V.

16. d. Ohm's law states V = IR, so $R = \frac{V}{I}$, which is $\frac{100,000\text{ V}}{0.1\text{ A}} = 1,000,000\ \Omega$, which is 1 M Ω.

17. a. Choice **b** is a capacitor; choice **c** is a voltage source, and choice **d** is a switch.

18. b. The power equation states P = VI, so $V = \frac{P}{I}$. $\frac{1000\text{ W}}{10\text{ A}} = 100$ V.

19. c. The broadcast antenna is used to broadcast the signal over the air. The mixer combines the signal and carrier wave. The de-mixer separates the carrier and the signal.

20. b. A conductor is a material with highly mobile electrons. Resistance is the opposition to current. A capacitor is a device that can store electrical charge.

Write your raw score (the number you got right) for each test in the blanks below. Then turn to Chapter 3 to find out how to convert these raw scores into the scores the armed services use.

1. General Science: _____ right out of 25
2. Arithmetic Reasoning: _____ right out of 30
3. Word Knowledge: _____ right out of 25
4. Paragraph Comprehension: _____ right out of 15
5. Auto and Shop Information: _____ right out of 25
6. Mathematics Knowledge: _____ right out of 35
7. Mechanical Comprehension: _____ right out of 25
8. Electronics Information: _____ right out of 20

How to Use
the CD-ROM

So you think you are ready for your exam? The LearningExpress's ASVAB Skills Tester AutoExam CD-ROM software, developed by PEARSoft Corporation of Wellesley, Massachusetts, is a great way to build your confidence so you *know* you are ready for the exam. The disk is included inside the back cover of this book and can be used with any PC running Windows 95/98/ME/NT/2000/XP. (Sorry, it does not work for Macintosh!)

First, install the program:

1. Insert the CD-ROM into your CD-ROM drive. The CD should run automatically. If it does not, proceed to Step 2.
2. From Windows, select **Start**, then choose **Run**.
3. Type D:/Setup
4. Click **OK**.

The screens that follow will walk you through the installation procedure.

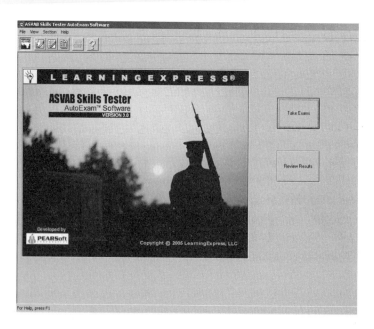

From the main menu (or on the right side of the screen), select **Take Exams**. (After you have taken at least one exam, click on **Review Results** to see your scores.)

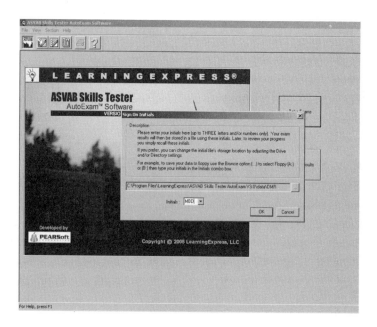

Notice that you can also change the drive and/or folder where your exam results are stored. If you want to save to a floppy drive, for instance, click on **Browse** (…) and choose the letter of your floppy drive. Now enter your initials. This allows you to record your progress and review your performance for as many simulated exams as you would like. Click **OK**.

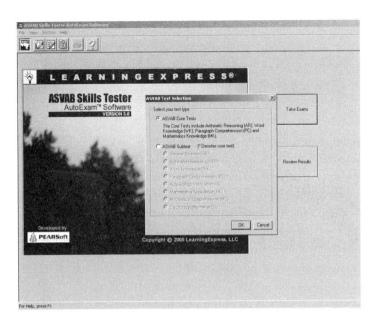

Now, since this CD-ROM supports the ASVAB core tests and subtests, you need to select your exam of choice. Let's start with the ASVAB core tests, as shown above.

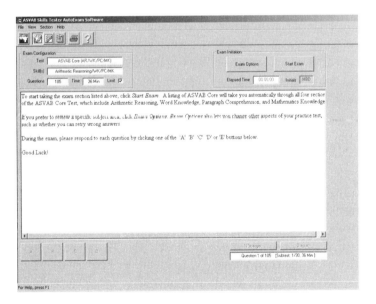

Now you are into the **Take Exams** section, as shown above. You can either choose **Start Exam** to begin your exam or **Exam Options**. The next screenshot shows you what your **Exam Options** are.

Instead of the core test, you could have selected a subtest. Choosing **Exam Options** will help you fine-tune your rough spots. How about a science warm up? Click on **Change Test,** select the **General Science** option, and click **OK**. Then, you can choose as many questions as you want to review right now. On the right, you can choose whether to wait until you have finished the exam to see your results (**Final Review & Score**) or have the computer tell you whether your answer is correct after each question (**Continuous Review & Score**). Please note: These options are only enabled when the time limit box is unchecked. By choosing **Retry Incorrect Responses,** you will get a second chance at questions you answered wrong. (This option works best with **Review Subject Area** rather than **Complete Test**.) If you have chosen the wrong exam or wish to select another, click on **Change Test** again and choose your exam. When you finish choosing your options, click **OK**. Then click the **Start Exam** button on the main exam screen, and you will see a screen like the one on the next page.

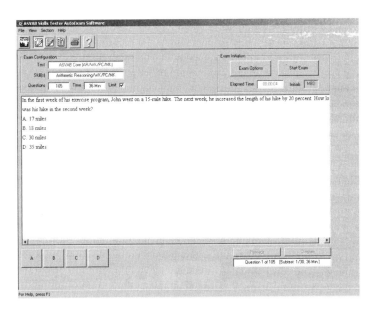

Questions come up one at a time, just as they do on the real exam. To answer each question, click on the A, B, C, or D at the bottom of the screen. If the question is long, you might need to use the left/right scroll to read the question in full.

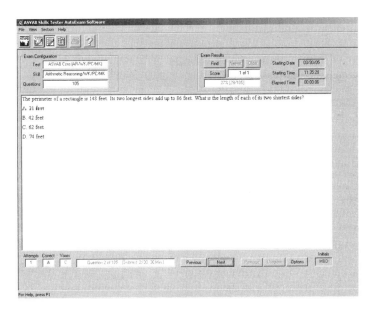

When you have finished your exam or subtest, you will receive a pop-up window that says, "Would you like to switch to the Review Process now?" (If you do not want to view your results now, you can always do it later by clicking on the **Review Exams Section** on the toolbar or by selecting the **Review Results** from the main menu.) If you choose "yes," you will see your score and whether you passed. The questions (with their answer explanations) come up one at a time. Under **Options** (found at the bottom-right of the screen), you can choose whether to look at all the questions or just the ones you missed.

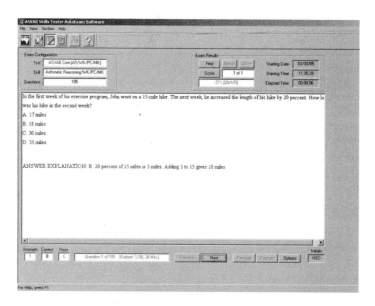

When you are in **Review Results,** click on the **Find** button to look at all the exams you have taken.

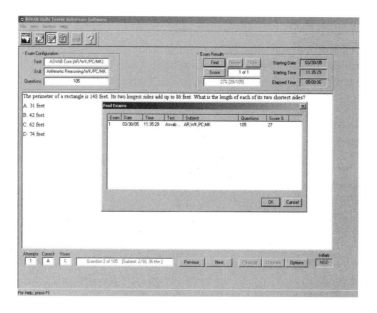

By default, your exam results are listed from newest to oldest, but you can sort them by any of the headings. For instance, if you want to see your results arranged by score, you can click on the **Score %** heading. To go to a particular exam you have taken, double-click on it.

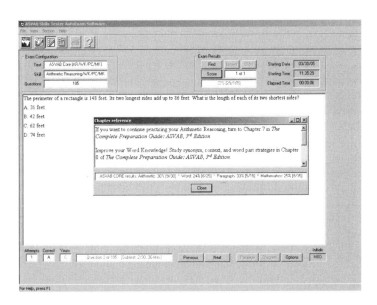

In the **Review Results** section, if you click on **Score**, you will see your score on the exam you're currently reviewing. This section also provides reference information to chapters or books that will help you improve your knowledge on the particular subject area.

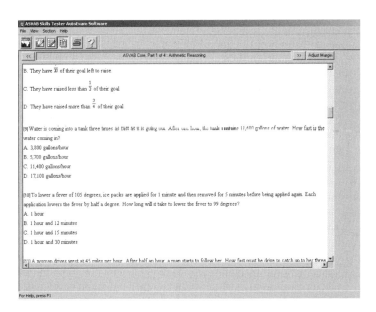

What's that? No time to work at the computer? For a quick printout of your exam, once an exam is in progress, simply click on the **Print** option of the file menu or the icon button in the toolbar. Your printed exam is only seconds away.

For technical support, call 212-995-2566 (ext. 2).